STONES INTO SCHOOLS

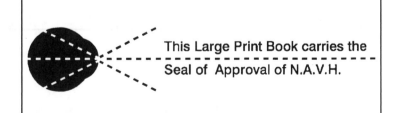

This Large Print Book carries the
Seal of Approval of N.A.V.H.

STONES INTO SCHOOLS

PROMOTING PEACE WITH BOOKS, NOT BOMBS, IN AFGHANISTAN AND PAKISTAN

GREG MORTENSON

LARGE PRINT PRESS
A part of Gale, Cengage Learning

GALE
CENGAGE Learning

Detroit • New York • San Francisco • New Haven, Conn • Waterville, Maine • London

LIBRARY OF CONGRESS CATALOGING-IN-PUBLICATION DATA

Mortenson, Greg.
  Stones into schools : promoting peace with books, not bombs, in Afghanistan and Pakistan / by Greg Mortenson. — Large print ed.
     p. cm.
  ISBN-13: 978-1-4104-2035-0 (hardcover : alk. paper)
  ISBN-10: 1-4104-2035-3 (hardcover : alk. paper)
  1. Girls' schools—Afghanistan. 2. Girls' schools—Pakistan.
  3. Humanitarian assistance, American—Afghanistan. 4. Humanitarian assistance, American—Pakistan. 5. Peace-building—Afghanistan.
  6. Peace-building—Pakistan. 7. Mortenson, Greg—Anecdotes.
  8. Taliban—History. I. Title.
  LC2330.M66 2009
  371.823'4209581—dc22   2009043336

ISBN 13: 978-1-59413-409-8 (pbk. : alk. paper)
ISBN 10: 1-59413-409-X (pbk. : alk. paper)

Published in 2010 in arrangement with Viking, a member of Penguin Group (USA) Inc.

Printed in the United States of America
1 2 3 4 5 6 7 14 13 12 11 10

To the noble people of Afghanistan and Pakistan and to the 120 million school-age children in the world who are deprived of their right of education

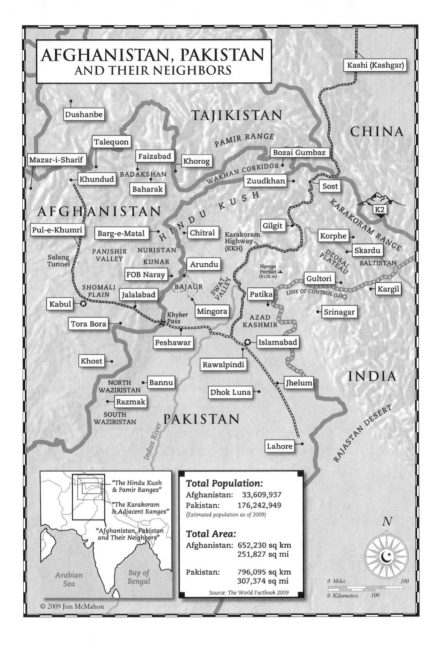

AFGHANISTAN, PAKISTAN
AND THEIR NEIGHBORS

Kashi (Kashgar)

CHINA

TAJIKISTAN

Dushanbe

Talequon

PAMIR RANGE

Mazar-i-Sharif

Faizabad

Khorog

Bozai Gumbaz

BADAKSHAN

WAKHAN CORRIDOR

Khundud

Zuudkhan

Baharak

Sost

AFGHANISTAN

HINDU KUSH

K2

KARAKORAM RANGE

Pul-e-Khumri

Barg-e-Matal

Chitral

Gilgit

Korphe

Karakoram
Highway
(KKH)

Salang
Tunnel

PANJSHIR
VALLEY

NURISTAN

Skardu

DEOSAI
PLATEAU

BALTISTAN

KUNAR

Arundu

Nanga
Parbat
(8126 m)

Gultori

FOB Naray

SHOMALI
PLAIN

BAJAUR

SWAT
VALLEY

Patika

LINE OF CONTROL (LOC)

Kargil

Jalalabad

Kabul

Tora Bora

Khyber
Pass

Mingora

AZAD
KASHMIR

Srinagar

Peshawar

Islamabad

Khost

Rawalpindi

INDIA

NORTH
WAZIRISTAN

Bannu

Jhelum

Razmak

Dhok Luna

SOUTH
WAZIRISTAN

PAKISTAN

Indus River

Lahore

RAJASTAN DESERT

"The Hindu Kush
& Pamir Ranges"

"The Karakoram
& Adjacent Ranges"

"Afghanistan, Pakistan
and Their Neighbors"

Arabian
Sea

Bay of
Bengal

Total Population:
Afghanistan: 33,609,937
Pakistan: 176,242,949
(Estimated population as of 2009)

Total Area:
Afghanistan: 652,230 sq km
               251,827 sq mi

Pakistan: 796,095 sq km
               307,374 sq mi

Source: The World Factbook 2009

N

0 Miles   100
0 Kilometers   100

© 2009 Jim McMahon

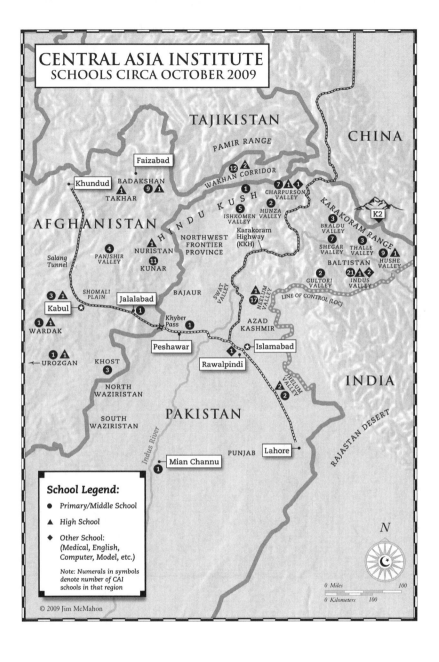

CENTRAL ASIA INSTITUTE
SCHOOLS CIRCA OCTOBER 2009

TAJIKISTAN

CHINA

PAMIR RANGE

Faizabad

WAKHAN CORRIDOR

Khundud

BADAKHSHAN

TAKHAR

H I N D U   K U S H

CHARPURSON VALLEY

HUNZA VALLEY

ISHKOMEN VALLEY

K2

KARAKORAM RANGE

AFGHANISTAN

BRALDU VALLEY

SHEGAR VALLEY

THALLE VALLEY

HUSHE VALLEY

NORTHWEST FRONTIER PROVINCE

Karakoram Highway (KKH)

Salang Tunnel

PANJSHIR VALLEY

NURISTAN

KUNAR

BALTISTAN

GULTORI VALLEY

INDUS VALLEY

SHOMALI PLAIN

BAJAUR

SWAT VALLEY

NEELUM VALLEY

LINE OF CONTROL (LOC)

Kabul

Jalalabad

WARDAK

Khyber Pass

AZAD KASHMIR

UROZGAN

KHOST

Peshawar

Islamabad

INDIA

NORTH WAZIRISTAN

Rawalpindi

JHELUM VALLEY

SOUTH WAZIRISTAN

PAKISTAN

Indus River

RAJASTAN DESERT

PUNJAB

Lahore

Mian Channu

School Legend:

● Primary/Middle School

▲ High School

◆ Other School:
(Medical, English,
Computer, Model, etc.)

Note: Numerals in symbols
denote number of CAI
schools in that region

N

0 Miles   100

0 Kilometers   100

© 2009 Jim McMahon

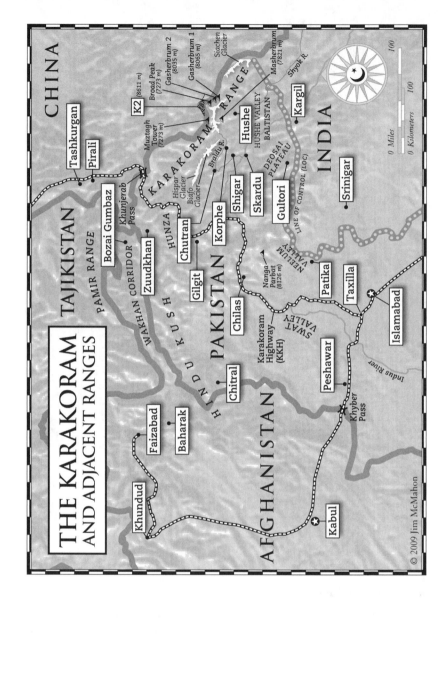

THE KARAKORAM
AND ADJACENT RANGES

CHINA

TAJIKISTAN

PAMIR RANGE

WAKHAN CORRIDOR

HINDU KUSH

AFGHANISTAN

PAKISTAN

INDIA

Tashkurgan
Pirali
Bozai Gumbaz
Zuudkhan
Khunjerab Pass
HUNZA
Gilgit
Chutran
Korphe
Chitral
Chilas
Karakoram Highway (KKH)
SWAT VALLEY
Peshawar
Khyber Pass
Kabul
Khundud
Faizabad
Baharak
Islamabad
Taxilla
Patika
NEELUM VALLEY
Nanga Parbot (8126 m)
Shigar
Skardu
Gultori
Srinigar
Kargil
LINE OF CONTROL (LOC)
DEOSAI PLATEAU
BALTISTAN
HUSHE VALLEY
Hushe
Masherbrum (7821 m)
Shyok R.
Siachen Glacier
Gasherbrum 1 (8065 m)
Gasherbrum 2 (8035 m)
Broad Peak (7273 m)
K2 (8611 m)
Muztagh Tower (7273 m)
Braldu R.
Biafo Glacier
Hispar Glacier
KARAKORAM RANGE

Indus River

0 Miles 100
0 Kilometers 100

© 2009 Jim McMahon

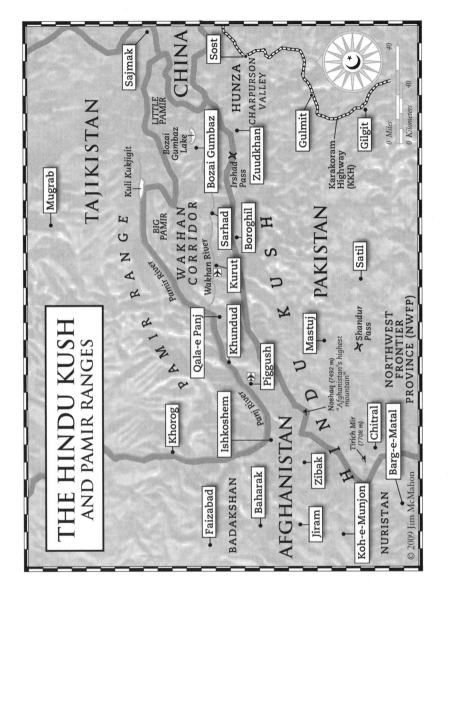

THE HINDU KUSH
AND PAMIR RANGES

TAJIKISTAN

CHINA

Mugrab

Sajmak

LITTLE PAMIR

Bozai Gumbaz Lake

Kuli Kukjigit

Sost

HUNZA

CHARPURSON VALLEY

Bozai Gumbaz

Zuudkhan

Irshad Pass

Gulmit

PAMIR RANGE

BIG PAMIR

WAKHAN CORRIDOR

Pamir River

Wakhan River

Sarhad

Kurut

Boroghil

Gilgit

Karakoram Highway (KKH)

Khorog

Qala-e Panj

Khundud

Piggush

Mastuj

Shandur Pass

Satil

PAKISTAN

Panj River

Noshaq (7492 m) "Afghanistan's highest mountain"

NORTHWEST FRONTIER PROVINCE (NWFP)

Faizabad

BADAKSHAN

Baharak

Ishkoshem

Zibak

Trich Mir (7708 m)

Chitral

HINDU KUSH

Jiram

Koh-e-Munjon

Barg-e-Matal

NURISTAN

AFGHANISTAN

© 2009 Jim McMahon

0 Miles 40

0 Kilometers 40

AFGHANISTAN PROVINCES
& FEDERALLY ADMINISTERED TRIBAL AREAS

ETHNIC DISTRIBUTION
WITHIN PAKISTAN AND AFGHANISTAN

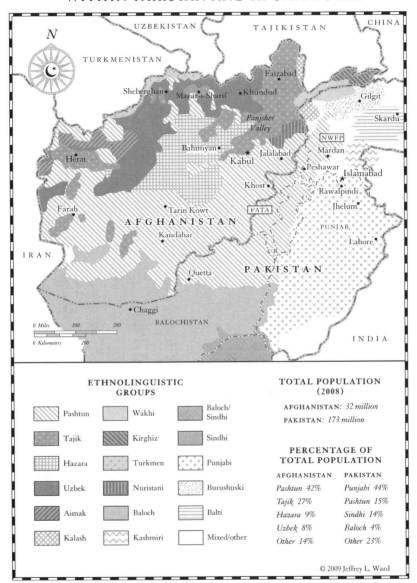

ETHNOLINGUISTIC GROUPS

Pashtun	Wakhi	Baloch/Sindhi
Tajik	Kirghiz	Sindhi
Hazara	Turkmen	Punjabi
Uzbek	Nuristani	Burushuski
Aimak	Baloch	Balti
Kalash	Kashmiri	Mixed/other

TOTAL POPULATION (2008)

AFGHANISTAN: *32 million*
PAKISTAN: *173 million*

PERCENTAGE OF TOTAL POPULATION

AFGHANISTAN	PAKISTAN
Pashtun 42%	*Punjabi 44%*
Tajik 27%	*Pashtun 15%*
Hazara 9%	*Sindhi 14%*
Uzbek 8%	*Baloch 4%*
Other 14%	*Other 23%*

© 2009 Jeffrey L. Ward

WHO'S WHO

Ali, Haji: Greg Mortenson's first mentor and chief of Korphe village, Pakistan; passed away in 2001

Ali, Jahan: Granddaughter of Haji Ali and Central Asia Institute's first female student to graduate from high school

Ali, Niaz: Spiritual leader of the Kirghiz in the Wakhan, Afghanistan

Ali, Twaha: Haji Ali's son and father of Jahan; from Korphe, Pakistan

Al-Zawahiri, Ayman: Egyptian physician; second in command of Al Qaeda

Baig, Faisal: Wakhi elder from Charpurson Valley, Pakistan, and the CAI's security manager

Baig, Nasreen: CAI student from Charpurson Valley who is now studying to be a maternal health-care worker

Baig, Saidullah: The CAI's manager in Charpurson Valley, Pakistan

bin Laden, Osama: Saudi Arabian leader of Al Qaeda who is now either in hiding or dead

Bishop, Tara: Greg Mortenson's wife and a psychotherapist

Boi, Tashi: Village chief of Sarhad, in the Wakhan Corridor, Afghanistan

Chabot, Doug: Climber, avalanche expert, and CAI volunteer

Chabot, Genevieve: CAI scholarship program manager; married to Doug Chabot

Chaudry, Shaukat Ali: Former Taliban member, now a teacher in the CAI girls' school in Azad Kashmir, Pakistan

Dostum, General Rashid: Uzbek ethnic leader based in Mazar-i-Sharif, Afghanistan

Ghani, Dr. Ashraf: Former minister of education of Afghanistan

Gulmarjan: CAI Afghan student killed by a land mine in 2003 at the age of twelve

Hoerni, Dr. Jean: Silicon transistor pioneer and cofounder of CAI with Greg Mortenson; passed away in 1997

Hosseini, Khaled: Physician, philanthropist, and best-selling author of *The Kite Runner* and *A Thousand Splendid Suns*

Hussain, Aziza: First maternal health-care worker in Charpurson Valley, Pakistan

Ibrahim, Haji Mohammed: *Shura* (elder)

leader from Uruzgan Province, Afghanistan

Karimi, Wakil: CAI manager for Afghanistan

Karzai, Hamid: President of Afghanistan

Khan, Abdul Rashid: *Amir* (leader) of the Kirghiz people in the Wakhan Corridor, Afghanistan

Khan, Sadhar: Tajik leader in Badakshan who was CAI's first supporter in the region

Khan, Sarfraz: CAI's remote areas project manager; from Pakistan

Khan, Shah Ismael: *Pir* (leader) of the Wakhi people in Afghanistan

Khan, Wohid: Badakshan border security commander in Afghanistan

Kolenda, Colonel Christopher: Former commander of Forward Operating Base (FOB) Naray and currently a key U.S. military strategist in Afghanistan

Kosar, Parveen: The first female high school graduate in the Wakhan, and now a maternal health-care worker there

Leitinger, Christiane: Director of Pennies for Peace

McChrystal, Major General Stanley: Commander of ISAF (and U.S.) military forces in Afghanistan; proponent of counterinsurgency methodology

Massoud, Ahmed Shah: Tajik military commander called the Lion of the Panjshir for his role in driving out the Soviets; assassinated by al Qaeda on September 9, 2001

Minhas, Suleman: CAI's Punjab Province manager, based in Islamabad; formerly a taxi driver

Mirza, Colonel Ilyas: Retired Pakistani military aviation officer and general manager of Askari Aviation, a civil aviation charter company

Mohammed, Mullah: Former Taliban bookkeeper and CAI accountant for the entire Wakhan region

Mortenson, Amira and Khyber: Children of Greg Mortenson and Tara Bishop

Mortenson, Christa: Younger sister of Greg Mortenson; passed away in 1992 when she was twenty-three

Mortenson, Irvin "Dempsey" and Jerene: Greg Mortenson's parents

Mughal, Ghosia: CAI student from Azad Kashmir

Mullen, Admiral Mike: Chairman of the U.S. Joint Chiefs of Staff and the military leader who inaugurated a CAI girls' school in Afghanistan in July 2009. Married to Deborah.

Musharraf, Pervez: President of Pakistan from 1999 to 2008; former Pakistani army chief of staff

Myatt, Major General Mike: Former commander of the Marine Expeditionary Force who led the invasion into Kuwait

Najibullah, Mohammed: Afghanistan's communist leader and former president; killed by the Taliban in 1996

Nicholson, Major Jason: U.S. military officer based at the Pentagon

Olson, Admiral Eric: SOCOM commander of the combined U.S. Special Forces. Admiral Olson and his wife Marilyn are advocates of girls' education and introduced Mortenson to several senior military commanders

Omar, Mullah: Afghan Pashtun tribal leader of the Taliban; thought to be hiding in Quetta, Pakistan

Parvi, Haji Ghulam: CAI's Pakistan-based manager and accountant, who has overseen the establishment of over fifty schools

Petraeus, General David: U.S. CENTCOM commander. It was from his wife, Holly, that General Petraeus first learned about *Three Cups of Tea*.

Rahman, Abdullah: Former medical librarian and CAI driver in Afghanistan

Razak, Abdul: Former expedition cook from Baltistan; eldest CAI employee; also known as Apo (old man)

17

Sen, Amartya: 1998 winner of the Nobel Prize in economics

Shabir, Saida: Headmistress of Gundi Piran girls' school in Pattika, Azad Kashmir, Pakistan, which was destroyed by the 2005 earthquake

Shah, Zahir: King of Afghanistan who fled to Italy in 1973 and returned to Afghanistan after 9/11, remaining there until his death in 2007

Shaheen, Farzana: CAI student in Azad Kashmir, Pakistan

Sipes, Jennifer: CAI's operations manager in Montana

CONTENTS

Part I
The Promise

Part II
Qayamat ("The Apocalypse")

Part III
The School on the Roof of the World

FOREWORD
BY KHALED HOSSEINI

The muddled war in Afghanistan is now in its eighth year, and has become the most urgent foreign policy challenge facing President Obama. Against a backdrop of rising conflict, respected think tanks like the Atlantic Council have published reports calling Afghanistan a failing state. The country indeed faces enormous problems: a violent, spiraling insurgency that is hampering the rule of law and developmental efforts, the growth of record crops of poppies, extreme poverty, criminality, homelessness, joblessness, lack of access to clean water, continuing problems with the status of women, and a central government that has struggled to protect its people and provide basic services.

But there are success stories as well in post-9/11 Afghanistan, and the most meaningful of them is education. If we accept the premise that education is the key to achieving positive, long-lasting change in Afghanistan, then it is impossible to overstate how encouraging it is that this year nearly eight and a half million children will attend school in Afghanistan, with girls accounting for nearly 40 percent of enrollment.

No one understands this better than Greg Mortenson, the founder of 131 schools in Afghanistan and Pakistan that provide education to nearly 58,000 students. No one grasps better the profound impact and ripple effect of even one child's education. And, arguably, no single individual or organization has done more to advance the American cause in Afghanistan than Greg Mortenson, a courteous, soft-spoken man who with his genial smile and warm handshake has shown the U.S. military how the so-called battle for the hearts and minds is fought. And how it is won.

Greg's philosophy is not complicated. He believes quite sincerely that the conflict in Afghanistan will ultimately not be won with guns and air strikes, but with books, notebooks, and pencils, the tools of socioeconomic well-being. To deprive Afghan children of education, he tells us, is to bankrupt the future of the country, and doom any prospects of Afghanistan becoming someday a more prosperous and productive state. Despite fatwas issued against him, despite threats from the Taliban and other extremists, he has done everything he can to make sure that this does not happen.

Very crucially, he has spearheaded efforts to educate girls and young women. Not an easy task in a region where parents routinely keep their daughters out of school and where long-standing cultural traditions have deprived women of the right to education. But in village after village, Greg has reached out to religious leaders and elders to help convince parents to send their girls to school. This is because Greg believes, as I do, that if Afghanistan has any chance to become a more prosperous nation, it will require the full engagement of its women as part of the process. And for that to happen, women have to be given access to schools, and their education has to be one of the cornerstones of national reconstruction and development. As he says repeatedly, mantralike, "If you educate a boy, you educate an individual, but if you educate a girl, you educate a community."

Lastly, Greg has done all this with charm, grace, patience, and unfailing humility. He has listened carefully, built relationships with village leaders based on trust and respect, and involved people in shaping their own future. He has taken the time to learn the local culture — courtesy, hospitality, respect for elders — and to understand and appreciate the role Islam plays in people's daily lives. No wonder the U.S. military has recruited Greg as a consultant on how to fashion better relationships with tribal leaders and village elders. They have a lot to learn from him. We all do.

Tashakor, Greg jan, for all you do.

Khaled Hosseini

www.khaledhosseinifoundation.org
Author of the international best sellers
The Kite Runner and *A Thousand Splendid Suns*

INTRODUCTION

*Every leaf of the tree becomes a page of
the Book
Once the heart is opened and it has learnt
to read*
— SAADI OF SHIRAZ

Nasreen at home in Zuudkhan village, Pakistan PHOTO: © 2009
TERU KUWAYAMA

In September of 2008, a woman with piercing green eyes named Nasreen Baig embarked on an arduous journey from her home in the tiny Pakistani village of Zuudkhan south along the Indus River and down the precipitous Karakoram Highway to the bustling city of Rawalpindi. The three-day trip — first on foot, then on horseback, and later by jeep and bus — took Nasreen, her husband, and their three small children from the sparsely populated Charpurson Valley, in the extreme northern part of Pakistan, directly into the heart of the Punjab, home to more than eighty-five million people. With the exception of a few farming tools, most of their worldly possessions, including a Koran, were crammed into a black suitcase that was cinched together with baling twine. They also carried a bulging burlap sack whose contents — every stitch of spare clothing they weren't wearing on their backs — were as jumbled and mixed up as the pieces of Nasreen's own story.

In 1984, at the age of five, Nasreen started attending one of the first coeducational schools to open up in the north of Pakistan, a region where women were traditionally denied the opportunity to learn reading and writing. Excelling at her classes, she distinguished herself as one of the smartest students in the school until 1992, when her mother unexpectedly died of pneumonia and Nasreen was forced to abandon her studies in order to care for her blind father, Sultan Mehmood, and her four siblings. Eventually her father remarried, and Nasreen's new stepmother, a woman who believed that girls had no business pursuing education, would taunt Nasreen late at night when she tried to continue her studies by the light of a kerosene lantern. "Women should work instead of reading books," her stepmother would rail. "Books will poison your mind and you will become a worthless wife and mother!"

Nasreen didn't see it that way. During her school years, she had acquired a rather bold dream for someone with resources as limited as hers: She had resolved that one day she would become a maternal health-care provider — a profession she had first been exposed to when roving government health-care teams would make their annual rounds through the local villages. She vividly remembers the joy with which she anticipated immunization shots, just so she could interact with the workers in their white cloaks. "My favorite smell was the antiseptic they would use," she says. "Also, I envied how they would write down all the babies' names, heights and weights, and immunization details in tidy rows in a spiral notebook."

Fueled by her dream, Nasreen studied relentlessly, despite her stepmother's harassment. "After tending to my brothers and sisters and doing all the household work," she recalls, "I would wait till everyone was asleep, and then late at night I would read." She persisted in this manner until 1995 when, at the age of fifteen, she received her metric diploma — the equivalent of a high-school degree — becoming one of the first of a handful of women from northern Pakistan's Hunza region ever to do so. As the brightest student and one of the first female graduates for miles around, she was now poised to make good on her ambition.

In 1999, Nasreen was offered an annual scholarship of $1,200 by our nonprofit Central Asia Institute, a stipend that would pay her tuition, room, and board for a two-year course of study and enable her to obtain her rural medical assistant degree. With these qualifications, Nasreen could then carry her skills north over a treacherous 16,335-foot pass into the Wakhan Corridor — a remote portion of Afghanistan just a few miles north of Zuudkhan where Nasreen's ancestors originally came from and where more women die each year during childbirth than anywhere else on earth.

By this point, however, Nasreen had been betrothed to a handsome but lazy young man from a nearby village, and her mother-in-law, Bibi Nissa, feared that Nasreen's scholarship would rob her household of the new daughter-in-law's labor. Even though there were no other qualified girls in the Charpurson Valley to replace Nasreen as a scholarship candidate, Zuudkhan's *tanzeem* — the council of elders who decide all matters of local importance — upheld Bibi Nissa's objections and forbade Nasreen from accepting her stipend, thereby consigning her to a life of near slavery that remains the destiny of so many promising young women in the remote villages of Pakistan and Afghanistan.

During the ten years that followed this decision, Nasreen toiled twelve- to sixteen-hour days tending goats and sheep in the mountains, tilling her family's potato fields, hauling water in metal jerricans, and gathering up eighty-pound bags of firewood and moist patties of yak dung — Zuudkhan's two primary sources of heating fuel during the six-month-long winters. During this time she also gave birth to three babies and suffered two miscarriages, all without the attendance of a maternal health-care worker.

Despite the drudgery and the frustration, Nasreen patiently waited out her decade of servitude. What's more, during her brief moments of respite, she kept her health-care dream alive by seeking out and caring for the sick, the elderly, and the dying within her community. "The lamp in my life refused to be snuffed out," she says. "God never let the kerosene of hope run dry."

Then, in the summer of 2007, the leadership of Zuudkhan's *tanzeem* changed and the elders decided to set aside their opposition. Nasreen spent a year in the town of Gilgit attending a preparatory school to build back her academic skills after the long hiatus. Finally, in the summer of 2008, with her scholarship in hand, Nasreen was free to travel to Rawalpindi to resume her studies.

Today, Nasreen is a year away from completing her medical training program, but she has decided to continue with her schooling in order to complete a full OB-GYN nursing degree. Sometime in 2012, she hopes to move her family to the Wakhan and begin providing the kind of medical care that this region, one of the most isolated and forbidding places on earth, so desperately needs. As for her "lost years," Nasreen harbors no bitterness whatsoever, mainly because she is convinced that her experiences imparted some essential insights.

"Allah taught me the lesson of patience while also giving me the tools to truly understand what it means to live in poverty," she says. "I do not regret the wait."

During the exact same time that Nasreen and her family were making their way down the Karakoram Highway toward Rawalpindi, I was paying a visit of my own to a small town in the heart of the Rocky Mountains. This was no different from any of the other 120-odd trips I make each year to cities across the United States and abroad in order to promote educational opportunities for women like Nasreen throughout Pakistan and Afghanistan. By the rather warped standards of my own schedule, September 18, 2008, was a fairly ordinary day. During the preceding week, I had given seventeen speeches at schools, churches, and libraries in nine other cities; and at three o'clock the following morning, I was slated to board a private plane that would take me from Durango to my next appearance, a children's peace rally in Rockford, Illinois. This would be followed by another eighteen lectures in eight more cities before returning to Pakistan on October 6. Somewhere in the middle of this, I was also hoping desperately for a one-day reprieve with my family.

In many other respects, however, September 18 was anything but ordinary. The previous weekend the federal government had permitted the investment firm Lehman Brothers to go bankrupt before attempting an $85 billion–dollar rescue of the insurance giant AIG. By the time the stock market had closed that afternoon, the Dow Jones was in free fall and the entire U.S. financial system seemed to be hovering on the brink of collapse. In short, I could not possibly have selected a worse time to stand in front of a group of Americans and ask them to pull out their checkbooks.

Fortunately, perhaps, my schedule allowed no time to contemplate the absurdity of this. It was a few minutes before 7:00 P.M. when, having already completed six back-to-back lectures, I dashed across the campus of Fort Lewis College to the gym, where more than four thousand people — almost a third of the town — had formed an impossibly long line. The fire marshal would eventually be forced to bar the door and prevent the final three hundred of these folks from entering the building. (Someone later told me that Durango hadn't seen a crowd this size since Willie Nelson last came to town.)

Although the talks I give in these kinds of settings tend to vary according to the composition of my audience, I always begin with the same words: *As-Salaam Alaaikum* — the Islamic invocation that means "May peace be upon you." And regardless of where I wind up steering the discussion, the heart of my presentation always includes the story of a promise.

This story begins in Pakistan in 1993, the year I attempted to climb K2, the world's second-highest mountain, only to be forced to turn back two thousand feet shy of the summit. After making my way back to K2 base camp, I then got lost while trekking down the thirty-nine-mile Baltoro Glacier and wound up staggering into a little village called Korphe (pronounced "KOR-fay"), a place so destitute that one in every three children perished before the age of one. It was in Korphe that I was provided with shelter, food, tea, and a bed. And it was in Korphe one afternoon during my recuperation that

I stumbled across eighty-two children sitting outside writing their lessons with sticks in the dirt, with no teacher in sight. One of those young students was a girl named Chocho, and somehow she got me to promise the community that I would someday return and build them a school.

The fulfillment of that promise involves a tale that recounts my fumbling efforts in Berkeley, where I worked as a nurse, to sell my car, my climbing gear, and all of my books in order to raise the necessary money — and the subsequent chain of events through which a lost mountaineer eventually came to discover his life's calling by fostering education and literacy in the impoverished Muslim villages of the western Himalayas.

A few years ago, I put these events together into a book called *Three Cups of Tea,* and as those who have read all 338 pages can attest, it's a rather long and unusual story. It is also a story that has always struck me as the chronicle of an ordinary man who inadvertently bumbled into an extraordinary place.

When it really comes down to it, I am nothing more than a fellow who took a wrong turn in the mountains and never quite managed to find his way home. My initial vision, if you could call it that, involved helping a village knock together a

2,218-square-foot schoolhouse without any plumbing or electricity in the middle of a barley field at 10,400 feet. In a world filled with bold dreamers and big ideas, it's hard to imagine a goal more humble than this. And it is the diminutive stature of this beginning that may help to explain why I now live my days beset by an almost continuous sense of wonderment and confusion.

Although I have, by my staff's estimate, completed a total of 680 appearances in more than 270 cities and towns from Miami and Los Angeles to Anchorage and Shreveport over the last three years, each time I travel somewhere new, I am still shocked by the sheer number of people who flock to hear this tale. Last summer in Boston, when the organizers of a talk I was giving at Northeastern University realized how many people wanted to learn about our schools in Pakistan and Afghanistan, they booked me into a hockey stadium and filled the place with 5,600 people. A week later at a basketball arena in Murfreesboro, Tennessee, 9,500 folks showed up and my speech had to be broadcast on a Jumbotron.

That's a big change for someone who once considered himself lucky to get the attention of half a dozen bored shoppers at a Patagonia or REI outlet, and perhaps the only thing that amazes me more than the size of these audiences is their dedication and interest. It is not unusual for people to drive six or even twelve hours to hear these presentations, then stand in line for another two hours simply to get their books autographed. But perhaps the most noteworthy testament to their commitment is the sort of thing that took place on that September night in Durango.

On the very same evening that Ben Bernanke, the chairman of the Federal Reserve, was informing members of the House Financial Services Committee that the entire global economy was days away from a complete meltdown, the citizens of Durango, population 16,007, presented the Central Asia Institute with checks totaling nearly $125,000. A single contribution of $50,000 was given by George Boedecker, the founder of the shoe manufacturer Crocs. But the rest of the money came from the sort of individuals who will never know what it means to own a brand or run a corporation. Ranchers, housewives, and salesclerks. Mechanics, teachers, and plumbers. Secretaries, dental hygienists, students, and retirees. People who embody the virtues, as well as the limitations, of a life that is fashioned from humble materials. People, in other words, as ordinary and as unremarkable as me and you.

In my view, that is amazing enough all by itself, but then consider this.

Very few of the people in Durango that night had ever been to Pakistan or Afghanistan. No more than a handful could have been Muslim. And it was doubtful that a single one would ever see, with his own eyes, the schools, books, pencils, and teacher salaries that his money would pay for. Still, they opened their hearts and gave. There, on the threshold of the greatest economic collapse since the Great Depression, in the midst of an era when so many of our leaders have encouraged us to subordinate our noblest impulses to our basest fears, a small community in Colorado responded in exactly the same way as every other city and town to which I have traveled in America since this whole saga got started.

"When you hand this money over to the folks over there on the other side of the world," said one local businessman, who had tears in his eyes as he spoke, "just tell them that it comes from a little town in the mountains of Colorado so that their daughters can go to school."

Here, then, is the source of my wonder and confusion. Why do so many Americans seem to care so deeply about people who live in a place that is so far away? Despite everything that has happened, how can our anger and our fear be transcended so consistently by our decency? And what is it about the promise of educating children — especially girls — that so often, and with such fervor, seems to evoke what is best in all of us?

In addition to being a profoundly bewildered man, I am an incorrigible introvert. I am awkward, soft-spoken, ineloquent, and intensely shy. I do not enjoy speaking in public, posing for photographs, or asking other people for money. I dream of privacy, I revere silence, and I loathe any action that involves drawing attention to myself. (Even creating these pages was painful: It took a supreme effort on the part of both my wife, Tara, and my editor, Paul Slovak, to force me to agree to write it in the first person — an approach that is emphatically *not* my cup of tea.) In the Christmas pageant of life, the characters I admire most — and the only roles for which I would ever consider auditioning — are the ox and the donkey.

Given these facts, the duties of speaking, promoting, and fund-raising into which I have been thrust during the last several years have often made me feel like a man caught in the act of conducting an illicit affair with the dark side of his own personality. For politicians and celebrities, a lifestyle that entails an endless schmoozefest of back slapping and elbow rubbing seems to come as instinctively (and as necessarily) as breathing. I, on the other hand, find this kind of thing extremely discomforting — partly because it sits so directly at odds with my deepest instincts about personal decorum, and partly because it so often leaves me wrestling with a sense of shame. All of which may help to explain why the unexpected and runaway success of *Three Cups of Tea* seems, at least in my view, to be charged with such a wicked irony.

As I write this in the summer of 2009, the book is currently logging its 130th week on the *New York Times* best-seller list for trade paperback nonfiction, has sold more than three million copies, and is being published in three dozen countries. As you might imagine, this has produced the kind of publicity and attention that I find intolerable. But it has also opened the door to some extraordinary opportunities.

Hard currency goes a long way in the impoverished hinterlands of the western Himalayas, where $20 is enough to educate a first grader for an entire year, $340 can send a girl to four years of high school on a full-ride scholarship, and $50,000 is sufficient to build and outfit an eight-room schoolhouse and endow the teachers' salaries for the first five years. During the four years since *Three Cups of Tea* was first published, our contributors have not only financed the construction of scores of new school buildings but have also funded scholarships, teacher-training programs, and women's vocational centers in remote villages extending from the glacier-carved valleys of the Karakoram to the wind-blasted reaches north of the Hindu Kush. Every bit as important as these projects, however, is the awareness that our donors have helped to raise about the vital importance of girls' education.

Studies from the World Bank indicate that just *one* year of primary school can result in an income bump of 10 percent to 20 percent for women later in life. According to Yale economist Paul T. Schultz, an extra year of secondary school may raise that same girl's lifetime wages by an additional 15 to 25 percent. And the effects don't end there. A number of studies indicate that in communities where a majority of the girls are educated through the fifth grade, infant mortality drops significantly after a single generation. At the same time — and somewhat paradoxically — basic education for girls correlates perfectly with lower, more sustainable population growth. In communities where girls have received more education, they marry later and have fewer children than their illiterate counterparts.

These premises, which I also encountered in the work of Nobel Prize–winning economist Amartya Sen, are now accepted by many development experts around the world. (The definitive short book on the general subject is *What Works in Girls' Education: Evidence and Policies from the Developing World,* by Barbara Herz and Gene B. Sperling.) Simply put, young women are the single biggest potential agents of change in the developing world — a phenomenon that is sometimes referred to as the Girl Effect and that echoes an African proverb I often heard during my childhood years in Tanzania: "If you teach a boy, you educate an individual; but if you teach a girl, you educate a community." No other factor even comes close to matching the cascade of positive changes triggered by teaching a single girl how to read and write. In military parlance, girls' education is a "force multiplier" — and in impoverished Muslim societies, the ripple effects of female literacy can be profound.

Take the issue that many in the West

would consider to be the most pressing of all. "Jihad" is an Arabic word referring to a "struggle" that is undertaken as a means of perfecting oneself, improving society, or defeating the perceived enemies of Islam. In Muslim societies, a person who has been manipulated into believing in extremist violence or terrorism often seeks the permission of his mother before he may join a militant jihad — and educated women, as a rule, tend to withhold their blessing for such things. Following 9/11, for example, the Taliban's forces suffered from significantly increased desertions; as a countermeasure, they began targeting their recruitment efforts on regions where female literacy was especially low.

Education, of course, offers no guarantee that a mother will refuse to endorse violent jihad, but it certainly helps to stack the odds against the men — and, yes, they are invariably men — who promote the lie that killing innocent people is in keeping with the teachings of the Koran. Although I am not an authority on the Koran, religious scholars have repeatedly emphasized to me during the last sixteen years that murder and suicide are two of the most unforgivable sins in Islam.

It is important to be clear about the fact that the aim of the Central Asia Institute is not indoctrination. We have no agenda other than assisting rural women with their two most frequent requests: "We don't want our babies to die, and we want our children to go to school." And in the process of addressing those wishes, it is certainly not our aim to teach the children of Pakistan and Afghanistan to think or to act like Americans. We simply want them to have the chance to attend schools that offer a balanced, nonextremist education. In this respect, we're also extremely sensitive to the difference between literacy and ideology. It is our belief that the first helps to thwart intolerance, challenge dogma, and reinforce our common humanity. The second does the opposite.

At the moment, female literacy in rural Afghanistan continues to languish in the single digits. In rural Pakistan, the figures are a little higher, but not by much. The demand for schools, teachers, books, desks, notebooks, uniforms, chalkboards, paper, and pencils in these two Islamic nations is immense, and the benefits of American investment in this "intellectual infrastructure" are indisputably clear. Nothing that has happened since my unsuccessful attempt to climb K2 — including 9/11 — has changed my conviction that promoting female literacy represents the best way forward for Pakistan and for Afghanistan.

Education is one of the many basic values that Americans of all faiths share with Muslim people everywhere.

When journalists write about the achievements of the Central Asia Institute, they often tend to trot out the same sets of figures. They are fond of mentioning that during the sixteen years since my failure as a K2 climber, I have completed thirty-nine trips to Pakistan and Afghanistan, where, without using a dollar of money from the U.S. government, the Central Asia Institute has established 131 schools that currently serve more than 58,000 students, most of them girls. These articles also claim that the response to my "message" cuts across the lines that traditionally divide politics, religion, and class in the United States. They point out that the fans of *Three Cups of Tea* include not only Bill Clinton, Laura and Barbara Bush, John Kerry, and Colin Powell, but also prominent military leaders such as CENTCOM commander General David Petraeus, chairman of the Joint Chiefs of Staff Admiral Mike Mullen, and SOCOM (Special Forces) commander Admiral Eric Olson. To my honor, *Three Cups of Tea* is now required reading for all officers enrolled in counterinsurgency courses at the Pentagon.

In some ways, these tidbits of information may be useful — if nothing else, they
convey a general sense of what we've been
up to and what others think of our work.
On a personal level, however, this approach
tends to miss the point. If there is a metric
by which I measure the achievements of the
Central Asia Institute, it is not the amount
of donations we receive each year, or the
number of people who have read *Three Cups
of Tea,* or even the number of schools we
have built. In fact, it really has nothing to
do with math and everything to do with the
girls whose lives have been changed through
education. In the end, the thing I care most
about — the flame that burns at the center
of my work, the heat around which I cup my
hands — are their stories.

And by God's grace, what marvelous stories these women can tell.

Take the case of Jahan Ali, whose grandfather, Haji Ali, was Korphe's *nurmadhar*
(village chief) and who became my most
important mentor. On the first day I met
Jahan in September of 1993, she extracted a
promise from me that if she graduated, we
would send her off to a maternal health-care
program — an IOU that she triumphantly
collected on nine years later. After finishing

grad school in Korphe, she went on to enroll in advanced studies in public policy administration. Meanwhile, back home, Jahan's father has been trying to marry her off — she is currently twenty-three years old, and her bride-price, thanks to her education, has now shot from five to fifty adult rams. Jahan, however, declares that she first intends to become a community leader and a member of Pakistan's parliament. "I am not going to get married until I achieve my goal," she recently told me. "*Inshallah* (God willing), someday I will become a super-lady."

Then there is the story of Shakila Khan, who graduated with the first class at our school in Hushe, a village in a valley to the south of Korphe that sits in the shadow of Masherbrum, one of the highest mountains on earth. Currently in her third year at Fatima Memorial Hospital in Lahore and scoring in the nineties, Shakila is slated to become the first locally educated female physician ever to emerge from Baltistan's population of 300,000 people. She is currently twenty-two years old and intends to return to the Hushe Valley to work among her people. "My main two goals," she says, "are that I do not want women to die in childbirth or babies to die in their first year."

Finally, consider Aziza Hussain, who grew

up in the Hunza Valley, not far from the point where the Karhuram Highway crosses into China. After graduating from Gulmit Federal Government Girls' High School in 1997 and completing a two-year maternal health-care program on a CAI scholarship, Aziza, too, insisted on returning home to ply her skills within her own community — a place where as many as twenty women perished each year during childbirth. Since Aziza came back in 2000, not a single woman in the area has died giving birth.

Thirteen years after we completed our first school in Korphe, the maiden generation of Central Asia Institute women have graduated and are preparing to launch their careers. These women are now making "first ascents" far more dramatic and impressive than the achievements of western climbers, such as myself, who have been coming into these mountains ever since Aleister Crowley, the British poet, spy, and yogic devotee, made the first attempt to climb K2 in 1902.

Already, these daughters have climbed so much higher than we mountaineers ever dared to dream.

Serious and worthy efforts to promote schooling for girls are currently taking place all over the world, from Guatemala and Egypt to Bangladesh and Uganda. The unusual twist that the Central Asia Institute applies to this enterprise, however, is encapsulated in the title of *Three Cups of Tea,* which refers to a Balti saying that Haji Ali invoked during one of my first visits to his village. "The first cup of tea you share with us, you are a stranger," he intoned. "The second cup, you are a friend. But with the third cup, you become family — and for our families we are willing to do anything, even die."

Of the many lessons that that old man imparted to me, this was perhaps the greatest. It underscores the paramount importance of taking the time to build relationships, while simultaneously affirming the basic truth that in order to get things done in this part of the world, it is essential to listen with humility to what others have to say. The solution to every problem, Haji Ali firmly believed, begins with drinking tea. And so it has proven.

After my first encounter with Haji Ali in 1993, I returned to the United States, raised twelve thousand dollars, and then went back a year later to Pakistan, where I purchased a massive load of cement, lumber, and other supplies in the city of Rawalpindi. This material was piled onto a Bedford truck and ferried up the Karakoram Highway to the town of Skardu, a trip that took three days. There it was transferred to jeeps and driven to the end of the road, eighteen miles from Korphe — where I arrived with the expectation of being greeted like a hero. Instead, I was informed (after drinking several cups of tea with Haji Ali) that before we could start construction on the school, we had to build a bridge. The reason? It would be impossible to ferry the construction materials over the roaring Braldu inside the only device spanning the river, a rickety wooden basket suspended beneath a 350-foot cable.

Perhaps I should have thought of this earlier; in any case, the unexpected turn of events seemed like a disaster. It forced me to retreat back to the United States, where I had to convince my main benefactor, Dr. Jean Hoerni, to contribute even *more* money, which was then used to purchase even *more* construction materials and transport these supplies to the edge of the Braldu, where the residents of Korphe built a 282-foot-long suspension bridge over the river. In the end, the whole exercise set the project back nearly two years.

At the time, I found this detour and its delays utterly maddening. Only years later did I begin to appreciate the enormous symbolic significance of the fact that before building a school, it was imperative to build a bridge. The school, of course, would house all of the hopes that are raised by the promise of education. But the bridge represented something more elemental: the relationships upon which those hopes would be sustained over time — and without which any promise would amount to little more than empty words.

Korphe's schoolhouse was finished in December 1996, and since then each and every school we have built has been preceded by a bridge. Not necessarily a physical structure, but a span of emotional links that are forged over many years and many shared cups of tea.

This philosophy means that some of our projects can grind along at a pace that mirrors the ponderous movement of the Karakoram glaciers. For example, in Chunda, a conservative rural village in Baltistan, it took *eight years* for us to convince the local mullah, an immensely cautious and pious man, to permit a single girl to attend school. Today, however, more than three hundred girls study in Chunda — and we take great pride in the fact that they do so with the full support of the very same mullah who once stood in their way. His change of heart affirms the notion that good relationships often demand titanic patience.

Like Nasreen Baig, the green-eyed nurse from the Charpurson, we do not regret the wait. As any wise village elder will tell you, anything truly important is worth doing very, *very* slowly.

The book that you are holding in your hands picks up where *Three Cups of Tea* left off in 2003 and is partly a chronicle of how that process has continued to unfold in Pakistan during the last several years. Mostly, however, this new book traces our efforts to take our work into a whole new region, the remote northeastern corner of Afghanistan. It is a place that has proved even more challenging than Pakistan, and the saga of what my staff sometimes calls our "Afghan adventure" is framed loosely in the context of a single school.

If *Three Cups of Tea* lays out the narrative of our first school — the seed with which we started our planting — then this is the tale of the most remote of all our projects, the flower in the farthest corner of the garden. No project has ever taken us so long or required such complex logistics as the little school we built next to the old Kirghiz burial grounds in the heart of the Afghan Pamir's

Bam-I-Dunya, the "Rooftop of the World." And next to Korphe itself, no school is closer to my heart, because, in ways both large and small, it was the most miraculous. It arose out of a promise made in 1999 during an unlikely meeting that seemed lifted from the pages of a novel set in the thirteenth century, when the horsemen of Genghis Khan roamed the steppes of central Asia. And it drew us into the land of the Afghans, the only place that has ever threatened to usurp the affection and the love I harbor for Pakistan.

Part of what has made this school such a surprise is that so many other urgent projects were demanding our attention during the ten years it took to make good on our promise. The fact that we refused to let it go, even amid an earthquake in Kashmir in 2005 and other challenges that are recounted in the pages that follow, is a testament less to me than to the vision and the persistence of the Central Asia Institute's staff, and in particular to a group of twelve men whom I affectionately call the Dirty Dozen. If there are any heroes here, it is they; and for the most part this book is their story, because without these men, none of it would have happened. If the daughters who flock to our schools represent the fire we've lit, then these men are the fuel that sustains the flames. They have guided, pushed, and inspired me in more ways than I can recount, and their commitment and sacrifices run so deep that whatever we achieve will ultimately belong not to me but to them. Without their example and their resourcefulness, I would still be nothing more than a dirtbag mountaineer subsisting on ramen noodles and living in the back of his car.

As you'll see, the story of the little gem of a school that we built in the most remote corner of central Asia is a roundabout tale — a thread that like the twisting roads we ply in our battered Land Cruiser through the passes of the Karakoram and the Hindu Kush can sometimes get lost amid the unexpected detours and the landslide of complications that cascade down upon anyone who ventures into that harsh and wondrous part of the world. But these digressions and dead ends may also provide something that readers of *Three Cups of Tea* have been requesting from me for years. What they've wanted, more than anything else, is a window into the day-to-day mechanics and rhythms of the Central Asia Institute. A sense of what it feels like to lay the physical and emotional foundation for girls' education, book by book and brick by brick, in the middle of Taliban country. If nothing else, this new work should fulfill that request.

I should also note that the first part of this story will cover some ground that may already be familiar to readers of *Three Cups of Tea*. I thought this was necessary and important because several of these early events began to shape themselves into a meaningful pattern only over time. Back when they took place, I did not understand the full significance of these experiences and lessons they imparted, nor did I realize where they fit into the larger story that it is my privilege to tell here.

In short, it was only after having moved forward a considerable distance that I was fully able to comprehend where we had been — a phenomenon that would not have surprised Haji Ali, who, to my sadness, passed away in 2001. Haji Ali never learned to read or write, and over the course of seven decades he left his home village only once, to perform a pilgrimage to Mecca. Nevertheless, he understood that hope resides in the future, while perspective and wisdom are almost always found by looking to the past.

Sometimes, it seems like everything I've

ever learned traces back to that irascible old man I first met in the barley fields of Korphe.

GREG MORTENSON
Baharak, Afghanistan
August 2009

PART I
THE PROMISE

PROLOGUE

The education and empowerment of women throughout the world cannot fail to result in a more caring, tolerant, just and peaceful life for all.
— AUNG SAN SUU KYI

Greg Mortenson in the Wakhan PHOTO: © 2009 TERU KUWAYAMA

The Irshad Pass is one of three great gaps leading north through the Hindu Kush into the most forgotten corner of Afghanistan. Along the crest of this pass the ground is free of snow for only four months each year, and the air is so thin that the traders who employ this route have been known to slice open the nostrils of their donkeys to help them breathe. Beyond the Pakistani high point, the track makes a long, talus-littered descent, at the bottom of which is a massive ravine that forces the trail to perform a sharp dogleg. This means that anyone waiting at the southern entrance to the Irshad cannot see who is coming through the pass until the very last minute — and that is how I came to miss the moment when the squadron of Kirghiz horsemen made their entrance into Pakistan in October of 1999.

It was the keen-eyed Sarfraz Khan — the hunter of the ibex, the ex-commando with the crippled hand — who spotted them first, just as they rounded the corner, from half a mile away. The second he caught sight of them, he leaped up from the blanket on which we were sitting, dashed over to our jeep, flung open the door, and started laying his fist into the horn.

"They are coming, they are coming!" he clamored in Wakhi, unable to contain his excitement. *"Wazdey, Wazdey!* Well done!"

I was about to take another swallow of the *nemek choi* (salt tea) that we had been sipping all morning to ward off the wind and the sleet, but my hand halted when the cup was halfway to my lips, then returned the cup to the ground and gently placed it there while I watched the horsemen advance.

It was not a spectacle one could witness in an offhand manner.

There were fourteen riders, coming fast through a scrim of cold rain, and even from the distance of nearly a thousand yards, the timeworn music of their cavalry — the hollow clomping of the hoofbeats and the metallic clanking of steel in the horses' mouths — cleaved the alpine air. We could hear, too, the muffled creak of wet leather under strain, and a faint patter as thick clods of dirt thrown up by the horses' hooves arced above the riders' heads and rained onto the

64

ground behind them.

The man in the lead was clad in a weather-beaten duster, black leather boots that rose to his knees, and corduroy pants that were dark and shiny with the smear of mutton grease. A battered British Lee Enfield rifle flopped along his back, his waist was belted with a strap of leather so wide that it spanned his belly, and on his head he wore a Soviet-era pile cap whose earflaps galloped with the movement of his horse. The men who followed him carried AK-47s and an abundance of other weapons, and their cartridge belts were slung heavily across their shoulders and chests. Their horses, like his, were short legged and shaggy and iridescent with sweat.

They thundered toward us in a headlong rush until, at the last possible second, they pulled to an abrupt halt and leaped in unison from their saddles with a catlike grace that seemed both cavalier and precise. It was the kind of careless perfection that only men who have spent their entire lives on horseback can achieve.

The leader, I could see now, was a young man with an ill-trimmed mustache and a flat, coppery, wind-burnished face. He was thin and ragged and hardened, and this combination of features made him seem to step directly from a stream of time that flowed unbroken from the forty or fifty generations of his nomadic forbears, who were among the greatest horsemen the world has ever known. Standing there in the mud, he reached into his coat pocket, removed a wad of moist green chewing tobacco, and greeted us with the customary *As-Salaam Alaaikum*. Then he remarked, softly and with great courtesy, that he and his men had been riding for six days without stopping.

They had been dispatched, it turned out, as emissaries from *Commandhan* Abdul Rashid Khan, the leader of the last group of Kirghiz left in the High Pamir. In the impoverished land from which these men had ridden, conditions were now so harsh that each winter their families and their herds of camels, sheep, and yaks seesawed on the threshold of starvation. Yet of all the things that Abdul Rashid's people lacked, what he desired most was the chance for their children to learn to read and write — and therein lay the errand that had drawn this horseman and his retinue over the Irshad Pass.

For the past several years, the horseman explained, strange stories had been filtering into the High Pamir from the southern side the Hindu Kush, tales of a mysterious American mountain climber who was said to be setting up schools in the most remote valleys of northern Pakistan, the places the government didn't seem to care about and where the foreign NGOs refused to venture. There were rumors, too, that in addition to educating the boys, the institutions this man was raising up would also open their doors to any girl who yearned for literacy.

When word had reached Abdul Rashid Khan that the American school builder was scheduled to pay a visit to the Charpurson Valley, he had sent out a platoon of his strongest riders and his swiftest horses to find this man and ask if he would consider coming into Afghanistan to build schools for the sons and the daughters of the Kirghiz.

Few things happen quickly in the hinterlands of the western Himalayas, but there was a special urgency to this man's mission. The first storm of the winter of 1999 was already descending upon the Hindu Kush, and if these horsemen failed to return before the snows blocked the crest of the Irshad, they risked being cut off from their homes and families until the following spring. Preferably right now, but no later than the following morning, they would need to race north over the pass with my answer.

"*Waalaikum-Salaam* (May peace be with you also)," I replied. "I understand that time is short, but first let us go to the home of my friend Sarfraz Khan so that you and your men can eat and take some rest," I told the leader of the horsemen. "Then later, we will talk of Abdul Rashid Khan's request, and we will discuss if it is possible to make a school."

Chapter 1
The People at the End of the Road

I don't know what your destiny will be, but one thing I know: the only ones among you who will be really happy are those who will have sought and found how to serve.
— Albert Schweitzer

Grand Trunk Highway near Jalalabad, Afghanistan. Photo: © 2005 Teru Kuwayama

Whenever I head for the airport to catch a flight to Pakistan or Afghanistan, my luggage usually includes a small plastic briefcase emblazoned with a green and white bumper sticker that reads THE LAST BEST PLACE. Those words were first put together as the title to an anthology of Montana-based writings that William Kittredge and Annick Smith edited back in 1988. Since then, "The Last Best Place" has become the unofficial motto for the state in which I have spent the last fourteen years living with my wife, Tara, our two children, Amira and Khyber, and our Tibetan terrier, Tashi. The slogan neatly sums up the stirring landscapes and the vast sense of openness that draw so many Americans to Montana, and the words are now as synonymous with my adopted home's identity as the silhouette of the mountains on our license plates.

For me, though, Kittredge's catchphrase

carries a radically different meaning.

If you look at the map of the schools that the Central Asia Institute has built since 1995, you will see that nearly every one of our projects is in a location that lacks an educational infrastructure because of geographical isolation, severe poverty, religious extremism, or war. These are areas that few people from the outside world even know about, the regions where almost nobody else goes. They are the places where we begin.

This approach is markedly different from the way development normally works. Most NGOs, for all sorts of sound and well-justified reasons, prefer to establish a base of operations in a region that enjoys favorable access to resources and communications, and only then will these organizations gradually expand into the harder areas. It's a sensible way to proceed. The problem, however, is that if you work in a way that is incremental and controlled, it can sometimes take a lifetime to get to the people who need your help the most. What is far more difficult — and sometimes more dangerous — is to start at the *end* of the road and work your way back. And for better or worse, that's exactly what we do.

The other thing that distinguishes us from some other development groups is that our aim is not to saturate a region with our presence by launching hundreds of projects. We simply want to plant a handful of schools in the hardest places of all, empower the communities in these areas to sustain those projects, and then step back in the hope that the government and other NGOs will start moving toward these points from the areas that aren't quite so rough, until the gap is eventually bridged. Surprisingly often, that's exactly what happens.

In Baltistan, the rugged and beautiful corner of northeastern Pakistan that lies in the heart of the Karakoram, we spent the second half of the 1990s targeting the villages at the farthest ends of the most remote valleys, places at altitudes of up to eleven thousand feet that are perched along the outer limits of human habitation. We broke ground on more than three dozen sturdy, stone-walled schoolhouses, providing construction materials and teachers on the condition that each village chip in free land and labor — and that they agree to increase female enrollment until the girls reached parity with the boys. The first school we established, in Korphe, is in the last human settlement in the Braldu Valley before you reach the Baltoro Glacier, which leads to K2. Our school in Hushe lies at the end of a valley that culminates at the base of Masherbrum, one of the most stunning of the world's great seven-thousand-meter peaks.

In similar fashion, we have also spearheaded projects in areas that are plagued by armed conflict and religious extremism. In 1999, at the request of the Pakistani military, we launched two projects in the Gultori region, where the armies of India and Pakistan were locked in fierce fighting along the contested border of Kashmir. The schools we put in were tucked into the slopes of mountains and featured pitched metal roofs capable of deflecting fallout from the Indian army's artillery shells. More recently, in 2008, we have helped communities in eastern Afghanistan's Kunar Province in building two girls' schools in the center of the volatile border region between Pakistan and Afghanistan that shelters many members of the Taliban. The Pathan tribal leaders who asked for these schools approached us with their initial request for assistance through the commander of an American military base that is located in the same area.

This "last place first" philosophy of ours is unconventional, and it occasionally provokes criticism; but sometimes there is simply no other alternative. If an organization like the CAI doesn't leapfrog directly into such places, another generation or two of girls will have lost the opportunity to attain literacy. In addition to these practical considerations, however, there's another reason why we do things this way — one that has little to do with pragmatism.

The good people who inhabit the frontiers of civilization do not, as a rule, tend to be the world's most sophisticated or cosmopolitan human beings. Often, they aren't especially well educated or refined, nor all that conversant with cutting-edge trends in areas like, say, fashion and current events. Sometimes, they're not even all that friendly. But the folks who live at the end of the road are among the most resilient and the most resourceful human beings you will ever meet. They possess a combination of courage, tenacity, hospitality, and grace that leaves me in awe.

What I have also discovered over the years is that with just a little bit of help, such people are capable of pulling off astonishing things — and in doing so, they sometimes establish a benchmark for the rest of us. When ordinary human beings perform extraordinary acts of generosity, endurance, or compassion, we are all made richer by their example. Like the rivers that flow out of the Karakoram and the Hindu Kush, the inspiration they generate washes down to the rest of us. It waters everyone's fields.

So for me, that THE LAST BEST PLACE sticker on my briefcase doesn't represent a slogan or a marketing campaign to promote the wonders of my home. Instead, those words affirm my belief that the people who live in the last places — the people who are most neglected and least valued by the larger world — often represent the best of who we are and the finest standard of what we are meant to become. This is the power that last places hold over me, and why I have found it impossible to resist their pull.

Back in 1993, when this whole school-building business first got started, the little village of Korphe struck me as the apogee of remoteness, the supreme expression of what it means to live in the very last place at the far end of the road. In the years that followed, it has been my privilege to work in some equally isolated and difficult places that thanks to the people who inhabit them are blessed by the same rough magic as Korphe. But until I met the Kirghiz horsemen who had ridden out of the Wakhan on that October afternoon in 1999, I had never encountered a group of people who came from a place so remote, so austere, that it didn't seem like the end of the road as much as the end of the earth itself.

A place that made even Korphe feel like a suburb of Los Angeles.

The Pashtuns say that when Allah was finished creating the world, he cobbled together all the leftover bits and pieces, and it was from this pile of rubble that he fashioned Afghanistan. The impression of a landscape that has been pieced together from discarded debris is evident in every part of this country, but nowhere is this sense of brokenness more acute than inside the panhandle of northeastern Afghanistan that thrusts between Pakistan and Tajikistan for nearly 120 miles until it touches the border of the People's Republic of China. Some of the loftiest mountain ranges on earth — the Kunlun, the Tien Shan, the Pamirs, the Karakoram, and the Hindu Kush — converge inside or near this region. The highest of their summits soars more than twenty thousand feet, and the inhabitants of the forbidding, desolate, bitterly cold alpine plateaus that stretch beneath those peaks refer to this place as *Bam-I-Dunya,* the "Rooftop of the World."

For more than twenty centuries, the Wakhan Corridor has served as a thoroughfare for traders, diplomats, invading armies, pilgrims, explorers, missionaries, and holy wanderers making their way between central Asia and China. The Corridor not only defined the meeting point between Inner and Outer Tartary — the realms that the Greek geographer Ptolemy called "the Two Scythias" — but also formed one of the most arduous sections of the Silk Road, the four-thousand-mile route by which the civilizations of India, Europe, and the Near East traded and communicated with those of the Far East.

Only a handful of westerners are known to have passed through the Wakhan, starting with Marco Polo, who spent four years making his way through Persia and across central Asia to reach the court of the Chinese emperor, Kublai Khan. While traversing the length of the Wakhan in 1271, the legendary Venetian traveler wrote of ridgelines so high that birds found it impossible to fly over them and a cold so intense that it stifled the heat of his campfires while robbing the flames of their color. Nearly 350 years later, a Jesuit priest named Benedict de Goes was chosen by his order to follow in Polo's footsteps in search of Cathay. Disguised as an Armenian trader, he joined a caravan of merchants and made his way to the Chinese city of Suchow, where he was detained, became ill, and eventually perished. De Goes's death, in the year 1607, roughly coincided with the Silk Road's final eclipse, as the great terrestrial thoroughfare of trade was supplanted by the sea routes that were being pioneered between Europe and the Far East — although a small but persistent trickle of commerce continued to dribble across the Pamir from Chinese Turkistan to Tibet and Chitral, the northernmost outpost of India.

The Wakhan did not reemerge on the world stage until the later part of the nineteenth century, when Great Britain and Russia began tussling for control of central Asia in the imperial contest known as the Great Game. During this period, Russia was expanding its southern borders toward the ancient cities of the Silk Road, while Britain was seeking to explore and protect the passes through the Himalayas and the Hindu Kush that led to India, the richest gem in Britain's imperial crown. An eccentric collection of explorers and military officers played a cat-and-mouse game along the high country of the Hindu Kush and the Pamirs. In 1895, after the two sides were brought to the brink of war, politicians in London and Saint Petersburg established the Wakhan as a buffer zone to ensure that the underbelly of the czars' kingdom would at no point touch the northernmost crest of the Raj.

Twenty-two years later, the creation of the Soviet Union shut down the Wakhan's northern borders, severing most of the remaining north-south commerce. Then, in 1949, Mao Zedong completed the Communist takeover of China and the Corridor's door to the east was slammed shut, permanently halting almost all east-to-west movement. Within a single generation, a place that had once served as the linchpin of the greatest trade route in history and had later come to demarcate the farthest borders of the world's two foremost imperial powers was transformed into the poorest and the most obscure dead-end road on earth.

Today, the residents of the Corridor are consigned to a state of quarantine that is impossible to imagine for anyone who inhabits a world whose borders are defined by e-mail, Twitter, and satellite phones. Implacably isolated and breathtakingly remote, the Wakhan is central Asia's Ultima Thule: a place so distant and so far beyond the margins of the known world that it seems to delineate not only the outer limits of geography but the edge of civilization itself.

The Kirghiz horsemen who rode over the Irshad Pass in the autumn of 1999 were descendants of nomadic tribes from the Tuva region of Russia who had migrated into central Asia in the thirteenth century, during the rise of the Mongol empire — and for the better part of eight centuries, these tribes' lives revolved around seasonal migrations across the mountain ranges separating what are now eastern Afghanistan, western China, and southern Tajikistan. Each year the tribes would rove freely across the grasslands of the High Pamir with their felt yurts and their flocks of goats, yaks, and double-humped Bactrian camels, unmolested by government officials, tax collectors, or security agents. The winters would be spent in the lower valleys of Tajikistan or western China, where they could shelter from the weather and protect their flocks from bears and wolves. In the summer, they would slowly move back into the alpine grasslands, where the only other inhabitants were Marco Polo sheep, ibex, and other wild animals.

Following the Bolshevik Revolution, the Soviet government devoted much of the 1930s to a policy of forcing the nomadic cultures who inhabited the USSR's central Asian republics to abandon their migratory traditions and settle on collective farms. A group of Kirghiz eventually rebelled against this effort and petitioned the king of Afghanistan for sanctuary in the Wakhan.

This protected them from the Soviets, but it reduced their migrations to a series of short shifts between the eastern Wakhan and China's Xinjiang Province. During the 1950s and 1960s, the Chinese Communists restricted these movements even further.

Then in 1978, just prior to the Soviet invasion of Afghanistan, roughly 1,300 Kirghiz led by an imam named Haji Rahman Qul decided to abandon the Pamirs and cross south over the Hindu Kush into Pakistan. They found life in this new home intolerable (the Kirghiz women were forced to follow the rules of purdah, and the heat caused many members of the group to fall ill). After trying unsuccessfully to acquire American visas and move his people to Alaska, Rahman Qul embarked on a new journey in 1982. Referred to as the Last Exodus, this odyssey eventually took his followers to eastern Anatolia, where they were given political asylum by the Turkish government and settled next to a group of resentful Kurds who had been forced out to make room for them. The community they established there continues flourishing to this day.

Meanwhile, a second group of roughly two hundred Kirghiz who refused to participate in the Last Exodus broke away from Rahman Qul and returned to the Wakhan, where they resumed the migratory lifestyle of their forebears. Lost within the immensity of the High Pamirs the descendants of these Kirghiz now struggle to uphold an ancestral lifestyle that represents one of the last great nomadic horse cultures on earth.

As romantic as that may sound, life has been exceptionally difficult for the Wakhan Kirghiz, and their capacity to survive seems to grow more marginal with each passing year. Unable to migrate to the warmer lowlands, they are exposed to the full fury of winters, which can last from September through June, with temperatures plummeting as low as negative twenty degrees. Despite the fact that the entire community often teeters on the threshold of starvation, especially during the early spring, they are cut off from even the most basic government services. As late as 1999, there was not a single school, hospital, dispensary, police station, bazaar, veterinary facility, post office, or doctor's clinic in the eastern sector of the Wakhan. Even by the extreme standards of Afghanistan, a country where 68 percent of the population has never known peace, the average life expectancy is forty-four years, and the maternal mortality rate is exceeded only by that of Liberia, the homeland of the Wakhan Kirghiz can be a desperate place.

The sole connection between the Kirghiz and the outside world is a single-lane dirt road that starts in the provincial city of Faizabad, in the Afghan province of Badakshan, and runs more than a hundred miles through the towns of Baharak, Ishkoshem, and Qala-e-Panj to the village of Sarhad, about halfway into the Corridor, where the road ends. Beyond Sarhad, all movement takes place on foot or on pack animals along narrow trails that hew closely to the Darya-i-Pamir and the Wakhan rivers and extend all the way to the easternmost end of the Corridor, where the frigid waters of a shallow, glassy blue lake lap at the edges of a grass-covered field known as Bozai Gumbaz. It was here, not far from the exact spot that Marco Polo spent the winter of 1272 recovering from malaria, that the Kirghiz leader who had dispatched his emissaries over the Irshad Pass to find me was hoping to build a school.

If any place met the definition of our last-place-first philosophy, surely this was it.

Needless to say, the logistics of even getting to such a location, much less constructing a place where teachers and students could gather to study and learn, were going to be daunting, especially for an organization as tiny as ours. Plus, there was enough work to keep us busy in Pakistan for the next fifty years. Prudence suggested that it might not be wise to spread our resources too thin by venturing into unknown territory at the far end of another country and attempting to work with communities we knew nothing about.

Then again, that's pretty much exactly what got us into this business in the first place. And besides, the team of people we've built up over the years tends to relish this kind of challenge.

As my wife often reminds me, I have a very unusual staff.

There are many unorthodox aspects to my style of operation, starting with my tendency to fly by the seat of my pants and extending through my willingness to fashion working alliances with unsavory characters who have included smugglers, corrupt government flunkies, and Taliban thugs. Even more un-usual is my preference for employing inexpe-rienced, often completely uneducated locals, whom I tend to hire solely on gut instinct — a practice, it turns out, that I learned from my father.

In the spring of 1958, when I was three months old, my parents moved our family from Minnesota to East Africa to teach in a girls' school and four years later helped establish Tanzania's first teaching hospital on the slopes of Mount Kilimanjaro. My sisters Sonja and Kari and I attended a school where the children hailed from more than two dozen different countries. Meanwhile, my father, Dempsey, struggled to lay the foundations for the Kilimanjaro Christian Medical Centre (KCMC). His greatest challenge was to overcome the expat community's fear of empowering local people. He was told repeatedly that getting anything done in Africa required a *muzungo* (white man) wielding a *koboko* (a hippo-hide whip). Despite these prejudices, he never wavered in his conviction that the key to success was listening and building relationships. In lieu of tea drinking, he would head over to the nearby town of Mamba, where after Sunday church, male and female elders would sit in circles, passing around a communal gourd of *pombe* (banana beer) while they celebrated their friendship and resolved their problems.

Over a decade, my father slowly put together a team that resembled a miniature United Nations. The construction firm that built the hospital were Zionists from Haifa. The engineering consultants were Egyptian Sunnis. The architect was a Roman

Jew, many of the senior masons were Arab Muslims from the Indian Ocean coast, the accountants were Hindus, and the project's inner circle of advisers and managers were all native Africans. Communication was a challenge during the early years, and there were several times when the whole thing almost fell apart. Nevertheless, my dad persisted, and by 1971 the KCMC was finally up and running — at which point he did something really interesting.

To celebrate the opening of the hospital, he built a giant cement barbecue in our backyard and held a daylong party, in the middle of which he stood up and gave a speech. After apologizing for all the hard work he had put everyone though, he thanked every single person who had been involved, from the top administrators down to the lowliest laborers, and praised them for a job well done. Then he said that he had a prediction to make. "In ten years," he declared, "the head of every department in the hospital will be a native from Tanzania."

There was an awkward moment of silence, and from the audience of expat aristocrats came a collective gasp of disbelief. *Who do you think you are?* they demanded. *How dare you boost these people's hopes with such unrealistic expectations and set them up for fail-*

ure? The explicit assumption was that it was naive and inappropriate to hold the Tanzanians to the same standards that westerners might expect of themselves. The implicit — and more insidious — assumption was that these Africans lacked ambition, competence, and a sense of responsibility.

Our family returned home to Minnesota in 1972, and in 1981 my father died of cancer. A year later, when the hospital's annual report for 1981 arrived in the mail, my mom showed it to me with tears in her eyes. Every single department head was from Tanzania, just as he had predicted — a fact that remains true today, twenty-eight years later.

One of my great regrets is that my father didn't live long enough to see that his instincts not only were vindicated, but also inspired some copycats. Because in my own way, I've adopted the very same approach in Pakistan and Afghanistan.

Altogether, the Central Asia Institute field staff totals about a dozen men, almost all of whom have appointed themselves to their positions. Even though I'm not the sort of person who normally travels with a security team, a hulking tribesman from the Charpurson Valley who once worked as a high-altitude porter on K2 (until his shoulder was torn to pieces in a car accident) insists on serving as my bodyguard. His name is Faisal Baig, and he embraces his duties with unapologetic fanaticism. In Skardu in the summer of 1997, Faisal caught a man leering through the window of the CAI Land Cruiser at my wife, Tara, as she was nursing our daughter, dragged him into an alley, and beat the poor man senseless.

Until a few years ago when he retired, the driver of that Land Cruiser was Mohammed Hussein. A gaunt-faced chain-smoker who could be moody and mercurial, Hussein took chauffeuring so seriously that he insisted on stashing a box of dynamite under the passenger seat — where I usually sit — so he could blast through the landslides and avalanches that often block the roads through the Karakoram. Our work was too important, Hussein believed, to waste time waiting around for government road crews.

Then there is Apo Abdul Razak, a tiny, bow-legged seventy-five-year-old cook who spent more than four decades boiling rice and chopping vegetables for some of the most famous mountaineering expeditions ever to climb in the Karakoram. Apo, who has fathered eighteen children and never learned to read or write, is so fond of tobacco that he smokes Tander cigarettes and uses chewing tobacco at the same time. (His few remaining teeth are the color of turpentine.) Apo's gift is his decency, which is infused with a sincerity so bottomless and so transparent that it endears him to everyone from Pervez Musharraf, the former president of Pakistan (who has taken tea with Apo on three different occasions), to the glowering security guards who are endlessly confronting us at airports, hotels, and highway checkpoints — and who often receive a hug from Apo after they are through patting him down for weapons. Also known as Chacha (uncle), Apo serves as the Central Asia Institute's senior statesman and diplomatic emissary, smoothing over disputes with recalcitrant mullahs, greedy bureaucrats, and bad-tempered gunmen.

It's true, I suppose, that our payroll includes one or two people whose qualifications might meet the definition of "vaguely normal." Haji Ghulam Parvi, for example, is a devout Muslim from Skardu who quit his job as an accountant with Radio Pakistan to become our chief operations manager in Baltistan. Mohammed Nazir, twenty-nine, an earnest young man with hooded eyes and a wispy goatee who manages several of our projects in Baltistan, is the son of a respected Skardu businessman who supplies food to the Pakistani troops bivouacked on the twenty-three-thousand-foot ridgelines looming above the Siachen Glacier, the highest theater of combat in the history of warfare. Most of our employees, however, are men whose résumés would never receive a second glance at a conventional NGO. The remainder of our payroll features a mountaineering porter, an illiterate farmer who is the son of a Balti poet, a fellow who used to smuggle silk and plastic Chinese toys along the Karakoram Highway, a man who spent twenty-three years in a refugee camp, an ex-goatherd, and two former members of the Taliban.

A third of these men cannot read or write. Two of them have more than one wife. And crucially, they are evenly divided between Islam's three rival sects: Sunni, Shia, and Ismaili (a liberal offshoot of the Shia whose spiritual imam, the Aga Khan, lives in Paris). I have often been told that under normal circumstances in Pakistan, it would be unusual to find men of such diverse ethnic backgrounds in the same room sharing a cup of tea. That may well be true. Yet with little pay and almost no supervision, they have somehow found a way to work together — and like the people at the end of the road whom they serve, they have accomplished some amazing things.

From the moment I set foot in Pakistan, I travel in the company of at least one or two of these men at all times. We spend weeks along the tortuous roads of Baltistan, Kashmir, and the Hindu Kush. Despite the long hours and the hard travel, they tend to exhibit the sort of behavior that makes me suspect they may actually belong to a roving Islamic fraternity. They often roar with laughter as they tease one another without mercy. Much of the humor is supplied by Suleman Minhas, a sharp-tongued, slickly mustached Sunni taxi driver who picked me up at the Islamabad airport one afternoon in 1997 and upon learning what I was up to, promptly quit his job and declared that he was now our chief fixer. Among the rest of the staff, Suleman is renowned for his symphonic snores, the gaseous emissions produced by his "other engine," and the mysterious splashing sounds that emerge whenever he's in the bathroom — a source of endless speculation and amusement among his colleagues.

Another popular source of diversion involves booting up our solar-powered laptop with SatLink capability and watching YouTube videos of firefights between the U.S. military and the Taliban. The hands-down favorite features a militant crying *Allah Ak-*

bhar! (God is great!) while loading a mortar shell in backward and accidentally blowing himself to pieces. Apo, a pious Sunni who detests religious extremism, is capable of watching this video ten or fifteen times in a row, cackling with glee each time the explosion takes place.

The other big pastime revolves around teasing Shaukat Ali Chaudry, an earnest schoolteacher with a shy smile, gold-rimmed glasses, and an enormous black beard who fought with the Taliban before becoming one of our part-time freelance advisers in Kashmir. Having recently turned thirty in a country where most men are married by their late teens or early twenties, Shaukat Ali is behind schedule on the important business of finding himself a wife and starting a family. By way of addressing the problem, he recently sent out marriage proposals to no fewer than four different women — and, sadly, was turned down by all of them. Among the staff, these rejections are explained by Shaukat Ali's fondness for launching into long-winded and rather tedious religious monologues that often last up to forty-five minutes. The fastest way to resolve the marriage situation, his colleagues solemnly advise Shaukat Ali, would be for him to start courting deaf women.

If there were a Muslim version of *Entourage*, it would probably be modeled on my staff.

I often refer to this group as the Dirty Dozen because so many of them are renegades and misfits — men of unrecognized talents who struggled for years to find their place and whose former employers greeted much of their energy and enthusiasm with indifference or condescension. But inside the loose and seemingly disorganized structure of the CAI, they have found a way to harness their untapped resourcefulness and make a difference in their communities. As a result, these men are performing a job that it would take half a dozen organizations to match, all of it fueled by their ferocious passion for women's education. To the members of the Dirty Dozen, schools are everything. Despite all the joking, they would lay down their lives to educate girls.

Even for a crew like this, however, the idea of setting up shop inside Afghanistan's Wakhan Corridor seemed, to put it mildly, somewhat insane. Pulling off such a feat would require a point man who possessed an unusual combination of physical courage and stamina, a mastery of at least five languages, and a willingness to travel on horseback for weeks at a time without taking a bath. A man who wouldn't mind cross-ing the passes of the Hindu Kush, unarmed and without fear, while carrying up to forty thousand dollars in cash in his saddlebags. Someone who could negotiate with war-lords, heroin dealers, gunrunners, corrupt government officials, and some very shady tribal leaders — and when necessary, charm the hell out of these people.

Fortunately, we were just about to hire someone who fit the bill — a man whom I refer to as our Indiana Jones.

CHAPTER 2
THE MAN WITH THE BROKEN HAND

Mountains can never reach each other, despite their bigness. But humans can.
— AFGHAN PROVERB

Widow in Kabul, Afghanistan PHOTO: © 2003 TERU KUWAYAMA

We met in the autumn of 1999 in the village of Zuudkhan, at the far end of the Charpurson, on the night before the Kirghiz horsemen came riding over the Irshad Pass. I had come to Zuudkhan ostensibly to inspect a project we had funded that involved laying a seven-kilometer-long pipe to provide the village with clean water and hydroelectricity. Normally, we don't involve ourselves in things like this, but it was the only way the government's inspector general would allow me into the Charpurson, which had been closed to foreigners since 1979 when the Soviets invaded Afghanistan. The real purpose of my visit, however, was to learn something about the Kirghiz, Wakhi, and Tajik communities just across the border in Afghanistan.

For the past two years I had been receiving sporadic reports that the people on the northern end of the Hindu Kush were desperate to begin educating their daughters. These messages suggested that several tribal leaders in the Wakhan Corridor had been attempting, without success, to get word to me — and Zuudkhan seemed like the most promising place to set up a communications link. In these same reports, I also kept hearing about a man in the Charpurson who might be able to help.

His name was Sarfraz Khan, and the stories that clung to him were both colorful and provocative. Some described him as a mishmash of contradictions: an ex-commando who was skilled in the arts of alpine combat, drove a "Taliban Toyota," loved music and dancing, and wore a peacock blue, Dick Tracy–style fedora in the mountains. Others hinted at a man with an unusual past: a smuggler of gemstones, an imbiber of whiskey, a trader of yaks. Outlandish claims were made about his marksmanship, his horsemanship, and his dentistry: It was said that he could take down an ibex with a high-powered rifle from a distance of up to a mile; that he could ride like a Cossack; and that when he took part in *bushkashi,* the violent central Asian version of polo played with the headless carcass of a goat, he did so with such passion and ferocity that his front teeth had been smashed to pieces, then replaced with dentures made of stainless steel.

There were some dark rumors of scandal, too: tales that spoke of a divorce from a first wife and, following on the heels of that disgrace, an even greater one arising from the unthinkable demand that he be permitted to gaze upon the face of his second betrothed before he would consent to marry her. Such a request was an appalling breach of propriety, yet if the stories were true, the request had actually been granted, the first and only time a demand so outrageous had ever been acceded to in the one-hundred-year history of Zuudkhan. What's more, no one could fully explain the reasons why — except, perhaps, as evidence of this Sarfraz Khan's prodigious charisma and his uncanny ability to command other men by bending their will to his own.

Who could say where the truth ended and the legends began? All I knew was that this was someone I needed to meet.

Snow was falling in earnest when I headed northwest from the town of Sost on the only road through the Charpurson. By the time I arrived in Zuudkhan, just before 9:00 P.M., the flat-roofed, mud-walled homes of the village were draped in white and the place looked like a scene out of *Doctor Zhivago*. I was traveling with Faisal Baig, the CAI's security man, who had been born and raised in Zuudkhan, and we were slated to spend the night with the family of Faisal's nephew, Saidullah, who was running several of our schools in the nearby Hunza Valley.

After ducking through the low doorway into Saidullah's home, we greeted his parents and settled cross-legged on some thick yak-wool rugs, leaning back against walls, which were coated in a layer of blackened soot that had the consistency of hardened molasses. Saidullah's sister, Narzeek, had just served a thermos of hot tea when the door swung open and in blew a man clad in a cavernous Russian tundra jacket who looked as if he had just clawed his way out of bed and run a salad fork through his hair. As he came swishing into the room, he seemed preoccupied with the dial on a plastic radio that was blasting a Uighur rock-and-roll station from Kashgar, in western China. Then he spotted me through the blue haze of the yak-dung fire and promptly forgot about the radio.

"Ah, Doctor Greg, you have arrived," he cried, flinging open his arms and flashing a wide grin that revealed a row of metallic teeth. "That is *baf* (excellent)!" He proceeded to wade across the sea of yak-wool rugs and envelop me in a massive bear hug before stepping back to shake hands.

It was then that I noticed the claw. Three of the fingers on his right hand had bent back on themselves in a manner that resembled the talons on a bird, and when we shook, he squeezed my hand with only his forefinger and thumb. I was curious about what could explain such an injury, but he had already performed an about-face, whipped back out the door, and disappeared into the night.

A moment later, however, he was back.

In his arms he carried an expensive red blanket from Iran that was apparently reserved for honored guests, and he insisted that I wrap myself in it. After I had settled the blanket around me, we shared our first cup of tea and I began to learn his story.

For the better part of the past forty-two years, Sarfraz had been, by his own testimony, "no much success." His first marriage had failed — a considerable embarrassment in Muslim culture — and his second marriage was approved only after he had lied to his prospective in-laws about not having children from his first marriage (in fact, he had two daughters) and then shocked them with the demand to see the face of their daughter prior to the wedding. He had also drifted through a series of marginal business dealings in locations stretching from the Karakoram to the Arabian Sea without managing to establish either a home or a solid future for himself. Most important, perhaps, he had failed to find a calling that drew out his innate abilities as a leader and an agent of change.

Born and raised in Zuudkhan, he would never get more than an eighth-grade education — acquired in a village at the opposite end of the Charpurson Valley that took five days to reach on horseback. The boarding expense at this school was a considerable burden for his father, Haji Muhamad, who drew a modest income as a border patrolman collecting customs levies. Nevertheless, Haji Muhamad and Sarfraz's mother, Bibi Gulnaz, were committed to their eldest son's education because an eighth-grade graduation certificate would qualify him to work as a primary-school teacher.

In accordance with this plan, Sarfraz finished his studies and duly went to work teaching first grade in Zuudkhan's very first elementary school. In good weather the students met outside, and in bad weather they gathered in the kitchen of the communal *jumat khana* (the Ismailis' place of worship). Within a year, Sarfraz had realized that he detested teaching and decided to enlist in the army, where he served as a commando in the Punjab Regiments' elite mountain force. Posted to Kashmir in 1974, he was wounded twice during a firefight with Indian troops. The first bullet grazed the side of his upper right arm, while the second passed directly through the palm of his right hand. The military doctors failed to repair the hand properly, and as paralysis set in, three of his fingers folded permanently around themselves to form the distinctive crook that is now his trademark. (Despite the impediment, he retains the ability to hold a pen, shoot a rifle, and manipulate the steering wheel of a speeding Land Cruiser while gabbing on his cell phone.)

Sent home with an honorable discharge and a four-dollar monthly pension, Sarfraz resumed teaching in Zuudkhan but lasted only a year because of his poor pay and expanding family. He then moved to the nearby town of Gilgit, where he became a minivan driver on the treacherous Karakoram Highway, often driving for thirty hours straight and rarely going home. Plagued by *no much success,* he moved on to Karachi, Pakistan's largest city and its commercial center, where he landed a job as a *chokidar* (security guard) for six months. Then it was north to Lahore, the country's academic and cultural center, to work in a Chinese restaurant. *No much success* there either, and by the early eighties Sarfraz was on the move again, this time to Peshawar, the capital of Pakistan's volatile Northwest Frontier Province, where he worked as a chauffeur, mechanic, and auto broker before deciding, once and for all, to give up on cars. Out of options, he returned home to Zuudkhan — completing a circle that is familiar to millions of men who come from Pakistan's tribal areas, where the unemployment rate hovers around 80 percent.

By this time, the Soviet Union's occupation of Afghanistan was in full swing. When the Soviets dispatched a squadron of helicopters across the border and into the skies above Zuudkhan, Pakistan's government responded by declaring the Charpurson Valley a security zone and closing it to all outsiders. Sensing an opportunity, Sarfraz decided to take up trading over the border with Afghanistan by leveraging his family's connections inside the Wakhan Corridor. (A century earlier, Sarfraz's ancestors had moved to the Charpurson Valley from the Wakhan, and many members of his extended family remained in the Corridor.)

He spent the next decade as a high-altitude trader. Three or four times a year, he would work his way over the Irshad Pass on horseback or on foot, ferrying rice, flour, sugar, tea, cigarettes, cooking oil, knives, batteries, salt, pots and pans, chewing tobacco, and anything else the inhabitants of the Corridor might need to make it through the winter. These items would be exchanged for butter and animals — mainly yaks and fat-tailed sheep — which he would drive back over the pass. He was also not averse to smuggling the occasional consignment of gemstones or whiskey, though he steered clear of opium and guns.

It was a hard way to make a living, even when it was supplemented with sporadic employment as a high-altitude mountaineering porter on K2 and other nearby peaks. Nevertheless, these experiences imbued Sarfraz with an impressive skill set. He came to know not only the nuances of the terrain and the movements of the Afghan and Tajik military patrols (which he avoided) but also the habits of the wild animals, especially the ibex and the Marco Polo sheep (which he took great pleasure in hunting). In the process, he gradually built up a dense network of business associates within the villages and settlements north of the Hindu Kush. By the end of a decade, his linguistic repertoire had burgeoned to the point where he could speak seven languages: Urdu, Punjabi, Dari,

Burushkashi, Pashto, English, and Wakhi.

Those gypsy years that Sarfraz had spent as an itinerant jack-of-all-trades and as an alpine peddler may have been rich in adventure, but when he recounted them before me that night in Zuudkhan, he did not romanticize this *no much success* period of his life. In his view, his aimless wanderings and his lack of financial success seemed to underscore how difficult it can be for almost any man (or woman) with a streak of independence to find his place within the poor villages and the teeming cities of Pakistan.

For my part, however, I perceived something quite different — and far more valuable.

By now the hour had grown late and the other members of Saidullah Baig's household had begun dropping off to sleep. When I realized just how much Sarfraz knew about the far side of the Hindu Kush, however, I tossed another clump of dried yak dung onto the fire and told him that I wanted him to give me a crash-course tutorial on the Wakhan. How many people were living there, what tribe did they belong to, and what were their religious and political affiliations?

Sarfraz chuckled and replied that it wasn't that simple. It was true, he acknowledged, that there were only about five thousand residents in the Wakhan. But inside the Corridor's 120-mile stretch — which in places is less than twelve miles wide — one encountered three different communities, each with its own distinctive customs, traditions, and ethnic identity, speaking three different languages and adhering to two separate branches of Islam.

At the far eastern end were the Kirghiz nomads, who move with their herds along the alpine pastures above twelve thousand feet. Descendants of the horsemen who founded the Ottoman Empire, the Kirghiz are Sunnis who speak a cognate of Turkish — attributes that differentiate them from their Wakhi neighbors directly to the west. The Wakhi people, Sarfraz explained, are ethnic Tajiks who trace their ancestry back to the Persian Empire in modern Iran. They are sedentary farmers who grow barley, buckwheat, and potatoes along the river valleys at altitudes considerably lower than those where the Kirghiz dwell. The Wakhi speak a cognate of Persian, and they belong to the Ismaili sect of Islam. Finally, at the far western end of the Wakhan, where the Corridor spills into Badakshan, the northernmost province of Afghanistan, one finds a third community. Like the Wakhi, they are ethnic Tajiks.

But instead of Ismaili, they are conservative Sunnis, and their languages, Tajik and Dari, are separate cognates of Persian.

When Sarfraz saw that I was struggling to make sense of these overlapping religious and linguistic characteristics, he seized a notebook, tore off a sheet of paper, and declared that he was going to draw a special map that would cut through the confusion. Like everywhere else in Afghanistan, he intoned, geography is far less important than relationships. If you want to understand the way things work in the Wakhan, the locations of the villages and the rivers and the roads really don't matter all that much. What *does* matter is who swears allegiance to whom. This is the key to grasping the way that power flows, he declared, and when you comprehend the dynamics of power, everything else falls into place.

Then he drew three circles across the page — left, right, and center — and in the middle of each circle he wrote a name. The Kirghiz were represented by the circle to the right (the east), and the name he wrote inside it was that of Abdul Rashid Khan. This was the headman who had refused to participate in the Last Exodus to Turkey in 1982 and elected instead to remain in the High Pamir with a small group of followers. The name inside the center circle (which represented the Wakhi people) was Shah Ismail Khan. His headquarters, Sarfraz explained, were in the village of Qala-e-Panj, halfway through the Corridor, and he took *his* orders from the Aga Khan, the supreme leader of the Ismailis. The left circle (the Tajiks) bore the name of Sadhar Khan, a mujahadeen commander who had spent ten years fighting the Russians and another five years fighting the Taliban.

Power flows from west to east, Sarfraz explained. The Tajiks have more money and better weapons than the Wakhi; the Wakhi are more productive farmers than the Kirghiz; and the Kirghiz have huge herds of sheep and yaks whose wool and meat are coveted by everyone else. Even though Sadhar Khan is the strongest leader in the entire Corridor, the civil affairs of the Wakhan hinge on a delicate balance between him, Shah Ismail Khan, and Abdul Rashid Khan, each of whom acts as a kind of supreme commander within his respective sphere of influence. Nothing takes place inside the Corridor that does not escape the knowledge of these three "big men." No new venture unfolds without their permission.

When Sarfraz had finished laying all of this out, he plunged into a topic that held far greater interest for him than the human dynamics of the Wakhan. "And now we will discuss horses," he announced, growing visibly animated. "Because for the people of the Wakhan, nothing is more important!"

As the night wore on, we talked of serious equine matters: the beauty of horses, their capacity to elevate the status of those who can master them, the importance of the violent games that the men of this region play on horseback in order to demonstrate their courage and prowess. By the time we had exhausted this topic, it was nearly dawn. Before breaking off for the night, however, Sarfraz said he had a suggestion to make.

"If you are truly interested in the Wakhan," he said, "then tomorrow let me take you to the entrance to Irshad Pass, and you will be able to see the route that leads into the Corridor." And with that, he bid me good night and slipped out the door to return to his home.

That was the first of what would eventually become an endless string of conversations between Sarfraz and me. At the time, I now believe, he regarded me as nothing more (and nothing less) than an eccentric American with a lust for adventure who offered the chance for him to earn some cash. What I saw in Sarfraz, however, was a man who possessed energy, ambition, and a rather flamboyant sense of his own theatricality — and who seemed to be genuinely intrigued by our last-place-first approach to building schools, perhaps because it mirrored something in his own soul.

I also knew that I was in the presence of a proud, innovative, frustrated, and immensely competent man who seemed to be conducting his life as if it were an endless *bushkashi* match. In short, I recognized a spirit that was not kindred to my own so much as its complement. In ways that neither Sarfraz nor I fully understood at the time, each of us seemed to round out and finish off something inside the other.

And so it was that our conversation on that snowy evening in Zuudkhan marked the beginning of the greatest friendship of my life.

The following day, after the elders of the village had taken me on a tour of their new water pipe and the hydroelectric generator whose construction the Central Asia Institute had financed, Sarfraz and I clambered into his cherry red Land Cruiser and drove north on a horrendous road whose surface was coated with a gelatinous soup of ice, mud, and loose boulders. Our destination was Baba Gundi

Ziarat, a small hexagonal shrine at the edge of Pakistan's northern border, on the threshold of the Afghan frontier.

It took an hour to complete the fifteen-mile trip, which took us through a barren landscape of treeless, rock-strewn hills that resembled the surface of the moon. The bleakness of the Charpurson (which translates to "place of nothing" in Wakhi) was hardened even further by the weather, a frigid mixture of sleet and snow that was periodically turned horizontal by the strong gusts of wind coming off the Hindu Kush.

As we drew near the shrine, we spied a herd of roughly twenty yaks, tended by five men on horseback. A group of Kirghiz had apparently just come through the Irshad Pass for a final trading session before winter set in.

These men were Sarfraz's friends and acquaintances, so after a round of introductions had been made, we gathered up several yak-wool blankets and spread them on the wet ground. It was while we were sitting there drinking salt tea that the squadron of fourteen Kirghiz riders, the men who had been sent out by Abdul Rashid Khan to find me, abruptly thundered around the corner at the entrance to the pass.

Their leader was Roshan Khan, the oldest

son of Abdul Rashid Khan, and when we had finished exchanging pleasantries, Sarfraz leaped into the back of his Land Cruiser and presented the Kirghiz with forty bags of flour as an early celebration of Id (one of the two biggest holidays on the Islamic calendar). When the cargo was unloaded, we headed back toward Zuudkhan, surrounded by the horsemen.

We were back at the village by early evening and converged on Sarfraz's mud-walled home. While the Kirghiz dismounted and tended to their horses, Sarfraz selected a fat *mai* (sheep), dropped it gently to the ground with its head pointing southwest toward Mecca, said a quick blessing, and drew a knife across its throat. When the animal had finished bleeding out, Sarfraz's wife, Bibi Numa, removed the skin from the carcass and set about preparing the meat.

By nightfall, nearly forty people had crammed into Sarfraz's one-room, sixteen by twenty-foot home and arranged themselves with their backs to the walls. The Kirghiz sat cross-legged in their enormous boots, from which they pulled out their riding knives to serve as silverware. (It is generally forbidden to wear shoes inside someone's home, but Sarfraz had given the Kirghiz a special dispensation because if they removed their boots, their feet would swell up as a result of the high-altitude crossing they had just completed, and it would be almost impossible to get their boots on again.)

Most of the mutton had been boiled in a large pot, although a small portion had been fried into kebabs in a pan. The real delicacy, however, was the *dumba,* the blubberlike fat from the animal's tail and its hind end. This was placed on a platter in the center of the room, where it sat quivering like a hunk of golden Jell-O.

The Kirghiz inhaled this feast with the harrowing relish of men who had been subsisting on rainwater and chewing tobacco. They scooped up the fat with their fists, they stripped the meat from the bones with their riding knives, and they snapped the bones in half and sucked the marrow into their mouths with moist slurping sounds. Everything was consumed — the head, the testicles, the eyeballs — and when they were through, the men took their hands, which were now slathered in grease, and carefully smeared them over their faces, their hair, and their beards.

Later, when everyone had pronounced himself sated, Chinese thermoses filled with salt tea were brought in, followed by large bowls of *arak,* fermented mare's milk. Then

116

it was time to prepare for bed, and as blankets were brought to Sarfraz's home from all over the village, the guests stepped outside to perform final ablutions.

By this time, the wind was settled, the snow had subsided, and the sky was littered with a spray of constellations so dense and so bright that the milky glow of the heavens defined every inch of the ridgelines along the peaks surrounding Zuudkhan. As the horsemen squatted in the starlight cleaning their teeth with matchsticks or the tips of their knives, Roshan Khan stood beside me for a moment, looking up at the night sky. Then, with Sarfraz translating so that I could follow, he said that he had a message from his father that he needed to recite:

For me, a hard life is no problem. But for our children, this life is no good. We have little food, poor houses, and no school. We know you have been building schools in Pakistan, so will you come and build the same for us in Afghanistan? We will donate the land, the stones, the labor, everything that you ask. Come now and stay with us for the winter as our guest. We will take tea together. We will butcher our biggest sheep. We will discuss matters properly and we will plan a school.

I replied that I was honored by this invitation, but I could not possibly return over the Irshad Pass to camp out with Abdul Rashid Khan for the next five months. First, I had no formal permission to enter Afghanistan — and the Taliban, who ran the government in Kabul, weren't exactly handing out visas to U.S. citizens. More important, my pregnant wife was expecting me home, and if I did not return soon, she would be deeply upset. Surely the Kirghiz could understand the seriousness and the magnitude of a wife's displeasure?

Roshan Khan nodded gravely.

However, I continued, I would definitely come to visit them when I got the chance, and when I arrived, I would do my best to help them. In the meantime, I needed some information. Could Abdul Rashid Khan perhaps give me a rough sense of the number of children, ages five to fifteen, who needed education?

"No problem," Roshan told me. "Soon we will give you the name of every single person inside the Wakhan."

This seemed a bit far-fetched. In the region that these men had just ridden out of, there are no phones, no faxes, no e-mail, no postal system, and no roads. Moreover, thanks to the snow and the storms, the area was about to be sealed off from the rest of the world for seven months.

"How in the world do they propose to get this information to us?" I asked, turning to Sarfraz. "And when it comes time for us to enter Afghanistan and make our way up to the Wakhan, how can we tell Abdul Rashid Khan when we're coming?"

"No problem, we do not need to tell," Sarfraz replied airily. "Abdul Rashid Khan will find a way of getting us the information. And he will know when we are coming."

Having no other alternative, I shrugged and took him at his word.

Now Roshan Khan and I enacted a ritual that I recognized from six years earlier, when Haji Ali had stood in the barley fields of Korphe and asked me to provide an assurance that I was coming back to him. The leader of the Kirghiz horsemen placed his right hand on my left shoulder, and I did the same with him.

"So, you will promise to come to Wakhan to build a school for our children?" he asked, looking me in the eye.

In a place like Zuudkhan, an affirmative response to a question like that can confer an obligation that is akin to a blood oath — and for someone like me, this can be a real problem. As those who work with me in the

United States understand all too painfully, time management is not my strong suit: Over the years, I have missed so many plane flights, failed to appear at so many appointments, and broken so many obligations that I long ago stopped keeping track. But education is a sacred thing, and the pledge to build a school is a commitment that cannot be surrendered or broken, regardless of how long it may take, how many obstacles must be surmounted, or how much money it will cost. It is by such promises that the balance sheet of one's life is measured.

"Yes," I replied. "I promise to come and build you a school."

The next morning by five o'clock, they were gone. It would be five years before we saw each other again.

CHAPTER 3
THE YEAR ZERO

But it was the women who burned the eyes with tears. The Taliban had hated them.
— COLIN THUBRON,
Shadow of the Silk Road

Girls' school bombed by Taliban in Baujur, NWFP, Pakistan
PHOTO: © 2007 TERU KUWAYAMA

121

If the band of Kirghiz horsemen riding north toward the Irshad Pass on that October morning seemed to belong to the thirteenth century, the Afghanistan they were returning to was trapped in a modern-day Dark Age in which civil society was under siege and time itself seemed to be moving backward.

Ten years earlier, the country had shattered into a patchwork of isolated fiefdoms as the rival mujahadeen militias who had been responsible for driving the Soviet army back beyond the borders of the USSR started battling one another for power. During the early 1990s, virtually every town and district in Afghanistan descended into unbridled lawlessness. The main roads connecting the cities of Quetta, Herat, Kabul, Jalalabad, and Mazar-i-Sharif were choked with hundreds of extralegal checkpoints, each manned by a petty chieftan or a band

of young fighters armed with a few Kalashnikovs who would demand payments from
travelers. In towns such as Torkham and
Kandahar, young boys and girls were regu-
larly abducted and pressed into servitude
or raped. Merchants and shopkeepers were
forced to contend with gangs that indulged
in looting, extortion, and murder. The arbi-
trary nature of these crimes and the chaos
they unleashed eventually gave rise to an
atmosphere of widespread public revulsion,
fear, and betrayal.

Then in October 1994, a group of about
two hundred young men, many of whom
had grown up in the squalid refugee camps
around the city of Peshawar, joined forces
to launch a new jihad. The vast majority
of these men had studied in hard-line madrassas, or religious schools, sponsored by
Saudi Arabian donors or the government
of Pakistan, where they had been indoctri-
nated with a virulent and radical brand of
Islamist ideology. Calling themselves the
Taliban, a Pashto word that means "student
of Islam," they crossed the Pakistan border
and swarmed into the Afghan truck-stop
town of Spin Boldak with the aim of restoring righteousness and stability by uniting
the country under the banner of a "true Islamic order."

The Taliban wore black turbans, flew a white flag, and swore allegiance to a reclusive, one-eyed Pashtun named Mullah Omar who made his headquarters in Kandahar and was rumored to anoint himself with a perfume he said was based on the recipe of the scent used by the Prophet Muhammad. During the next several weeks, their ranks rapidly swelled with new recruits until their numbers reached more than twenty thousand fighters. Aided by weapons, ammunition, and communications technology supplied by Pakistan's most powerful intelligence agency, they achieved a series of decisive victories against their mujahadeen rivals. Within a month they had stormed Kandahar and captured the town's airport, where they commandeered six MiG-21 fighter jets and four Mi-17 transport helicopters. By the following September, their motorized cavalry of Japanese pickup trucks mounted with machine guns had overrun the western city of Herat. A year after that, they took the eastern town of Jalalabad and then Kabul itself, where they seized Afghanistan's Communist leader and former president, Mohammad Najibullah, castrated him in his bedroom, tied him to the back of a Land Cruiser, and dragged him round and round the compound of the palace before hanging his body from a traffic post for all the city to see.

By the end of 1996, the Taliban controlled over two-thirds of the country and had established a draconian regime that blended sadism with lunacy. Bizarre edicts where issued that forbade people from listening to music, playing cards, laughing in public, or flying a kite. Marbles and cigarettes were taboo. Toothpaste was banned, along with sorcery and American-style haircuts — especially those that mimicked the look sported by Leonardo DiCaprio in the movie *Titanic*.

These new rules were enforced by thuggish officials from the "Department of the Promotion of Virtue and the Prevention of Vice," who patrolled the streets in pickup trucks wielding AK-47s or whips made of radio antennae. In their zeal to impose a new moral order, they created an atmosphere so austere that the only acceptable form of public entertainment was attending executions in which criminals were stoned to death in soccer stadiums or hung from street lamps. All across the capital city, a place once beloved for the songs of its nightingales, thrushes, and doves, anyone who dared to keep birds was imprisoned and the birds were slain.

In addition to their many other targets, the

Taliban fiercely opposed anything deemed *bid'ah,* the Arabic word for innovation that leads to deviation from the Koran. As part of their campaign to sever virtually all contact with the outside world, they banned movies and videos, destroyed television sets by running them over with tanks, strung spools of music cassettes from lampposts, and decreed that anyone caught carrying a book that was "un-Islamic" could be executed.

Eventually, this violent catechism spilled over into an assault on the social and cultural fabric of Afghanistan itself. At the National Museum, which contained perhaps the world's finest collection of central Asian art, virtually every statue and stone tablet was smashed to pieces with hammers and axes — an expression of the Taliban's conviction that artistic depictions of living creatures help to promote idolatry. For the same reasons, they blew up two mammoth Buddhist statues in the province of Bamiyan that had been carved into the side of a sandstone cliff during the third and fifth centuries. Inside Kabul's presidential palace, the head of every peacock on the silk wallpaper was painted over in white, and the stone lions guarding the building's entrance were decapitated.

By the late 1990s, this inferno had begun

to warp and consume even the most sacred principles at the heart of the Taliban's vision — the spirit of Islam itself. Islam is not simply a religious faith based upon the words of the Prophet Muhammad and founded on the principle of absolute submission to the will of Allah. Islam is *also* the framework of a civilization created by the community of Muslim believers — a framework that includes not simply theology but also philosophy, science, the arts, and mysticism. Whenever Islamic civilization has achieved its fullest and most beautiful levels of expression, it has done so in part because its leaders permitted the societies over which they ruled to be enriched by tolerance, diversity, and an abiding respect for both the divine *and* the human. By deliberately seeking to destroy this tradition, the Taliban — like many other contemporary Islamic fundamentalist groups — abandoned the message of the Koran to build a society that is just and equitable and whose rulers are directly responsible for the welfare of all their citizens.

Of the many ways in which the Taliban perverted and brutalized the tenets of Islam, however, nothing quite matched the crimes that they visited upon their sisters, daughters, mothers, and wives.

■ ■ ■ ■

During the early 1970s, the women of urban Afghanistan enjoyed a level of personal freedom and autonomy that was relatively liberal for a conservative Muslim society. According to the U.S.-Afghan Women's Council, a significant percentage of the women in Kabul worked for a living — tens of thousands of them serving in medicine, law, journalism, engineering, and other professions. In the country's rural areas, of course, the opportunities for female education and employment were far more limited; but in Kabul itself, unveiled females could be seen inside factories and offices, on television newscasts, and walking the streets wearing Eastern European–style dresses and high heels. Within the first week of taking Kabul, the Taliban stripped away these privileges and summarily rendered the female population silent and invisible.

In every major city and town across the country, women were now forbidden to go outside their homes unless accompanied by a close male relative and clad in an ink-blue burka. The few who dared venture out in public were not allowed to purchase goods from male shopkeepers, shake hands with or talk to men, or wear shoes whose heels made a clicking sound. Any woman who exposed her ankles was subject to whipping, and those who painted their nails could have the tips of their fingers cut off. Young girls were banned from washing clothing in rivers or other public places, participating in sports, or appearing on the balconies of their homes. Any street or town that bore the name of a female had to be changed.

As these injunctions against women piled up, unforeseen contradictions gave rise to even more grotesque levels of absurdity. Women who were ill, for example, could be treated only by female doctors — yet during the first week after the Taliban seized Kabul, all women physicians were confined to their homes and denied permission to go out, thereby severing half the population's access to health care. Those same restrictions also meant that the capital city's war widows who had no living male relative — a group whose numbers the USAID estimated to exceed fifty thousand — suddenly had no way of earning a living except through begging, stealing, or prostitution. Those enterprises, of course, were violations of the law that merited punishments ranging from beating and amputation to being stoned to death, depending on the whims of the religious police.

One of the primary targets in this war against women was, quite naturally, education. The moment the Taliban captured Kabul, every girls' school and university in the country was abruptly closed, and the act of teaching girls to read and write was outlawed. In the capital city alone, this resulted in the immediate suspension of 106,256 elementary-school girls and more than 8,000 female university students. In the same moment, 7,793 female teachers lost their jobs. To enforce this policy, the vice-and-virtue squads started carrying rubber whips made from bicycle tires that were specifically designed to be used on girls attempting to attend class. Any teacher caught running a clandestine girls' school was subject to execution, sometimes directly in front of her students.

In response to such outrages, a handful of women resisted by setting up an underground network to provide health care, education, and a means of communicating with the outside world. Groups that included the British government's Department for International Development, Save the Children, and the Swedish Committee for Afghanistan helped courageous women set up secret schools for girls in houses, offices, and even caves. By 1999, some thirty-five thousand girls around the country were being home-schooled. Despite these developments, however, the experience of finding themselves imprisoned in small apartments and cut off from all aspects of public life began to take an appalling toll. In a health survey of Afghan women conducted by Physicians for Human Rights in 1998, 42 percent of the respondents met the diagnostic criteria for post-traumatic stress disorder, 97 percent displayed symptoms of major depression, and 21 percent revealed that they experienced thoughts of killing themselves "quite often" or "extremely often."

Under the sorts of conditions imposed by this fanatical theocracy, the idea that an ex–mountain climber from Montana might consider venturing into Afghanistan in order to start building schools and promoting girls' education was, quite simply, unthinkable. By the summer of 2001, however, the Taliban's fortunes were poised to suffer a radical reversal.

Several years earlier, having already been evicted from his native Saudi Arabia, Osama bin Laden had been expelled from his base in Sudan along with his wives, his children, and scores of his closest followers. With the blessing of the Taliban leadership and the government of Pakistan, Bin Laden and his entourage had been permitted to settle in Afghanistan, where he had proceeded to plan and finance a series of terrorist operations, including the August 1998 bombings of the American embassies in Kenya and Tanzania, which the U.S. State Department reported killed more than 230 people and wounded more than 4,000.

Although the Taliban leaders were clearly uneasy about Bin Laden's terrorist activities, they had rebuffed repeated demands by U.S. government officials that he be expelled from the country or handed over for trial. The Taliban's reasoning was straightforward: Bin Laden was a fellow Muslim who had fought with them against the Russians, and to turn him over to the Americans — or anyone else — would have violated the Pashtun code of *nenawatay,* the right of refuge and protection that is afforded all guests. This is where matters stood during the second week of September, 2001.

At the time, I had returned to Zuudkhan, Sarfraz Khan's village in the western part of the Charpurson Valley, in order to check up on a women's vocational center that we had recently established. On the second night of my visit, I stayed up quite late meeting with a group of community elders and didn't make it to bed until after 3:00 A.M.

Sarfraz, as he often does, remained awake, fiddling with his Russian shortwave radio in the hope of catching his favorite radio station out of the Chinese city of Kashgar, which broadcasts the reedy Uighur music he loves to listen to. Instead, he picked up a disturbing news broadcast about an event that had just taken place on the other side of the world. Shortly after 4:30 A.M., Faisal Baig shook me awake.

"I'm sorry," he said. "A village called New York has been bombed."

The American response to the attacks on the World Trade Center and the Pentagon was swift and devastating. Operation Enduring Freedom, launched on October 7, involved both a massive aerial bombardment and a ground offensive spearheaded by a loose coalition of mujahadeen militias from northern Afghanistan who received the support of several hundred Central Intelligence Agency operatives and U.S. Special Forces. By November 12, the Northern Alliance had seized nearly all of the territory controlled by the Taliban and retaken Kabul. A month later, Taliban fighters abandoned their last stronghold in Kandahar, the southern city from which they had launched their original campaign to conquer the country. As the leaders scattered and ordinary fighters melted back into the villages or fled across the border to seek refuge in Pakistan's Tribal Areas, the movement of bearded clerics and earnest madrassa pupils that had swept across all but a tiny sliver of northern Afghanistan seemed to vanish into thin air. And so it was, in the second week of December, that I was finally able to pay my first visit to Kabul.

The road from Pakistan to the Afghan capital is on the western end of the 1,600-mile Grand Trunk Highway, which is one of South Asia's longest and oldest major roads, dating back to the Mauryan Empire that began in 322 B.C. The Grand Trunk was originally a series of trade routes that linked the Bay of Bengal and present-day Pakistan to Afghanistan and the Persian Empire. Over centuries, dozens of successive empires used this route to move armies ranging from foot-soldier infantries and elephant-mounted cavalries to mechanized tank divisions.

My trip started out with Suleman Minhas driving me through the western suburbs of Peshawar and past a check post featuring a twenty-year-old signboard that declared NO FOREIGNERS ALLOWED BEYOND THIS POINT. From there, the road heads up into the Safed Koh Mountains, a perilous twenty-three-mile stretch that needs to be navigated with precision to dodge oncoming traffic from both front and rear. (Some locals call this section of the Grand Trunk the Martyr's Road because so many drivers have been killed in accidents or by bandits.) This segment concludes at the town of Landi Kotal, which features a smuggler's bazaar where one can purchase everything from tires to television sets to heroin. Directly off the road in Landi Kotal is a colonial cemetery where hundreds of British soldiers who were slaughtered during the Second Afghan War (1879–90) and the Third Afghan War (1898 and 1919) are buried — a graphic reminder of the fate that has befallen every foreign army that has ever attempted to invade and control Afghanistan.

From there, the Grand Trunk begins a dramatic descent toward the Afghan border. Along this steep and narrow incline, overladen supply trucks shift down to their lowest gears as they thread through the rust red limestone walls that mark the legendary Khyber Pass, through which armies from Alexander the Great and Genghis Khan to the Persians, the Moguls, and the British have passed. From the Khyber Pass, it is only about three miles to the Afghan border and the town of Torkham.

In December 2001, Torkham was a frenzied circus of thousands of Afghan refugees, some of whom were returning to Afghanistan while others were heading back to Pakistan. One elderly Afghan man with a wispy beard told me he was fleeing Afghanistan due to the U.S. bombing campaign, while a woman with a handful of kids declared that she was evacuating because her land had been seized by squatters and she had nowhere to go. The actual border was an open circular area crowned on both sides by massive metal gates. The Pakistani immigration clerks' office featured dozens of official-looking filing cabinets. On the Afghanistan side, the arrangements consisted of a desk, a chair, and a single courteous official who gave me one look and performed a staccato of stamping on the surface of my passport. "Most welcome to Afghanistan," he declared with a big smile. "Can I give you some tea?"

So far, so good, I thought. *The first Afghan I meet offers a cup of tea.*

I politely tried to decline, but he insisted, and after he barked an order out the back door, two small cups of steaming green tea were handed to us by a disheveled boy. After thanking him for his hospitality and bidding him farewell, I drove through the checkpoint and entered Afghanistan, where I found myself greeted by a mile-long line of metal shipping containers whose sides were pockmarked with bullet holes. From the interior of each container, entrepreneurs were hawking televisions, kites, music cassettes, and a host of other products that had been forbidden under the Taliban.

Driving past this Afghan-style shopping mall, I was offered a more sobering reminder of the wars that had been raging unchecked here for the past twenty-two years. As far as my eye could see, the sides of the Grand Trunk Highway and the surrounding hills were littered with the carcasses of tanks, artillery launchers, and armored personnel carriers. Amid the detritus, I could pick out a scattering of rusted helicopters. They resembled the broken skeletons of dead birds.

Twelve hours later, when I finally reached the capital, the devastation was everywhere. Kabul in the winter of 2002 was effectively at "year zero": its population traumatized, its infrastructure destroyed, its suffering and its horrors etched upon the gray and shattered surfaces of what had once been its architecture. Regardless of which direction one looked, it was impossible to pick out a single building whose facade had not been honeycombed with blackened holes punched by grenades and rockets. Two decades of virtually uninterrupted fighting had made even the most dignified structures appear drunken, wounded, or lost. The entire city seemed to affirm the notion that warfare is a disease.

Amid this destruction, government officials conducted their business under burlap or plastic sheets tethered to the remains of the various ministerial buildings. Passing the airport, I could spot pieces of bombed planes lying by the runway, and demining crews were clearing the edges of the taxiways with armored bulldozers. The national airline, Ariana, was in shambles: After the U.S. bombs had knocked six of its old planes out of business three months earlier, only a single aging Boeing 727 remained operational. In the months to come, I would learn that Ariana's pilots and stewardesses who flew to New Delhi or Dubai were forced to sleep on the plane at night because the crew could not afford hotel rooms. The flight engineers used a slide rule to calculate weight and balance, and each flight had to carry cash in order to pay for fuel.

Eventually I made my way to a crumbling building on Bagh-e-Bala Road called the Peace Guest House. Snow had fallen, and there was no heat, electricity, or running water. The sparse surroundings reminded me of being in a remote mountain village in Pakistan, except that I was in a bustling city of 1.5 million. That first night, I lay in bed listening to the sporadic bursts of automatic weapon fire resounding across the city. After each volley, there was a brief lull of silence that was filled by a shrill chorus of howling dogs.

Over the next few days, I moved about the capital city with the help of a taxi driver named Abdullah Rahman, a man whose eyelids had been scorched away by an exploding land mine and whose hands had been so badly burned that he was unable to close them around his steering wheel. One of Abdullah's several jobs involved safeguarding three locked cases of books at the Military Hospital library. Every morning, Abdullah, along with six other librarians, would sign in to the register to mark their presence, sit together at a long desk for about an hour, and then leave at the directive of their boss. Abdullah had been doing this six times a week for twelve years, and for his services he was paid $1.20 per month. He told me that on average, about one book a week was checked out.

During the next week and a half, I toured around the city with Adbullah in an effort to get a sense of how much damage had been done to the capital's education system. Despite the fact that classes were scheduled to reopen later in the spring, only a handful of the 159 schools were prepared to receive students, and even these were in horrendous condition. In some cases, the buildings were so unstable that classes would have to be held outside or moved to metal shipping containers. In other cases, the students would have to scale crude ladders built from logs after the stairways had been destroyed.

Toward the end of my stay, I paid a visit to Dr. Ashraf Ghani, who was Afghanistan's minister of finance and a personal adviser to Hamid Karzai, who would soon be appointed to serve as the country's interim president. Dr. Ghani had received his graduate degree in anthropology from Columbia University and later pursued a successful career with the World Bank, but after 9/11 he had given up everything to return to Afghanistan and help his country get back on its feet.

When we met in his office, the minister informed me that less than a quarter of the aid money that President George W. Bush had promised to his country had actually been delivered. Of those funds, Dr. Ghani explained, $680 million had been "redirected" to build runways and bulk up supply depots in Bahrain, Kuwait, and Qatar for the upcoming invasion of Iraq. Afghanistan was now receiving less than a third of the per-capita assistance that had been plowed into reconstruction efforts in Bosnia, East Timor, or Rwanda — and of that, less than half was going to long-term development projects such as education. Moreover, to administer this inadequate stream of cash, a massively expensive bureaucracy had sprung up.

As bad as this sounded, I learned later that the situation was even more bleak. A significant amount of the development money offered by the United States was, it turned out, simply recirculating into the hands of American contractors, some of whom were paying Afghan construction workers five or ten dollars a day to construct schools and clinics whose price tags could exceed a quarter million dollars per building. Equally disturbing, almost none of the tiny amount of money that was actually reaching Afghan citizens in Kabul was flowing beyond the capital and into the rural areas, where the devastation was even greater and the need for assistance even more desperate. Twenty miles beyond Kabul's suburbs, most of the country was largely on its own — a state of affairs that seemed to be lost on Dr. Ghani, overwhelmed as he was by the devastation at his feet.

"Look around you — Kabul is a mess," he exclaimed. "We don't have enough buildings to live in, not to mention electricity, food, communications, plumbing, or water. At least in the countryside the people have land on which to grow crops and rivers to drink from. They can sleep in a tent under the stars wherever they please, and they have animals to eat."

He reached for a black book filled with contact information.

"So you should begin your work right here in the city," he continued, opening the book and running his finger down a list of names. "I know many good contractors that can help you."

Clearly, there was a compelling case to be made that the CAI should devote its limited resources to working in Kabul. Serving the girls of Afghanistan's ravaged capital city would be enough to keep us busy for the next two decades. The problem, however, was that I already had given my word to the Kirghiz — and in order to honor that commitment, I was going to have to find a way to disengage from Kabul and begin making my way toward the Wakhan.

"I'm sorry," I told him, "but our mission is to serve remote areas and to set up schools where none already exist."

"Well, young man, have it as you wish," said Dr. Ghani, clearly disappointed. "But as you will find out, the last thing the people in the remote areas want is schools."

"Thank you for the information," I replied. "But I still need to head north."

CHAPTER 4
THE SOUND OF PEACE

Traveling in Afghanistan was like wandering through the shadows of shattered things.
— CHRISTINA LAMB,
The Sewing Circles of Heart

Greg with schoolgirls in Lalander village, Afghanistan PHOTO: ©
2007 TERU KUWAYAMA

When the Kirghiz horsemen and I had met for the first time in the fall of 1999, I had told them I needed a rough count of the number of school-age children in the eastern Wakhan. More than a year later, a group of traders crossed over the Irshad Pass, rode into Zuudkhan, and delivered up to Sarfraz a sheaf of several dozen pages of yellow, legal-sized notebook paper, bound between two pieces of cardboard and wrapped in a purple velvet cloth. The pages contained the first comprehensive census of every single household in the Afghan Pamir, painstakingly recorded by hand with a black fountain pen. According to this document, in a total population of 1,942 Kirghiz nomads, there were more than nine hundred children under the age of nineteen who were cut off from any access to education and whose families spent the year roaming over an area of approximately one thousand square miles. Farther west, along the banks of the Amu Darya, the river that delineates the Russian and Afghan frontiers, there were also more than six thousand Wakhi farmers scattered among twenty-eight villages who, having received word of our pledge to the Kirghiz, were now apparently clamoring for schools for their own children.

When Sarfraz showed me this census, I was dumbfounded not only by its thoroughness but also by what the numbers revealed about the true scope of the demand for education in the Wakhan.

By this point, it was clear to me that Sarfraz's many years of wheeling and dealing throughout the Corridor qualified him as the perfect point man to ramrod this initiative — so I decided to offer him a job as the Central Asia Institute's "Most-Remote-Area Project Director" with a salary of two thousand dollars a year. It would be his responsibility, I explained, to coordinate our most far-reaching ventures at every level, from drinking tea with the elders in each community to hiring the masons and carpenters who would do the work. He accepted with enthusiasm, exclaiming that he was finally about to embark on an enterprise that would involve *much success.*

"So if we want to put things in motion in the Wakhan," I then said to him, "how do we figure out where to actually put the schools that we need to build?"

Sarfraz — who as always was one step ahead of me — promptly whipped out another sheet of paper with a list of eight locations. Langhar, Bozai Gumbaz, and Gozkhon I had heard of; the other five were new to me. Then he unfolded a map of northern Afghanistan and started pointing with his index finger.

"We will build *here* and *here* and *here* and *here* and *here* and *here* and *here* and *here*," he declared. "And once these schools are finished, the children will come."

That sounded straightforward enough, but he went on to explain that we had two problems. First, if we wanted to set up operations inside the Wakhan, it was necessary to enlist the permission and support of the network of "big men" who ran the affairs of the Corridor, which meant that we needed to figure out a way to get from Kabul to the northernmost part of Afghanistan and start building relationships.

The second problem was that Sarfraz did not yet have a passport — which meant that for the first phase of this new venture, I was going to be flying solo.

■ ■ ■ ■

The northern province of Badakshan has always stood somewhat aloof from the rest of Afghanistan — an isolated region, cut off from the south by the soaring escarpments of the Hindu Kush, whose deepest cultural and historical links extend north into Tajikistan and Uzbekistan. Between Kabul and Badakshan, the dry, rust-colored plains of southern Afghanistan give way to the Pamir Knot, the great tangle of peaks that marks the point where the Himalayas collide with the Karakoram. It is an implacable geographic barrier, and thanks to this great divide, Kabul can sometimes seems more distant — and more foreign — than the remote central Asian khanates of Bukhara, Bishkek, and Samarkhand.

Harshly beautiful and horrendously poor, Badakshan has historical ties to the kingdoms beyond its borders mainly because some of the most popular trade routes linking China, Kashmir, and central Asia passed through this area — and it was along these thoroughfares that one of the province's few treasures was shipped to the outside world. For more than six thousand years, the mines of Sar-e Sang, forty miles north of the Panjshir Valley, have provided the world's most important source of lapis lazuli, the gemstone that lent its intense blue fire to the death mask of Egypt's King Tutankhamen, the official seals of Assyrian and Babylonian governments, and the paintings of Renaissance Europe. (The stone was ground into a powder to make the pigment the Venetians called ultramarine.) In ancient times, Badakshan's seams of lapis were mined by lighting fires in the tunnels and then cracking the hot rock by packing it with ice. In recent years, the mujahadeen commanders who control the mines have preferred the use of military explosives.

Until recently, Badakshan's only other source of wealth was opium. The terrain and climate qualify this as perfect poppy country: suitable soil, steep and well-drained hillsides, long hours of sunshine, and the right amount of rainfall. The province sits directly in the middle of the "heroin highway" that transports raw opium north into Tajikistan, then Tashkent, Moscow, and points beyond.

As in other remote parts of Afghanistan, Badakshan's political and economic power has traditionally rested in the hands of local warlords, or *commandhans,* who fulfill many of the functions of a centralized government: guaranteeing security, providing small-business loans, maintaining roads, digging wells, sitting as judge and jury, supporting education, and, of course, levying taxes. It was the *commandhans* who led the mujahadeen struggle against the Soviets from the moment the first Russian tanks clattered across the borders of Uzbekistan and Tajikistan in the winter of 1979; and it was these men who kept the resistance alive when the Taliban swept over the rest of the country during the mid-1990s.

Since Hamid Karzai was first appointed interim president in 2002, this hierarchy has remained unchanged. Nothing takes place inside Badakshan's rocky gorges, lush valleys, and highland plateaus — no business venture, no marital alliance, no negotiation with outside authorities — without the express permission and the blessing of the *commandhans.*

For the previous five years, the reigning *commandhan* in eastern Badakshan had been a mujahadeen by the name of Sadhar Khan, a man who possessed the mind of a West Point military tactician and the soul of a poet. Born in a tiny hamlet not far from the mouth of the Wakhan Corridor, he had hoped to become a historian and scholar but was forced to abandon those plans when the Russians invaded in 1979 and virtually every able-bodied man and boy within a hundred miles of Baharak fled into the surrounding mountains to join the resistance.

During the early years of the war, Sadhar Khan's speed and cunning often got him picked to lead quick, dangerous raids deep into enemy territory. Thanks to these exploits, he rose swiftly through the mujahadeen ranks and eventually emerged as a lieutenant of Ahmed Shah Massoud, the famous "Lion of the Panjshir," who was perhaps the most gifted and formidable mujahadeen to fight against the Soviets. In addition to his leadership and planning skills, Khan also acquired a reputation for ruthlessness and ferocity. Inside the northeastern corner of Badakshan, his power was absolute.

Khan's base lay just outside of Baharak, a town of about twenty-eight thousand people where the roads arriving east from the regional capital of Faizabad and north from the Panjshir Valley converge. There is also a third road in Baharak that provides the only motorized means of accessing the Wakhan — and thanks to this, Sadhar Khan was effectively the gatekeeper for the entire Corridor. Without him, it would be impossible to drive a nail or lay a single brick for a school anywhere between the Pamirs and the Hindu Kush.

"Before you do anything, you must first go to Baharak and speak to Sadhar Khan," Sarfraz advised. "He is the *chabi*."

He twisted his wrist — the key.

Northeast of Afghanistan's capital city, nearly every mountain pass through the Hindu Kush is over ten thousand feet and thus is locked down by snow for six months of the year. In the 1960s, however, a three-mile-long tunnel was drilled by Soviet engineers below the Salang Pass to create an all-season route linking Kabul with Badakshan. The tunnel is reached by a winding road on which Soviet military convoys were ambushed repeatedly by mujahadeen units that specialized in dismantling trucks, artillery cannons, even tanks, and hauling them, piece by piece, over the mountains and back to the Panjshir Valley. In the spring of 2003, I headed through the Salang in a rented Russian jeep driven by Abdullah Rahman, the taxi-driving librarian with the scorched hands and eyelids, in the hope of paying my first visit to Baharak.

In the years to come, I would look back on the obstacles I encountered during that first trip north and understand that together they represented a kind of metaphor for what our

"Afghan adventure" would be like. When we were driving through the tunnel, the dust and the fumes became so dense that we were forced to stop the jeep and get out. Hoping to find an exit, I climbed through a viaduct leading to the outside, stumbled into a field where the rocks had been painted bright red, and realized I was surrounded by land mines. (After I carefully retraced my steps and descended back into the tunnel, Abdullah and I eventually blundered through and resumed our drive.) Later on that same journey, we found ourselves caught in a firefight between opium smugglers and were forced to take cover in a roadside ditch. When the shooting subsided, I told Abdullah that it was too dangerous for him to continue, jumped onto the back of a truck, and hid myself beneath a pile of putrid animal hides headed to a leather-tanning factory.

In the end, I made it to Baharak but was forced by my schedule to turn around without having met Sadhar Khan, return to Kabul, and fly home to the United States. A few months later, however, I was back in Afghanistan, repeated the same journey, and upon arriving in Baharak, immediately started casting around for the *commandhan.* Standing in the middle of the market, I spotted a white Russian jeep packed with gunmen rolling toward me and flagged it down on the assumption that anyone who could afford such a vehicle in Baharak would probably know Sadhar Khan.

The driver, a small, elfin man with refined features and a neatly trimmed beard, got out to address me.

"I am looking for Sadhar Kahn," I said in broken Dari.

"He is here," the man replied, in English.

"Where, exactly?"

"I am *Commandhan* Khan."

Having anticipated being forced to spend a week waiting for a meeting with a man who did his business from behind a wall of gatekeepers and armed guards, I was momentarily at a loss for words.

"Oh, I am sorry," I stammered, realizing that I had failed to introduce myself in proper Afghan fashion. *"As-Salaam Alaaikum,* I have come from America —"

"I apologize, but right now it is time for prayers," interjected Khan. "Please get in and I will take you to a safe place while I go to the mosque."

He drove us through the bazaar and to the northern end of the town's center and parked in the middle of the road next to the Najmuddin Khan Wosiq mosque. While a handful of plainclothes guards surrounded the jeep and whisked Khan into the mosque, I was led by a single uniformed guard to the second story of a nearby office building. When the guard ushered me into a dingy, windowless room, I requested to be permitted to go up to the roof. He was a bit puzzled but ushered me up the stairs and invited me to sit on a reed mat, where I had a dramatic view of the Hindu Kush range. Turning my gaze down into the street, I watched as several hundred men streamed out of the bazaar and into the mosque for their afternoon prayers.

About thirty minutes later, the procession of men emerged from the mosque, led by Sadhar Khan and the local *ulema* (religious leader). As he stepped into the street, Khan looked up, spotted me on the roof, and pointed. I watched, startled, as several hundred pairs of eyes followed the motion of his hand toward me. Then Khan gave a wave and cracked a smile.

When he had joined me on the roof, I introduced myself and began to tell him the story of the Kirghiz horsemen and our meeting at the southern end of the Irshad Pass. Before I was halfway through, his eyes lit up with astonishment and he wrapped me in a fierce bear hug.

"Yes! Yes! You are Doctor Greg!" he

cried. Word of the promise to the horsemen had already filtered out of the Wakhan and reached Sadhar Khan. "This is incredible. And to think, I didn't even arrange a meal or a welcome from the village elders. Forgive me."

Later that evening, after eating dinner, Khan invited me to the roof of his own house so that we could discuss plans. He told me how eager the communities in his jurisdiction were to have schools, as well as many other services that his people so desperately lacked. He told me about all the girls who had nowhere to study, not only in the Wakhan but also in Baharak and across eastern Badakshan. He spoke of the destruction that had been wreaked over the course of two wars — the first against the Soviets and the second against the Taliban — and how much rebuilding needed to be done.

"Look here. Look at these hills," he said as he pointed toward the mountains looming over the town, whose lower slopes were strewn with countless rocks and boulders. "There has been far too much dying in these hills. Every rock, every boulder that you see before you is one of my mujahadeen, *shahids*, martyrs, who sacrificed their lives fighting the Russians and the Taliban. Now we must make their sacrifice worthwhile."

He turned to me with a look of fierce determination. "We must turn these stones into schools."

The implication was clear. Sadhar Khan was more than happy to allow us to assist the Kirghiz, and he was eager to help this effort in any way he could. But before we could work our way out to the farthest reaches of the Wakhan, we needed to start by helping him to address the needs of his own community, right here in Baharak.

That was how our relationship began.

Over the next two years, I made several more trips to Baharak in order to cement our ties with Sadhar Khan and plan the school that would open the door for us to enter the Wakhan itself. Each of these visits took place inside his headquarters in the tiny village of Yardar, about three miles outside of Baharak. Here Khan maintained two compounds. The first was a modern, two-story, Soviet-style bunker with discreet defensive features that included false doors and hidden holes through which gunfire could be directed. This is where Khan entertained his guests. The other dwelling, a cluster of three mud-brick buildings five hundred yards east of the guesthouse, which featured dirt floors covered with dozens of tribal rugs, was his actual family home.

Inside the confines of the meager boundary wall that ran around the perimeter of this property, the numerous members of Sadhar Khan's extended family all lived together, the same kind of "village within a village" that can be found anywhere in rural Afghanistan or Pakistan. The buildings were surrounded by fields of wheat, barley, spinach, and okra, while the edges of the irrigation canals were lined with neat rows of walnut, pistachio, almond, cherry, mulberry, apple, and pear trees. In the summer and fall, Khan would delight in plucking some of the choicest fruits and nuts from the trees and pressing them on his guests.

"Forget about war — farming is much better than fighting," he once declared when he grew tired of my endless questions about his years during the Soviet occupation. On another occasion, he apologized for the fact that the pear he had selected for me was not as sweet as he thought it should be. "Most of my trees are too young," he explained. "I am trying to catch up for the twenty-five years we lost when we were too busy with fighting to be able to farm."

Whenever I rolled through the entrance gate to Khan's compound, glassy-eyed after yet another harrowing thirty-hour drive from Kabul, I found myself surrounded by a scene that offered an incongruous blend of the ancient and the modern. It was almost always late afternoon or early evening when I arrived, and as smoke from the evening cooking fires filtered through the rays of the setting sun, the call of the muezzin resounded across the fields, punctuated by the tinkling of the little bells tied to the necks of cows and goats as small boys herded the animals home for the night. Meanwhile, a group of up to a dozen young men dressed in combat boots and army fatigues might be kicking a soccer ball near the entrance gate while their older comrades stood beneath the satellite dishes mounted to the thatched roofs, cradling AK-47s in the crooks of their arms and muttering into their cell phones.

If it was still daylight, Sadhar Khan usually met me beneath the branches of a massive walnut tree, where he held court on a cement platform that his men had built directly over the irrigation canal. He was a busy man, and there was almost always a line of several dozen people squatting at the edge of the dirt driveway patiently waiting for an audience. These petitioners might include a group of farmers who had fallen into a boundary disagreement and were hoping the *commandhan* could resolve their dispute or the widows of fallen soldiers coming to collect cash. Yet whenever I arrived, he would get up to exchange embraces, then usher me onto an enormous red Persian carpet, where we settled ourselves, cross-legged, in a nest of maroon pillows. Then the *commandhan* would pour green tea into a set of tiny porcelain cups while his bodyguards passed around dishes filled with raisins, pistachios, walnuts, and candy as a prelude to whatever business we needed to discuss.

Later, as darkness descended over the valley, I would be invited to walk with the rest of his visitors and family members across the compound and into the guesthouse's long, narrow dining room. Only men were admitted, and after everyone was properly seated, Sadhar Khan would walk in and we would all stand up to formally shake his hand, then wait until he was seated before we resumed our places. (If another guest or male family member arrived, the same ritual would be repeated.) Once these courtesies had been properly observed, a group of three or four younger men, led by the host's oldest son, would unfurl a red plastic tablecloth across the length of the floor, and upon this surface the banquet would be laid out. The dishes served were simple and delicious: lamb, chicken, dal, spinach, okra, tomatoes, cu-

cumbers, and rice.

When the meal was finished, the oldest guest would offer up the *dua,* a blessing of thanks. As the words were spoken, everyone would cup his hands together, palms raised, and when the blessing was complete each guest would sweep his hands over his face and intone, *"Alhamdulillah"* ("praise be to God" in Arabic). Finally, cups of green jasmine tea with a small sprig of mint would be served, and then we would talk deep into the night.

These discussions could sometimes last until the muezzin sounded the morning call to prayer at 4:30 A.M., and it was during these rituals that I began to learn about Sadhar Khan's past and to gain a sense of the experiences that had shaped him, especially the war against the Soviets.

In the first several years following the Soviet invasion of Afghanistan, Khan and his mujahadeen had deployed a host of desperate guerrilla tactics in the hope of countering the Soviets' overwhelming technological superiority. Along the narrow mountain roads to the east of Baharak, for example, his men would leap from ledges or boulders onto the tops of passing tanks and smear handfuls of mud over the drivers' viewing ports, then fling Molotov cocktails fashioned from Coke bottles into the hatches. They also adopted ruses that included broadcasting the tape recordings of prayer chants on loudspeakers as a way of luring Russian infantry patrols into ambushes. During those early days of the struggle, they fought with whatever weapons they had — scythes, rocks, and sharpened sticks. Striking when they were able, they fled into the mountains, where they hid in caves, surviving on roots or dried cheese and, when necessary, eating grass.

For this resistance, they were made to pay dearly. Anytime a Russian soldier was killed, civilians were forced to flee as their homes were bombed by helicopters conducting reprisal raids. During the first five years of the war, it was not unusual for mujahadeen units like Sadhar Khan's to suffer 50 percent casualties in battle, but the reprisals against their homes and families could be even more devastating. While women and children spent weeks living in caves in the hills around Baharak, animals were machine-gunned, crops were torched, and fields were seeded with land mines in an effort to force the population into submission through hunger and starvation. Today many of the trails leading down to the streams are adorned with small stone cairns marking the places where children who were sent to collect water were killed by Soviet snipers.

As one of the most important commanders, Sadhar Khan featured prominently on the Soviets' target list. During the decade in which the Soviets occupied eastern Badakshan, the village of Yardar was shelled more than sixty times. Even though every building in Khan's compound had been completely destroyed by 1982, the Soviets' Mi-24 helicopter gunships continued bombing what he called "my dead land" and seeding it with land mines more than a dozen times.

It was those helicopters, which the Afghans called *Shaitan-Arba* ("Satan's chariots"), that wreaked the greatest destruction on the mujahadeen. The Mi-24s would conduct "hunter-killer" sorties, flying in formations of up to eight gunships, attacking mujahadeen positions with a range of weapons that included S-8 rockets mounted with fragmentation warheads and 30 mm high-explosive grenade launchers. No amount of bravery or guile on the part of the rebels could overcome such overwhelming firepower — until 1986, that is, when the American Central Intelligence Agency started supplying the Afghan insurgents with shoulder-mounted Stinger missiles equipped with heat-seeking guidance systems that were shockingly effective at taking out the slow-flying Mi-24s. During the next three years, the CIA flooded Afghanistan with over one thousand Stingers, resulting in hundreds of helicopters and Soviet transport aircraft being shot out of the sky.

In eastern Badakshan, the first mujahadeen to succeed in shooting down a helicopter with a Stinger was one of Sadhar Khan's most important subcommanders, a man named Haji Baba, who is now married to one of Khan's daughters. During our visits under the walnut tree, I was given the chance to hear Haji Baba himself recount the saga of his exploit, in exhaustive detail, on several different occasions. Each telling was slightly different, and the longest of them lasted more than an hour.

From Sadhar Khan I also learned about the sacrifices that the residents of Baharak and the surrounding countryside had made, after having fought the Russians from 1979 to 1989, in order to prevent the region from being overrun by the Taliban between 1994 and 2001. Out of these conversations I came to know a man who seemed to embody many of the contradictions and complexities of his torn and ravaged landscape, and also a man who was not ashamed to express his love of poetry, solitude, and flowers. Early one morning, he invited me to walk with him five or six hundred yards to the bank of the Warduj River, where two enormous boulders are suspended over the rushing water. Here, he explained, he often retreated to spend a few minutes alone before walking to the mosque to perform his evening prayers. As we sat there on the rock, I asked him if he would mind answering a question.

"Please," he said, "ask anything."

"You are a busy man with enormous responsibilities," I said, "so why is it that you spend so much time just sitting here watching the river run by?"

Khan smiled to himself and said that I wouldn't understand the answer to my question because I had never fought in a real war. "You may be a veteran, but you are not a warrior because you have never fought in battle," he gently explained. Then he began to describe, in graphic terms, some of the horrors he had witnessed: the concussive shock of a grenade as it tears apart the body of a man he had shared breakfast with only thirty minutes earlier; the nauseating odor emanating from the flesh of another comrade incinerated by a rocket; the sound that escaped the lips of a man who was dying from infections because his commander lacked even the most rudimentary medical supplies to treat his wounds.

Unlike other mujahadeen, such as Haji Baba, who often cackle with delight when they recount the glorious struggle waged by the mujahadeen, Sadhar Kahn was neither gloating nor boastful. Instead, he described what it felt like to have a friend whom one has known since grade school bleed to death in one's arms and then dump his body into a shallow grave. He talked of the impossibility of a normal life for women and children during war. He spoke of the mounting litany of loss as a life that should have been devoted to worthwhile pursuits, such as reading or music or the cultivation of pear trees, is given over to the business of death.

We talked — *he* talked — for almost two hours that afternoon, and in the end, he said this: "Sitting here watching the water rush past is the only way that I can justify having gone to war. The reason that I fought the Soviets and then the Taliban was for moments such as the one we're having right now. Unless you have been inside the fire of a battle, this is something that you will never understand."

About a year later, during another one of our encounters, Khan said that he had been thinking of our conversation next to the river that morning and was worried that he had failed to answer my question. Then he handed me a piece of paper. He explained that he had written a poem that might, perhaps, have succeeded in capturing the sentiments that he had been trying to express.

Here is the translation, from Dari:

You wonder why I sit,
here on this rock,
by the side of this river,
doing nothing?

There is so much work to be done for my
* people.*
We have so little food,
we have so few jobs,
our fields are in shambles,
and still there are land mines everywhere.

So I am here to listen to
the quiet,
the water,
and the singing trees.

This is the sound of peace
in the presence of Allah.
After thirty years as a mujahadeen,
I have grown old from fighting.
I resent the sounds of destruction.

I am so weary of war.

CHAPTER 5
STYLE IS EVERYTHING

"Greg is very important to me. Without him, I'd be nothing more than a guy who trades yak butter."
— SARFRAZ KHAN

Wakhi family hearth in Sarhad, Afghanistan PHOTO: © 2005 TERU KUWAYAMA

During our many encounters, Sadhar Khan was invariably a model of gracious and refined hospitality — and yet, for me at least, his wry smile and his elaborate rituals of courtesy somehow never quite managed to soften the intensity of his stare. His eyes were a merry shade of green and his laugh had a high-pitched timbre, but when he saw or heard something that displeased him, his face could darken into the kind of expression that made one want to take a step back. In such moments, he seemed to bear a disquieting resemblance to one of the Russian land mines he so despised: a small container, lying just below the surface, that housed the potential for enormous violence.

Despite this sense of menace, Khan ultimately personified the kind of man that I would encounter over and over again during my time in Afghanistan: a former mujahadeen who had emerged from the savageries of the Soviet occupation and the atrocities of the war against the Taliban with a desire to spend his remaining years repairing the damage to his community. Like almost all *commandhans,* he was savvy and shameless in the way he went about this, installing supporters and family members in plum jobs, dipping his hand into the lapis lazuli mines sixty miles south of Yardar, and exacting a stiff tariff from the heroin traffickers whose mule trains moved a significant chunk of Badakshan's opium supply through his territory on the way to the Tajik border. Unlike his more corrupt colleagues, however, he was implacably determined to plow the bulk of these profits directly back into the welfare of his people. For the veterans who had served under his command, he had constructed a thriving bazaar in Baharak. He disbursed small loans so they could start businesses, helping to ease the transition from soldier to merchant, and handed out seeds and tools to almost any farmer who even hinted at needing help.

His special passion, however, was education, especially for girls. For almost twenty-five years there had been virtually no schooling in the rural villages of his region, and the loss this represented to the current and upcoming generations weighed on him deeply.

"War has forced us to starve not only our bodies but also our minds," he once said to me. "This should never again happen to my people."

Unbeknownst to Sadhar Khan, the Central Asia Institute was about to be hit by a tsunami of cash that would enable us to take a dramatic step forward. In April 2003, *Parade* magazine ran a cover story about our school-building initiatives in Pakistan, and during the ten months following the publication of that story, our Bozeman office was flooded with more than nine hundred thousand dollars in donations. I had wired most of those funds to our bank in Islamabad and ordered the Dirty Dozen to embark on a score of new projects inside Pakistan, but I had also reserved a portion of the *Parade* money to launch our Wakhan initiative. In the spring of 2004, I informed Sadhar Khan that we were ready to begin building in Baharak.

As we sat on the red carpet under his walnut tree, I laid out exactly how the finances and other matters would be handled, explaining that these aspects of the project would not be subject to negotiation, even with a *commandhan* of his stature, because they were the only ways of guaranteeing that our projects are properly supervised and accounted for. The *shura* (local council of elders) in Baharak would be in charge of the funds, I told him, and he and his neighbors would be required to donate the land for the school. We would hire exclusively from within the local community for the basic labor, and we had budgeted fifty thousand dollars for construction and teachers' salaries, plus another ten thousand dollars for supplies, furniture, and uniforms. We would deliver one-third of this financing up front, in cash. Another twenty thousand dollars would be paid only after the workers had finished the construction to roof level, and the last payment would be delivered upon completion. As a final condition, at least 33 percent of the students would have to be female from the first day of class, and this number would need to increase each year until the girls' numbers reached parity with the boys'.

"Only 33 percent female enrollment?" Khan exclaimed, shaking his head and chuckling. "The number of girls waiting to attend this school is already almost double that, so perhaps you should consider giving our local council of elders a performance bonus for already exceeding your quota, no?"

I handed over the first down payment to the *shura* that morning, and work started immediately. By midafternoon the grid lines of the outer walls had been marked with twine and a crew of laborers was digging the trenches for the foundation with picks and shovels. Toward the evening, a series of explosions echoed between the walls of the surrounding mountains as the masons began dynamiting the granite boulders that would yield the stones for the walls. For Sadhar Khan, the reverberation of those blasts — which sounded eerily similar to Soviet or Taliban artillery — must have offered a deeply satisfying confirmation that we were truly turning stones into schools. For me, however, those concussive bursts signaled something else.

The door to the Wakhan Corridor was now unlocked, and it was time for Sarfraz and me to plan our next move.

When Sarfraz and I drew up our 2004 plan for northeastern Afghanistan, it was fairly straightforward. Since the only road into the Wakhan began in Baharak and ended halfway through the Corridor at the village of Sarhad, we decided on a two-pronged attack in which we would hit the beginning and end of the trail first, then literally build our way toward the middle until the literacy gap was closed. Once this process was complete, we would embark on the far more challenging task of leapfrogging into the roadless reaches at the far end of the Wakhan and fulfilling our commitment to the Kirghiz.

By this point, we had finally managed to get Sarfraz his first passport, and he had flung himself into a series of grueling trips from Kabul to Faizabad, through Baharak, and into the Wakhan in order to negotiate, launch, and supervise the first wave of school projects. Many of these journeys were solo undertakings, but whenever I flew into Kabul, Sarfraz and I would travel together — and it was during these ventures that our connection and our friendship began to deepen into something we both found rather remarkable. The chemistry we shared enabled us to understand each other so well that before long, each was able to anticipate the other's moves and complete his sentences. Eventually, we even got to the point where we communicated using a nonverbal vocabulary of glances and facial expressions. This did not happen immediately, however — and before we achieved this level of synthesis, it was first necessary for me to pass through a kind of cultural version of Afghan boot camp: a series of tutorials, run by Sarfraz, that I now refer to as Style School.

Starting with our very first trip north

from the capital, I learned that traveling with Sarfraz through Afghanistan would be a far more complex and perilous affair than in Pakistan. Among the new concerns we faced, the biggest involved getting kidnapped. At the time, the going rate for bribing someone to help set up the abduction of an American citizen was around five million Afghans, or roughly $110,000. (Today, that number has increased tenfold.) To avoid this danger, Sarfraz was willing to go to extraordinary lengths, starting with camouflage.

Afghanistan is one of the most ethnically complicated countries on earth, a place where the overlapping cultures, languages, religions, and tribal loyalties have bedeviled historians, anthropologists, and military strategists for centuries. Understanding these distinctions was an essential precondition to safe travel, and this accounted for Sarfraz's obsession with a word that normally applies to the sartorial and behavioral nuances displayed on the streets of Manhattan or Paris, as opposed to the deserts and mountains north of the Hindu Kush. "To have much success in Afghanistan, you must understand style," he would patiently lecture me again and again. "Style is everything here."

In any given situation, regardless of whether it involved an all-night negotiation with a group of conservative mullahs or a five-minute break at a roadside tea stall, he paid keen attention to the body language of everyone involved. Who sat where and why? Who sipped his tea first and who hung back? Who spoke and who remained silent? Who was the most powerful person in the room, who was the weakest, and how did their respective agendas influence what they were saying? There can be many layers and shades of meaning within each of these distinctions, and by responding to them all with equally subtle adjustments of his own, Sarfraz strove to avoid drawing unwanted attention either to himself or to me. As a means of blending in as we moved from one region to another, for example, he often adopted different headgear, donning a *lunghi* (a Pashtun wrap-around turban) in the Taliban areas of Wardak province, exchanging it for a mujahadeen's *pakol* (woolen hat) in the Tajik-dominated areas of Badakshan, and eventually discarding that for a *kufi* (a white skullcap) as we entered the mosque in Baharak. Among his network of trading partners and relatives in the eastern part of the Wakhan, he was also fond of putting on his favorite hat of all, a dashing peacock blue fedora — an expression, I suppose, of style in the more conventional sense of the word.

Sarfraz's chameleon-like qualities included the spoken word as well as dress. His mastery of the seven languages at his command extended beyond lexicon and grammar to embrace a smorgasbord of accents and inflections. In Kabul his Dari might sound crisp and gentrified, but as soon as we were in the mountains, he would gradually downshift, like a truck descending a long grade, through a series of increasingly less refined accents and dialects until he abandoned Dari for Wakhi before finally sliding into Burushkaski — the patois of his Wakhan ancestors. (He kept his Pashto in reserve for the Pashtun-dominated territories east of Kabul, and his Urdu, Punjabi, and English for Pakistan.) Perhaps the only thing Sarfraz would not do in order to be as local as possible was to grow a beard. Other than that, he freely adopted any ruse he could conceive — including telling elaborate lies about where he was from and what he was up to — in order to fit in and avoid hitting people's trigger points.

My job was to follow his lead by copying his mannerisms and his demeanor. I would mimic the manner in which Sarfraz crossed his legs as he sat, the angle at which he held a teacup, even where he permitted his gaze to fall. Under these circumstances, of course, I wasn't deluding myself into thinking that I'd actually be mistaken for a local. But by following Sarfraz's mannerisms and body language, I was hoping to avoid giving myself away as a wealthy American interloper. The goal was simply to make anyone whom we encountered experience a moment of confusion in which they dwelled, however briefly, on the possibility that in some strange way that they didn't quite understand, I might actually belong. And as we moved around the countryside north of Kabul, this often worked surprisingly well — a tendency helped by the fact that Afghanistan is a vast melting pot in which green eyes, brown hair, and Caucasian features are not at all uncommon.

The second part of Sarfraz's kidnap-prevention strategy involved transportation, and it was here that things started to get exciting.

Moving from one destination to the next inside Pakistan was a fairly simple matter. Suleman Minhas, the CAI manager in Islamabad, ferried us around the city in a company-owned Toyota Corolla, and for the mountains of Baltistan we relied on a twenty-eight-year-old, four-wheel-drive Land Cruiser. When none of these vehicles was available, we would hire one from a pool of local Pakistani drivers whom we had known for years. Afghanistan, however, was quite different. Because we had neither a fleet of our own vehicles nor a network of trusted chauffeurs, we were usually forced to rent a car and driver on the spot, an arrangement that placed us at the mercy of people we'd never met and whose loyalties were unknown.

The process began with Sarfraz's paying a visit to a roadside bazaar in Kabul and negotiating an arrangement without actually telling anyone where we were heading. If there were a bunch of men standing around the rental place, Sarfraz might ostentatiously declare that he was looking for someone to take us to, say, Mazar-i-Sharif or Kandahar or Bamiyan — anywhere but our true destination. After he had completed his negotiations and we had piled into the vehicle, he would announce that our plans had changed, divulging as little information as possible about the "new" destination — often no more than the name of a village twenty or thirty miles up the road.

Once we were heading in the correct direction, he would begin sniffing the air for signs that something might be wrong, and if his suspicions were aroused, all bets were off. If the driver seemed to be asking too many questions or spending too much time on his cell phone or simply didn't look right, Sarfraz would abruptly exclaim that we needed to pull over at the next roadside truck stop, explain that he was dashing inside for a cup of tea, and once inside set about arranging for another car and driver. When he found someone new, he'd dash back out, open the door, and start flinging our bags into the parking lot. Then he'd toss a handful of money at the driver and tell him to get lost, and off we'd go — until it was time to fire the new driver. When it came to such precautions, he was unapologetic and completely ruthless.

Sarfraz also preferred to hire and fire drivers based on ethnicity and tribal affiliation. At any given point on the road, the goal was always to place ourselves in the hands of someone local, a man whose face and name would be known in the event that we were stopped at a roadblock or pulled over. Hiring local was also, in his view, the best way to obtain accurate information about road conditions, the weather, and the likelihood of being robbed.

This approach differed markedly from the conspicuous transport arrangements preferred by the larger humanitarian organizations and the international consulting groups, most of whom were easily distinguished by their shiny SUVs equipped with tinted windows, air-conditioning, and twelve-foot-long radio antennae. "That big antenna makes them a perfect target for the Taliban!" he would exclaim. He was also contemptuous of the disconnect that such equipment created between the employees of those organizations and the locals on whose behalf they were working.

The greatest likelihood of our being abducted or attacked was during the thirty-hour drive from Kabul to Baharak, and on this stretch of the drive, Sarfraz's concerns about security occasionally placed him at odds with my desire to get to know ordinary Afghans — a point of contention that he and I still wrestle with even today. This difference first surfaced during one of our earliest trips together in the spring of 2004.

As usual, we had left from Kabul late in the afternoon in order to pass unimpeded through the Salang Tunnel, which was only open to civilian traffic at night. Just north of the tunnel, the rattletrap jeep we had hired emitted a loud sizzle, and steam began pouring out of the engine. Sarfraz ordered the driver to drift down the hill about a mile and pull into a roadside mechanic shop. There, a boy who was no older than eleven stepped up in a pair of flip-flops to ask what we needed. His head was shaved and covered with a black woolen cap, and he wore an oil-stained *shalwar kamiz* that was coated with grease. His name was Abdul, and he walked with a limp.

Abdul jumped into the engine compartment like an acrobat, and by the time Sarfraz and I had eaten a quick meal and had a cup of tea at a nearby canteen, our young mechanic had deftly replaced our radiator and hoses. He told us the price was fourteen hundred Afghans (about twenty-eight dollars), and as Sarfraz counted out the money, I tried to get a sense of who Abdul was and what his story entailed.

"Where is your father?" I asked. "It is nearly midnight and you are working alone?"

"I am an orphan from Pul-e-Khumri," he replied matter-of-factly. "I have no father because the Taliban killed my entire family."

"Where do you live?"

"I live here — I sleep in the truck trailer over there where we keep our spare parts." He pointed to a rusting metal container.

"How much money do you make?" I asked as I searched in my pocket to offer him a small tip.

"None," he replied. "I don't get paid — I only get some food, tea, and a place to sleep. I work day and night, every day, and sleep when there is no customer. And if my boss finds out I have taken any money, he will beat me with the iron rod over there."

By this point our driver was revving the engine to signal that we needed to get moving, and Sarfraz had lit up a cigarette and was glaring at me with impatience. It was the middle of the night on a dangerous road, we were behind schedule, and it was time to go.

"Sarfraz," I pleaded, initiating an exchange that he and I were to repeat endlessly over the next several years, "can't we please do something here?"

"Greg, this is Afghanistan — you cannot help everyone!" Sarfraz barked. "If he works hard, this boy might eventually own his boss's garage. But for now he has food and a place to sleep, and that is better than half of the orphans in Afghanistan."

"Okay, but how about if we just —"

"No, Greg!" he declared, cutting me off. "I promise that when I pass through here again, I will stop to check on Abdul. But we really need to go now, or we will become *shahids* on the highway, and for that your wife will never forgive me."

Knowing that he was right, I pulled out my camera to take a picture of the boy mechanic, and then we drove away.

On his next trip north, Sarfraz did indeed stop to check on Abdul and discovered that another young boy was working in his place. Sarfraz asked what had happened to Abdul, but no one in the shop could offer any information. Perhaps he had gone north to Faizabad, or maybe south to Kabul. No one knew anything except that Abdul, whose story seemed to mirror that of so many others in this nation of orphans, had simply disappeared.

In the black-and-white image I shot that night, Abdul is standing in the garage, covered in grease and oil, with a flat expression of resignation and loss that no eleven-year-old boy should ever feel. The photo sits on my desk in Bozeman, and I see it every day that I am home.

Once we finally reached Baharak and were traveling through territory controlled by Sadhar Khan, Sarfraz's concerns about security began to drop away. They were immediately replaced, however, by a whole new set of challenges connected to the terrain.

The rutted dirt track through the western half of the Wakhan Corridor followed the

Panj River, and during the spring and summer months the runoff from the glaciers and snowfields in the Hindu Kush created a series of channels that spilled directly across the roadbed. These flood zones could be up to half a mile wide, consisting mostly of loose gravel interlaced with braided streams of varying widths and depths. Upon reaching the edge of a new series of streams, we often were forced to cruise up and down the shoreline for half an hour or more before finding a spot that seemed to offer a promising place to cross. Then Sarfraz would order the driver to gun his engine and blast into the water with as much speed as possible. If we were lucky, we'd smash through to the other side. If not, we might wind up in waist-high water that would gush through the floorboards and fill up the inside of the car. Then we'd have to pile out, make our way to the edge of the stream, wait for a truck or a jeep to come by, and pay them to haul us out.

It's fair to say that Sarfraz and I treated our drivers without mercy. We goaded them into pushing their vehicles to the point where the axle seized or the transmission dropped out or the muffler was torn to pieces. If the driver himself had been forced beyond the point of exhaustion, Sarfraz would order him into the back and one of us would get behind the wheel. In the spring and the fall we'd hydroplane through acres of mud (which can be two or three feet deep in the Wakhan) until the vehicles would bog down and gurgle to a stop. Then, while the driver headed off to find a team of yaks to pull his car out, Sarfraz and I would take off our shoes, and sometimes even our pants, and start walking. (The tunic top of a *shalwar kamiz* extends well below the knees, so exposure was not a problem.)

Sooner or later, we would reach our goal — whatever stretch of the Corridor formed the focus of the trip. And it was at this point that our real work would begin.

Over the years, Sarfraz and I gradually developed a routine to which we would adhere once we had arrived in a particular "project zone." Each day would begin well before dawn, when we would wake up, blinking, in the same clothes we'd been wearing for more than a week, surrounded by the components of our mobile office: one small black backpack, a wheeled compact carry-on, and my black Pelican case bearing the THE LAST BEST PLACE bumper sticker. Together these pieces of luggage held all the paperwork for our schools in the Wakhan, along with several extra copies of *Three Cups of Tea* (which made excellent presents to the mujahadeen), our sat phone, a Nikon battery charger, one spare 28 mm camera lens, a spare *shalwar kamiz,* a Sony laptop, three cameras, several large bricks of cash, and our GPS unit.

First on the agenda were morning ablutions, which basically consisted of me smearing some aloe-scented hand sanitizer into my hair and Sarfraz scratching himself in the right spots. (Showers, bathtubs, and wet wipes were extremely scarce in the Wakhan.) Then we would pop the cap on our jumbo-size jar of ibuprofen, and each of us would take two or three tablets as a prebreakfast appetizer. (When we were going hard, we'd each go through about twelve or fifteen pills a day in order to help dull the aches and pains induced by the arduous travel and the lack of sleep.) At this point, one of us might put on the pair of reading glasses that we shared — we both have the same prescription — while the other stepped outside with the toothbrush. (Yep, we shared that, too.)

The spectacle of two men passing personal grooming items back and forth was bizarre enough that one morning a reporter from a national magazine, who was traveling with us in order to write an article about the Wakhan, asked me to provide a list of everything that Sarfraz and I used in common.

191

"Well, let's see," I replied. "We share our jackets, our razors, our hairbrush, our soap, our socks, our hats, our *shalwar kamiz*, our undershirts —"

"How about your underwear?" the reporter interjected. "Do you guys share that?"

"Look, I'm not sure I want to reveal this," I said, squirming with embarrassment, "but there's really no sense in lying about it either." Then I explained that having spent the first fifteen years of my childhood in rural Tanzania — where underwear is not a big priority — I have sort of gone "alpine style" for my entire life.

"And what about you, Sarfraz?" demanded the reporter, who was diligently writing all of this down.

"Alpine style for me, too."

When we had completed our morning ritual, it was time to pile back into the car, hit the road, and head off toward that day's destination. Upon arrival, the first item on the agenda called for an inspection of the school — usually surrounded by a scrum of children tugging us by the hands. (One of the greatest joys in my work is spending time with the students and teachers, and at every school, I make it a priority to greet each child, one by one, and encourage them to give me an update on how their studies are progressing.)

At every stop where there was a project, the bricks of cash that we were carrying were brought out and Sarfraz would balance the accounts with Mullah Mohammed, sixty-three, a former Taliban bookkeeper from the village of Khundud who served as our accountant for the entire Wakhan (and who usually traveled with us). Our ledgers were kept according to the old British double-entry system and were laid out by hand, from right to left, in Persian script. Every transaction was recorded down to the penny, and at the end of each accounting session, which could take hours, Sarfraz would "seal" the ledger by drawing a line in ink along the edge of the page so that no additional expenses could be written in later. Then he would solemnly warn Mullah Mohammed that if any errors later emerged, Mullah Mohammed would be shipped off to rejoin the Taliban.

While this business unfolded, I often found myself besieged by people submitting requests for assistance. In Khundud, there might be a man asking for money to set up a grocery store in exchange for providing tutoring services to our students. In the town of Ishkoshem, I might be approached by a pair of local officials seeking funds for a water-delivery system. In the tiny hamlet of Piggush, the school principal might claim to need additional cash to purchase desks and filing cabinets for her teachers. The pleading was always polite, but the needs were endless: more books, more pencils, more uniforms, another classroom. I would get proposal after proposal, and unfortunately, I would have to say no to dozens of them, even though many of the petitioners might have traveled for days on foot or by public transport to present me with their requests.

As the day progressed, Sarfraz and I would also find ourselves passing the sat phone back and forth in order to keep in contact with the rest of the CAI staff who were scattered throughout the Punjab, Baltistan, and eastern Afghanistan. There were hourly chats with Suleman in Islamabad, who served as our communications hub and who would keep me abreast of who among the staff was arguing with whom — an inevitable by-product of an organization staffed with members of half a dozen different tribal and religious backgrounds.

Finally, as evening drew near, we would be invited to gather at the home of a village leader and convene with the local heavyweights for a *jirga,* or council session. A *jirga* is a formal gathering of elders sitting in a circle on a carpet, or under a tree, and as a rule the participants are forbidden from adjourning until consensus has been achieved around a decision. As a result, *jirgas* can go on for hours and often extend through much of the night. They invariably feature long speeches, periods of intense deliberation conducted in absolute silence, and prodigious amounts of tea drinking.

Toward dawn, Sarfraz and I would snatch a brief nap in an empty room in someone's house or bunk down on the floor of the school. Two or three hours later, it would be time to pack up, pile into our hired vehicle, and race off to the next project. And so it would go, school by school and village by village, until we had worked our way through the places we needed to visit and it was time for me to fly home to Montana and for Sarfraz to head back to the Charpurson Valley.

These trips were long and grueling, and during the course of them my respect and affection for Sarfraz continued to deepen. By the end of that first year, he had impressed me with his intelligence, his diligence, and his work ethic. He was culturally savvy, constantly on the move, and able to switch between charming and harsh as the

195

situation demanded. For our point man in the Wakhan, I do not think there could have been a better choice than Sarfraz Khan.

There was one area, however, in which both he and I were an absolute disaster.

Thanks to Sadhar Khan's support and protection, we were making fair progress inside the Wakhan itself. Eventually, however, we would need to make contact with the government in Kabul and obtain official permission for our projects. With this in mind, Sarfraz and I set up meetings with a number of government officials during the course of three separate visits to the capital city — and it was in those offices that we achieved a whole new level of *no much success*.

To be fair to the officials with whom we collided, the country they were attempting to govern had been at war for more than two decades, and virtually every aspect of civil society was in shambles. Nevertheless, the people we tried to work with in Kabul didn't make it easy for us to help them rebuild their own school system. On the contrary, I'd say. Never have we drunk three cups of tea so many times to so little purpose.

In that part of the world, if an office doesn't have its own tea, someone has to go for takeout, which can sometimes take up to half an hour. As often as not, we would wait for the tea and only after it had arrived be informed that the individual we needed to see wasn't in. Once or twice, we announced the name of the official we needed to see and were told "no problem," invited for tea, eventually served, and then informed that this person wasn't actually in the office after all, and could we come back tomorrow? To some degree you get used to this in central Asia, but in Kabul such tendencies were more pronounced than usual.

During one of our first meetings, we ran into trouble at the offices of the Interior Ministry, to which we had been shuttled from the Education Ministry. Interior occupied a decrepit multistory building in downtown Kabul, and the guards at the entrance and in the hallways were all armed with AK-47s. We trudged up the stairs to the reception area on the second floor, where I told the young man behind the desk that I had with me letters from the education officials in Badakshan Province stipulating that the Central Asia Institute had received approval to build schools inside the Wakhan Corridor. We had confirmed our appointment in advance by phone, and all we needed were the proper federal certificates.

"You have arrived unannounced," declared

the official after running his finger down the day's list of appointments and failing to find our names. "And now you are asking us to give you permission to build some schools? Who instructed you to come here?"

"Well, our letters are from the authorities at the village, district, and provincial level," we explained. "But now we need federal approval, and that's why we're here to see you."

"But why are you proposing to build schools in the Wakhan?" he exclaimed. "We already have hundreds of schools there! Why don't you instead propose to build some schools in Kabul or Kandahar — for that I would be happy to give you permission."

"But there is not a single school in the eastern half of the Wakhan Corridor," I responded.

"That is not true!" he said.

At this point, Sarfraz unfurled a map and began pointing out the places in the Wakhan that needed schools.

"But this is not even part of Afghanistan!" the man cried. "Why are you proposing to build schools in China?"

"The fact of the matter, sir," said Sarfraz, "is that this is *your* country."

"Well, even if it *is* Afghanistan," he continued, "schools are not necessary in this area because no one lives there."

Within the span of a single five-minute exchange, this official had asserted that the Wakhan was filled with hundreds of schools, that the Wakhan was not part of Afghanistan, and that no one actually lived in the Wakhan.

Needless to say, we left that office empty-handed.

In the following months, our exchanges with members of the various government ministries to which we were dispatched were equally fruitless. That was the norm in Kabul. Out in the countryside, the main concern of the education directors, the *commandhans,* and the local religious leaders who had already provided us with stamped and signed authorizations was that we continue with our work. And yet, by the beginning of 2005, we had failed even to register as an officially approved NGO working in Afghanistan, much less to receive retroactive permission for the schools that we had already started constructing.

As Sarfraz would say, "paper side" was never our strong suit.

On the "project side," however, we were doing reasonably well. By now, Sarfraz and I had launched five projects in the Wakhan, with another dozen in the works. There was much to be pleased about — yet one concern continued to prod at the back of my mind. There was still the matter of the unfulfilled promise that I had made to the Kirghiz concerning the most remote school of all.

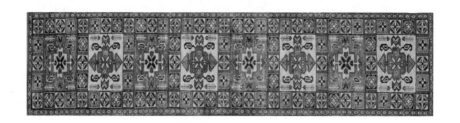

Chapter 6
The Seal of the Kirghiz Khan

But I know, somehow, that only when it is dark enough, can you see the stars.
— Martin Luther King Jr.

Teacher in Afghanistan Photo: © 2009 Teru Kuwayama

As I have mentioned, the construction of Sadhar Khan's school had started in 2004. The general contractor was Haji Baba, the mujahadeen who claimed the honor of having taken out a Soviet helicopter in Badakshan with a Stinger missile. Under his supervision, the foundation, walls, roof, and interior framing were completed by winter. When the snow began to melt, his crews raced to complete everything else — the finishing carpentry in the classrooms, the latrines, the kerosene stove heaters, and the boundary wall. By spring, the little white schoolhouse with the lime green trim in the village of Yardar was the pride of the entire valley and was almost ready to open its doors to its first class of 358 students. Just as Sadhar Khan had promised, more than two hundred of them were girls, including two of his own daughters.

In early May, I arrived in Kabul and

caught a UN flight into Faizabad, where Sadhar Khan's oldest son, Waris, met me in his Soviet-era jeep and shuttled me to Baharak, where Sadhar Khan was waiting to take me on a tour of the new school. With only twelve classrooms, it was hardly our biggest or most elaborate project. But even so, I had to admit that it was a real beauty. Its most impressive feature was the intricate stonework, chiseled and carved from the blasted boulders in the mountains. It was clear that Sadhar Khan was enormously pleased and proud, and together we basked in a sense of accomplishment over this, the very first school we had built in Badakshan.

During the coming week, Waris was planning to enlist the help of several men in the surrounding community to build the desks and chairs — a smart move that would avoid the high cost of purchasing the furniture from Kabul and paying the exorbitant shipping costs. In the meantime, my plan was to head into the Wakhan and meet up with Sarfraz so that we could attend the inauguration of our school in the village of Sarhad. If everything went as planned, I'd be able to toast the opening of the projects on either end of our two-pronged "literary pincer movement."

A day later, traveling with a jeep and driver

provided by Sadhar Khan, I arrived in Sarhad. It was a gorgeous morning — the sky was a soft robin's-egg blue and the shadows of swiftly moving clouds were playing across the lemon yellow contours of the enormous peaks that rise abruptly to the north and south of Sarhad. Sarfraz and I rode to witness the opening day of school by squatting in a wooden trailer pulled by a red tractor. The lurching and bumping was so violent that we had to brace ourselves against the sides of the trailer to avoid being pitched out.

The stone-walled school had been constructed in the shape of a circle, a local design, and it boasted nine classrooms with a sunroof that would permit streaming sunlight to illuminate the interior while providing warmth. Waiting in the courtyard were 220 eager students and their teachers. The girls were clad in traditional crimson tribal dresses with woolen stockings wrapped around their legs, while the boys wore the drab, gray *shalwar kamiz* that is standard attire in the region.

As often happens at such events, the kids were just beside themselves with anticipation. As Sarfraz and I hopped out of the trailer, they gathered in a line to welcome us. One of the students at the front of the line, a wispy third grader named Aisha, displayed the knock-kneed gait that is a by-product of rickets, an ailment common to the remote interior of the Wakhan, where the diet is deficient in vitamin D. Unlike most of the girls, who shyly greeted me with a traditional kiss to the back of my outstretched hand, Aisha gave me an enormous hug and refused to let go.

The entrance to the school's interior compound was guarded by a pair of myrtle green metal gates, and the honor of taking the first official steps inside was given to a group of the village's most respected elders, all of them men. Then one by one, the children gingerly stepped through. Some were clad in rubber boots, others wore sandals, and several were in their bare feet. All of them were closely watched by Tashi Boi, the village chief, who recited the name of each child as he or she walked through the gate and gave a crisp nod of approval.

As I watched the children step into the school courtyard, I couldn't help but notice that the gray, lunar-looking dust now bore the imprints of a mosaic of footprints, and I was reminded, oddly enough, of the moment when Neil Armstrong had stepped onto the surface of the moon. *One small step for a brave young girl,* I thought as the knock-kneed Aisha tottered into the courtyard, *one giant leap for this community.*

Standing beside me was Doug Chabot, the husband of Genevieve, CAI's international program manager, who has volunteered to help us over the years and who had arrived a few days earlier with Sarfraz. "This is really something to watch," murmured Doug, turning to me with a look of subdued amazement that suggested that he was beginning to fathom what the promise of education meant to a village like Sarhad. "They are just *hungry* for this, aren't they?"

I nodded silently and could not help but think back to the afternoon in 2002 when Afghanistan's minister of finance had told me that "the last thing the people in the remote areas want is schools."

The following morning, I bade farewell to Sarfraz and, together with Mullah Mohammed, the CAI's ex-Taliban bookkeeper, began heading back to Baharak. By this point, word of our arrival had spread throughout the Corridor, and as we bounced along the rutted jeep track, we were unable to travel more than a couple of miles without encountering a cluster of people waiting by the side of the road to flag down our vehicle and invite us inside for a cup of tea so that they could submit a special request.

The message was always the same: We have heard about the *maktab* (school) that you have just opened in Sarhad, and we know that you plan to build new schools next year in Wargeant, Babu Tengi, and Pikui. What about us? Will you not consider helping our children by building a *maktab* for them, too? With all the stopping and starting, it took more than forty-eight hours before we made it back to Baharak and somewhere along that stretch of road, the outside world caught up with us.

Several days earlier, *Newsweek* magazine had published an article that suggested that an American soldier stationed at the U.S. prison in Guantánamo Bay had taken a copy of the Koran and flushed it down a toilet. The editors would soon retract the story, but the damage had already been done, and as word of this alleged desecration reverberated throughout the Muslim world, events quickly began spinning out of control.

In Afghanistan, the first riots took place in Jalalabad on Wednesday, May 11. At about 10:00 P.M. that night, Mullah Mohammed and I arrived in Baharak. After driving to Sadhar Khan's home and being informed that he was not there, we headed into the center of town with the intention of spending the night on the floor of a crowded public "guesthouse." On the way there, however, I was approached by a guard who worked for Wohid Khan, a former mujahadeen commander and a colleague of Sadhar Khan's who is in charge of the Border Security Force in eastern Badakshan. After warning us that trouble was brewing in town, the guard urged Mullah Mohammed and me to proceed to a building owned by Wohid Khan, where we could join a group of travelers who were spending the night under his protection.

Happy to comply, we headed over to the two-story apartment building, where a cluster of perhaps twenty Afghans had gathered. By now it was nearly midnight, and just as we were preparing for bed, in strode Wohid Khan. In a typical demonstration of Afghan hospitality, he insisted on feeding everyone dinner. We all filed into another room and sat cross-legged on Persian rugs while platters of roast lamb and Kabuli rice were served.

I found myself sitting next to two dignified but ragged figures with Mongolian features. The gentleman to my immediate left, who was wearing thick eyeglasses and a black robe made of dense cloth, looked to be about seventy years old. He politely introduced himself as Niaz Ali and explained that he was the imam, or spiritual leader, of a group of Kirghiz nomads who lived in the High Pamir, at the far eastern end of the Wakhan.

My pleasure at making Niaz Ali's acquaintance was quickly overtaken by a sense of astonishment and delight when he introduced me to his companion, who was sitting to my right — a dusty, disheveled elder clad in corduroy breeches and high leather boots who was draped in the exhausted demeanor of a man who had been on the road far longer than he might have wished. This was none other than Abdul Rashid Khan, the very man who had sent his son, Roshan, over the Irshad Pass to find me in the fall of 1999.

It was an extraordinary coincidence. Here in Baharak, Abdul Rashid Khan and I had finally been brought together around a plate of roast lamb, long after midnight on the eve of a full-blown religious riot. But even more remarkable, as I was about to discover, were the events that had drawn this man from his home in the mountains at the far end of the Wakhan. As we tucked into the food laid before us, he told me the story of the arduous journey he had just completed to meet the president of Afghanistan in Kabul, and the reasons why he was now returning, empty-handed and nearly broke, to his people in the High Pamir.

During the mid-1990s, the Afghan forces that had defeated the Soviet army found themselves grappling with the impossible challenge of rebuilding a war-shattered nation without any significant assistance from their former allies abroad, including the United States. In the absence of outside aid, one of the few reliable sources of wealth was opium — a crop that had offered a lucrative source of income to a number of cash-strapped mujahadeen commanders during the Soviet occupation. By the early 1990s, so much heroin was flowing out of the country that Afghanistan rivaled Southeast Asia as the prime source of the world's opium supply. Then in 1994, as one province and city after another fell to the armies of Mullah Omar, many members of Badakshan's beleaguered mujahadeen found themselves turning to drug dealing as their primary means of financing their war against the Taliban, sending enormous quantities north through new overland routes developed by organized crime groups in Russia, who would transport it to Moscow and European cities beyond.

In addition to taxing the growth and export of opium from within their own territory, these mujahadeen had also played a role in selling drugs to peasants in remote villages, especially the Wakhi and Kirghiz of the Wakhan. In village after village, the pattern repeated itself: Within the tight confines of a close-knit household, addiction would spread from an ailing husband or a rebellious teenager to every member of the family, including the women, the elderly, and even toddlers. From there the scourge would spread to members of the extended community, enveloping entire villages. Starting in the late 1990s, Ismaili and Kirghiz communities all across the Corridor began reporting opium addicts in every stratum of society, with estimates as high as a quarter of the entire adult population.

The results were devastating. Families suffering from advanced levels of addiction wound up selling everything they owned to finance their three-times-a-day habit. First to go were their possessions — mainly the goats, sheep, and yaks — followed by their land, and in the most extreme circumstances, even their daughters, who came to be known as opium brides. (It is not uncommon to find entire families sold into servitude.) Those who remained were reduced to a diet of tea and bread, making them vulnerable to sickness and diseases.

By early 2005, things had become so desperate that Abdul Rashid Khan decided to form a delegation of leaders from northeastern Afghanistan and travel to Kabul to lay these grievances before the newly elected president, Hamid Karzai. In addition to making Karzai aware of the problems stemming from heroin addiction, the representatives intended to present evidence that their sector of the country lacked virtually any semblance of a functioning federal government.

For Abdul Rashid Khan, the trip to the capital took an entire month and involved traveling by horse, jeep, and public transport. Upon reaching Kabul in early March, he and Niaz Ali spent several weeks moving around various government ministries in an effort to meet with officials who were responsible for services such as education, transportation, health care, and post offices. During these encounters, they got the same kind of runaround that Sarfraz and I had met with during our own visits. Meanwhile, they set themselves up in a rundown apartment with no heat or electricity and petitioned for an audience with President Karzai. They waited two months before receiving a reply.

When they were finally granted an audience, the president permitted Abdul Rashid

Khan to get halfway through his itemization of the problems among his people before cutting him off. "Don't worry," Karzai interrupted. "I am going to arrange food — I will send you back with food on helicopters. You will not go home without a solution to your problems. We will arrange what documentation is needed for the clinics, and we will get your food."

With that, the meeting was over.

There was no follow-up from Karzai's office on the matters of food, helicopters, medical services, or anything else. In early May, Abdul Rashid Khan and Niaz Ali realized that the president's promises were not going to be fulfilled and started their journey home to the Wakhan empty-handed — and by road.

By the time Abdul Rashid Khan and I met at Wohid Khan's supper in Baharak, the two Kirghiz leaders had been away from home for more than four months and had squandered much of their personal fortune. Upon reaching the Pamirs, they would be faced with the duty of informing their people that it had all been for naught.

When he had finished relating this tale, Abdul Rashid Khan confirmed that he knew all about my meeting with his son at the entrance to the Irshad Pass and expressed his amazement that we were now, on the heels of his brutally disappointing sojourn in Kabul, finally meeting for the first time. It was a very emotional exchange: He declared that he was deeply honored to meet me; I protested that it was a far greater honor to meet *him*. Then the *duas* began to flow from his hands, one after the other, and he and Niaz Ali began a Koranic recitation out of sheer joy.

A *dua* is a prayer invoked as a blessing or thanks to Allah, and in the case of Abdul Rashid Khan's invocation, it was partly an expression of gratitude over the miracle that we had finally met and partly an expression of his hope that the humiliating and fruitless quest on which he had embarked might actually result in something positive.

"All I really want for my people is a school so that we can provide education for our children," he said. "To achieve that, I am willing to give up all of my wealth — all of my sheep, all of my camels, all of my yaks — everything I have, if only Allah will grant this one request."

"But you have nothing to worry about," I said. "I have already promised your son that we will build you a school."

"If that is truly the case," he replied, "then

let us start now — this very minute!"

Ooba (yes), I told Abdul Rashid Khan, but first I have to call someone. I stepped into the cool evening outside, turned on my sat phone, and punched the number for Karen McCown, one of our directors, who lives in the Bay Area. Seeking permission from our board to fund a particular school is not the way we normally do things at the CAI. But I was excited and overwhelmed, and so was everyone else, and the emotions of the moment took over.

"Karen," I blurted, "do you remember the Kirghiz tribesmen who rode across the border and found me in Zuudkhan in October of 1999? Well, I am finally here with Abdul Rashid Khan, and he is in desperate straits, and we have to start the school for him and his people."

My excitement was apparently contagious, even over the phone.

"Go ahead, Greg," Karen declared. "I'll check with the board and get retroactive approval, but let's get this show on the road!"

When I returned to the dining room and announced that we had the funding for the school, Abdul Rashid Khan declared that he wanted to draw up a formal agreement right then and there. As the leader of the Kirghiz, it was his duty to provide a guarantee that his people would donate the land and the labor in order to ensure that this project would go forward.

Wohid Khan summoned a guard to give me a spiral notebook and a pen, and I drew up a standard CAI contract, the document that codifies our arrangement with any new community. I then handed the paper to Niaz Ali and he transcribed it into Kirghiz with a vintage fountain pen. It was only eight sentences long, and in English it read as follows:

Bismillah ir-Rahman ir-Rahim

In the name of Allah, the Merciful, the Beneficial

With the witness of Commandhan Wohid Khan, Abdul Rashid Khan, Mullah Mohammed, and Greg Mortenson

Whereas, the Kirghiz people of the Wakhan have no school, teacher, or education

And Whereas, the Afghanistan government has not provided us schools as promised

The Kirghiz people, under the leadership of Abdul Rashid Khan, hereby sign this agreement to build a four-room school at Bozai Gumbaz, Wakhan, with the assistance of registered charity NGO Central Asia Institute.

Central Asia Institute will provide building materials, skilled labor, school supplies, and help with teachers' salary and training.

Abdul Rashid Khan agrees to provide free land, subsidized manual labor, and support for teachers.

The exact terms of the budget and agreement will be worked out after a jirga is convened in Bozoi Gumbaz.

Abdul Rashid Khan

Wohid Khan

Greg Mortenson

Mullah Mohammed

Then Abdul Rashid Khan did something that I had never seen. He reached inside his jacket and pulled out a tiny brown leather satchel. Inside was a very old wooden stamp with the official seal of the Khan of the

Kirghiz of the Little Pamir. On this seal was emblazoned a pair of Marco Polo sheep horns, twisted in a spiral. He also had an ink dipper, and with this he carefully blotted ink onto the stamp, which I noticed had a tiny crack running down the middle, then placed this mark upon the contract. When he was through, he took a red candle, dribbled a small circle of wax at the bottom of the stamped seal, and with ponderous gravity, pressed his thumbprint into the wax.

When this formality was complete, Niaz Ali launched into a lengthy prayer that apparently included half of Kirghiz history and that petitioned, among many other things, that

Allah the Compassionate, Allah the Merciful, Allah the Beneficent, might watch over Wohid Khan, whose food had brought these humble servants of Islam together for this miraculous meeting . . . and the men of the eastern Badakshan border security force, who were protecting us on this most dangerous night . . . and, yes, even President Hamid Karzai, who may not have kept his promise but who bore the weight of a shattered nation on his shoulders, which surely is a greater burden than any man ever should be called upon to bear . . . and this school-building American mountaineer, who is attempting to honor the first word of the Holy Koran, Ikra ("to read") by lighting a lamp for the illiterate daughters of Islam . . . and this American's strange band of employees — first of all, bless the Sunnis among them, of course, but the Shiites, too; and yes, even this crazy Ismaili from Pakistan with the broken hand named Sarfraz Khan. . .may Allah shower his blessings upon them all . . .

Praise be to God . . .
There is no God but God . . .
And Muhammad is His Prophet . . .
La Ilaha Illa-Allah . . .

This went on for quite some time. When it was finally over, everyone clapped. Abdul Rashid Khan and I embraced. And then Wohid Khan solemnly declared that if it became necessary, he would personally travel to Kabul to ensure that no corrupt bureaucrat or misguided government official dared to interfere with the construction of this school for the Kirghiz of the Little Pamir.

Thus ended one of the most memorable encounters I have experienced during the twelve years since I failed to climb K2 and wound up stumbling into the village of Korphe. It was remarkable on its own terms, to be sure — but it was rendered even more astonishing, it now seems to me, by virtue of the events that were about to unfold.

At about ten o'clock the following morning, Mullah Mohammed and I bade farewell to our Kirghiz friends and left Baharak, heading west for Faizabad. It was now Friday the thirteenth, and as we made our way through town we could see that a large group of men had gathered around the Najmuddin Khan Wosiq mosque, which was located just off the bazaar. They looked angry, and many of them were carrying hoes, shovels, and sticks.

We kept driving, reached Faizabad about three hours later, and immediately checked into the Marco Polo Club, a former Soviet guesthouse on an island in the middle of the roaring Amu Darya River that currently functions as a decrepit hotel. By now, the *Newsweek* story about the desecration of the Koran had filtered into every corner of the Muslim world, and enraged imams from Morocco to Islamabad were preparing to launch fiery sermons on the subject during Friday prayers, which typically begin around 1:30 P.M. Fearing that things might get out of hand, the employees of almost every foreign NGO in eastern Badakshan appeared to be evacuating Faizabad, either by getting a seat on the one UN flight at the airport or by heading south on the road to Kabul in their Land Cruisers.

My thinking in these matters has always been different. When things get tense, I'd rather be with local people than with foreigners, even if the foreigners have guns. So I stayed put at the Marco Polo.

That evening, a group of aid workers who were fleeing from Baharak to Kabul stopped in Faizabad and brought word that a pair of conservative mullahs had given especially inflammatory speeches that afternoon at the Baharak mosque in which they had declared that the insult to the Koran that had taken place at Guantánamo Bay was an unpardonable offense that needed to be met with violence. In response, several hundred men had swarmed out of the mosque into the streets of Baharak and headed southeast toward a street that houses the offices of nearly every foreign aid agency in town.

During the next several hours of rioting, each of these offices was ransacked. The windows were smashed, the doors broken down. While every piece of furniture and equipment inside was destroyed, the vehicles parked outside them were pummeled with sledgehammers and crowbars, then set on fire. In the process, four local residents who had been employed by these organizations were murdered and the entire bazaar was smashed to pieces. Wohid Khan and the Border Security Force were eventually able to restore order and quell the violence, but only after shooting down two rioters, wounding at least a dozen more, and arresting more than fifty.

When word of these events reached me in Faizabad, my heart sank. Under most circumstances, I remain optimistic that things will work out for us in Asia, but on that evening, I was convinced that our new school just outside Baharak, which is less than a mile from the street where the NGO offices were attacked, had been gutted and destroyed. If that had indeed happened, it would be a setback for our entire Wakhan initiative, one from which we might not recover. Years of work and patient negotiation might spiral down the drain, along with our newly lit hopes of finally making good on our promise to Abdul Rashid Khan and his people in the Pamirs. In short, if this new school in the backyard of our strongest supporter in the entire province — Sadhar Khan himself — had been sacked by the mob, we could be out of business in the Wakhan.

I had no confirmation that this had actually taken place, of course, but my fears were getting the best of me. Not helping my frame of mind was Mullah Mohammed, who at some point that Friday had bolted from the Marco Polo and gone into hiding, apparently concluding that he'd be safer without me. I wasn't angry — who could blame him? But his actions seemed to underscore the extent to which everything was spinning out of control.

Two days later, Mullah Mohammed reappeared at the Marco Polo Club, apologizing profusely for having abandoned me. I wanted to ask him why he had violated the most sacrosanct of tribal codes and deserted me, but I noticed he was still terrified, literally trembling, and I reassured him we both were quite fine — but I added that we needed to line up some transportation and head for Baharak, where by now the rioting had subsided, in order to find out what had happened to our school. He quickly found a minivan for hire, and we were off.

As we drove into the outskirts of Faizabad, I began to see piles of burned wood, twisted rebar, and other remnants of the rioting piled at the north end of town. Near the main mosque, a firebombed Land Cruiser still smoldered and was missing its big antenna. Nervous men and curiosity seekers lingered on all sides of the locked-down bazaar stalls. A few local chai stands were doing a brisk business, with men congregating around them to sort out fact from fiction among the rumors that were flying through town.

Beyond Faizabad itself, there was no evidence of rioting or destruction on the sides of the roads. The farmers were in their fields weeding and rerouting irrigation channels; the small shops along the road were mostly open for business. For lunch we stopped at a local tandoori shop to get warm chai and fresh naan, hot out of a clay oven. The baker there complained that most of the vehicles that day were in a hurry to get out of the area and raced by his stand without stopping. He was amused when we told him where we were headed.

"You two are fools to be headed for Baharak today," he declared. "You should be going the other way."

Just before the entrance to Baharak, the road sweeps over a plateau and offers a stunning view of the town with the distant Hindu Kush in the south. As we topped the rise, we failed to spot anything unusual — but upon crossing the final bridge into Baharak and entering the main bazaar where the mosque and the government offices are located, it seemed as if we were passing into a war zone. Rubber tires still smoldered in the streets, which were covered with sticks, bricks, and stones.

In the middle of the bazaar, where the NGO offices began, there were gutted Land Cruisers, smashed computers, and broken glass everywhere. The mob's fury had clearly been directed at these buildings, which housed the Aga Khan Development Network, FOCUS, East West Foundation, Afghan Aid, and other NGOs. Their offices lay in ruins, and even the safes and desks had been smashed to pieces.

As we made our way down past the south end of the bazaar toward Yardar, I was braced for the worst. But when we pulled up in front of the boundary wall of the new school, I could hardly believe my eyes. No windows were broken. The door was intact. The fresh coat of lime green paint that the building had received only a week earlier was as bright as a newly minted dime.

"Allah Akbar," mumbled Mullah Mohammed, and cracked a smile.

As we stood surveying the building, Sadhar Khan's son Waris walked up and explained that during the peak of the riots, a faction of the mob that was attacking the bazaar had stormed down the road in the direction of the school. Before reaching the boundary wall, however, they had been met by a group of elders who had donated the land for the school, organized the laborers who had built it, and participated in the laying of the cornerstone. These elders, or *pirs,* informed the rioters that the Central Asia Institute school belonged not to a foreign aid organization but to the community itself. It was *their* school, they were proud of it, and they demanded that it be left alone. And with that, the rioters dispersed.

Not a stone had been hurled, Waris told me.

Later, after all the damage had finally been tabulated, the cost of the Baharak riots was assessed at more than two million dollars. The CAI school was one of the few buildings associated with an international aid organization that was left standing, and the reason for this, I am convinced, was that our school wasn't really "international" at all. It was — and remains — "local" in every way that counts.

The outcome seemed to vindicate our three-cups-of-tea approach while simultaneously filling me with a sense of tremendous relief and pride — emotions that might well have gotten the best of me, had the journey home not served up a rude reminder of how much work remained to be done in this part of the world.

Waris was kind enough to offer Mullah Mohammed and me a ride back to Faizabad, where we were scheduled to catch a UN flight to Kabul. We were about an hour west of Baharak just outside the village of Simdara when I looked to my right and saw an old earthen hut twenty yards from the side of the road that appeared to be filled with children. At least that's what I thought I saw, but I couldn't be sure.

"Would you mind stopping?" I asked Waris. "I think there was a school back there."

Waris and Mullah Mohammed both laughed. "No, Greg, that's actually a public toilet," explained Waris. "It was left over from the Russian occupation, when it was used by the construction crews who widened the road to accommodate the Soviet tanks."

He kept driving.

"That might be true, Waris, but it seemed to be full of kids. What were they doing there? We need to go back and find out."

Waris refused to believe me, and the debate continued until I finally became adamant and basically ordered him to turn around. When we got back to the hut, I got out, walked over to the open door, and peered in. Sure enough, it was a toilet — or at least it had been at one time. The roof was now gone and the four toilet pits had been covered by old boards. There were twenty-five children between four and five years old, plus one teacher, and a slate board leaning against the wall.

The students were quite happy to chat with Waris, Mullah Mohammed, and me about their class and their curriculum. After about ten minutes the teacher, a polite young woman who looked to be about twenty years old, asked if we might like to see "the rest of the school." Curious to discover what sort of other classrooms might have been paired with an erstwhile public toilet, we nodded and followed her up the hill.

Just over the crest, at a spot that was invisible from the road, were a pair of tattered UN refugee tents, each of which featured a single chalkboard and at least thirty children, all of whom were sitting on the ground. These students were a little older, second and third graders, and they were terribly excited because, unlike their colleagues down at the toilet school, no one *ever* visited their tent class. After a few minutes of chatting, one of the two teachers turned to me and asked, "Do you want to see our upper school?"

"By all means — please lead the way."

Down the other side of the hill was a structure that appeared to be an old toolshed. This building had a roof, a small window, and a piece of tarpaulin over the doorway. It was slightly larger than the toilet — perhaps ten feet wide by eighteen feet long — and very dark inside. It was also quite noisy because nearly one hundred students were packed in like sardines. These were the fourth, fifth, and sixth graders, and according to the two women who were teaching them, they were doing extremely well — although it might have been helpful to have some books, some paper, and some pencils.

This was my introduction to the education system serving the region of Simdara, an area with a population of roughly 4,000 people. For more than two decades, the district had been attempting to keep its schools running without any assistance whatsoever. The students had neither books nor school supplies nor uniforms, and the teachers had not been paid in more than two years — although they had been receiving weekly rations of flour in compensation for their services.

We were forced to get back on the road and catch our plane, but later I telephoned Sarfraz and asked him to look into this situation with the education office in Faizabad. The officials in Faizabad, which is less than forty miles down the road, said they had never even heard of the Simdara school district — but they would be delighted if we would consider putting in a proper school for the valley.

By this point we had committed most of our current funding in Afghanistan to the new schools inside the Wakhan, but we did manage to scrape together enough cash to begin paying the salaries of the Simdara teachers. Our hope was that within a few months, we might be able to figure out a way to get the students out of the toilet and the tents and into a structure that at least vaguely resembled an actual school.

By the time autumn arrived, however, the world had shifted on its axis, and the lives of Sarfraz, me, and the other members of the Dirty Dozen had been swept up in — and consumed by — the disaster that took place on the morning of October 8, 2005.

PART II
QAYAMAT
("THE APOCALYPSE")

CHAPTER 7
A DARK AND DISTANT ROAR

On October 7, I was Prime Minister of Azad Jammu & Kashmir. On October 8, I was Prime Minister of a graveyard.
— SARDAR SIKANDAR HAYAT KHAN

Widow in refugee camp after Pakistan earthquake PHOTO: © 2005
TERU KUWAYAMA

235

One hundred and fifty million years ago, the landmass of India belonged to a super-continent known as Gondwana that splayed across much of the southern hemipshere and was bounded by a primordial ocean called the Tethys Sea. Sometime between the Jurassic and the Late Cretaceous periods, Gondwana started breaking apart, and this geologic partition cast loose India's moorings and sent it plowing northward through the sea like an immense terrestrial barge until it rammed into the southern edge of Eurasia. The impact generated plate-tectonic forces powerful enough to crush and contort the bottom of the Tethys Sea, then thrust the entire ocean bed high into the sky. The result was a soaring arc of snow-draped peaks that now stretches for more than 1,500 miles, from the lunar-looking escarpments of eastern Afghanistan to the dripping, flower-draped forests of Bhutan.

Today, the fossilized skeletons of the trilobites, crinoids, and other marine creatures that were once suspended in the warm currents of the Tethys Sea can be found littering the summits of the Himalayas, which continue to rise at a rate of ten meters each century as the Indian subcontinent sustains its slow-motion crash into central Asia. At irregular intervals, the stresses and pressures generated by this concussion cause earthquakes to ripple across the axis of the Himalayas, one of the most active fault zones in the world. Most of these temblors are minor events that scarcely draw notice. Every few decades, however, the earth's crust is seized by a cataclysmic convulsion that sets the greatest peaks on the planet to shaking like the branches of an apple tree in a strong wind.

This is what took place in northeastern Pakistan around 8:50 A.M. on the morning of Saturday, October 8, 2005.

Because it was still Ramadan, the ninth month of the Islamic calendar, when devout Muslims are forbidden to eat or drink between sunrise and sunset, many adults were inside their homes that morning, doing chores or napping after their predawn meal. Saturday is also a school day in Pakistan, however, so most schoolchildren had already gathered inside their classrooms by the time the quake struck.

The seismic shock wave originated more than sixteen miles beneath the surface, deep under Kashmir's Neelum Valley at a point whose surface coordinates corresponded almost exactly with the Government Boys' Degree High School in the village of Patika, about twelve miles northeast of the city of Muzaffarabad. The school was a two-story brick structure, and at 8:30 A.M., eighty-one tenth-grade boys had assembled at their desks in room number six. Their first class was an English lesson conducted by a twenty-four-year-old teacher named Shaukat Ali Chaudry, a former Kashmiri guerrilla fighter and an ex-member of the Taliban whose past was as convoluted as the geography of Kashmir.

Shaukat Ali was born in Patika in 1981, and at the age of twelve, when his father died, he was forced to complete his own studies while simultaneously working as a private tutor to support his mother and his eight younger siblings. His home lay just beyond the twenty-mile range of India's Swedish-manufactured Bofors artillery cannons, but throughout his teenage years he could hear periodic Indian bombardments of nearby villages in the Neelum Valley. It was during this period, in the late 1990s, that he found himself drawn into Kashmir's burgeoning independence movement — a campaign that drew inspiration from the Afghan mujahadeen's victory over the Soviets in 1989. Not long after his sixteenth birthday, Shaukat Ali joined the Jammu Kashmir Liberation Front (JKLF), where he received guerrilla training before being assigned to quick forays to raid Indian army convoys inside the portion of Kashmir that was controlled by the Indian government.

Around this time he also made the first of several trips to Kabul to observe the Taliban's efforts to impose strict Islamic law in Afghanistan, and from there he was able to roam across portions of central Asia and Chechnya. He initially found himself impressed by the Taliban's ideological fervor and decided to join the movement, but later grew deeply troubled by the Taliban's many atrocities against civilians, and especially by their attitude toward women. Thanks to his command of Arabic — a skill that many of his illiterate fellow militants did not possess — Shaukat Ali understood that they were violating the teachings of the Koran and did not hesitate to tell them so. "If that woman was your mother or your sister," he would demand, pointing to a woman who was being persecuted by one of his colleagues, "would you dare to beat or kill her in the name of Islam?"

Torn between his relationship with a group of men who were committing crimes in the name of Islam and his longing to return to his duties as a teacher, he eventually sided with the latter. "One of the happiest days of my life," he once told me, "was when I finally put down my gun forever and took up the pen. This is the jihad that is Allah's calling for me."

He took a job at the Government Boys' Degree High School in Patika, where he also joined the faculty of the Gundi Piran Higher Secondary School for Girls, an eighth of a mile down the road, tutoring three hundred female students in English, economics, and mathematics — the first man in the history of the district permitted to teach girls. Sporting round, gold-rimmed glasses and a long black beard, he looked like a cross between an Afghan mujahadeen and a Berkeley philosophy professor. And by the fall of 2005, this young, earnest, and talented Islamic rebel was passionately devoted to empowering Kashmir's first generation of science-educated girls to enter college and eventually move into the workforce.

On the morning of October 8, Shaukat

Ali's lesson plan called for him to read a passage to his English class that began with the sentence, "Sports and games are very important for physical health." Before he started reading, he looked up and spotted a student named Tarik, who had been absent the previous day.

"Tarik," he demanded, "where were you yesterday?"

Tarik shot to his feet.

"Sir, I was sick and unable to come," he explained. "Would you please repeat yesterday's lesson?"

Before Shaukat Ali could respond, a dark roar engulfed the entire Neelum Valley and the walls of the school building began to shake violently.

"Run!" cried Shaukat Ali.

He held the door tightly as the boys threaded through one by one, then followed after them while reciting the words of the First *Kalima*, one of the five pillars of the Islamic declaration of faith — *La ilaha illal-Lah, Muhammadun rasulula-Lah.* "There is no god but Allah, and Muhammed is his Prophet."

Teacher and students raced along the hall and down the stairs to join the rest of the school in the courtyard, where everyone watched in disbelief as the walls supporting the second story crumbled and the top floor of the building fell apart. Shaukat Ali and his colleagues immediately started counting heads to determine if anyone had been left behind and quickly realized that the headmaster, Akbar Ahwan, and the history teacher, Professor Khalid Husmani, were nowhere to be seen. The two men were later found dead in the rubble, along with the body of Khoshnood Ali Khan, the school clerk, who apparently had been checking the classrooms to make sure the students had all evacuated before attempting to flee himself.

It was during the brief interlude required to complete this initial roll call that several things happened. Roughly 450 miles to the southeast, tremors caused panic in the streets of the Indian cities of Amritsar and Delhi, while in the district of Poonch, the two-hundred-year-old Moti Mahal fort abruptly collapsed. Far off to the northwest, a wall in the Afghan city of Jalalabad tumbled onto a young girl, who became one of the quake's only two casualties inside Afghanistan. Meanwhile, fifty-five miles southwest in Islamabad's Blue Area, the Margalla Towers residential apartment building disintegrated, killing seventy-four people according to the Associated Press. None of those events, however, could compete with the carnage and destruction that greeted the teachers of Shaukat Ali's school when, upon completing their head count, they looked up to survey their surroundings.

Along the hills beyond the town, landslides had severed every road and buried entire villages. The bridge across the Neelum River had twisted sideways. In Patika itself, there was barely a house, *dukan* (shop), or office left standing, and people were running through the streets, many of them screaming and covered with blood.

Shaukat Ali started to rush across to the town bazaar but was brought up short when his gaze turned toward the Gundi Piran Higher Secondary School for Girls, where all that was left was pile of gray and white rubble. The entire structure had failed, trapping three hundred girls inside. Many were already dead, but some were still alive, and when the parents of these students beganing running into the schoolyard, they were greeted by the muffled cries of their daughters coming from under the wreckage.

Shaukat Ali's own home in the village of Batangi was eight miles away, and as the head of his household, he knew that his family would be looking to him for leadership in this moment. His responsibilities as the oldest son demanded that he leave immediately, but there was another set of obligations that required him to do the opposite. "I knew every girl inside that building," he later told me. "These were my students — they were like sisters and daughters to me, and I could not leave them."

The streets were impassable, foreclosing any possibility of getting heavy equipment to the school, and the aftershocks were already triggering new spasms of vibration. Amid the dust and debris, the parents and the teachers could spy arms and legs and bits of clothing, so they went at the rubble with their bare hands. Muffled voices and screams helped guide the frantic rescuers to those who were still alive. Although the students who were pulled out were in shock, many of these survivors set to work separating the dead from injured, laying the corpses of their classmates out in the courtyard while caring for the stricken and the broken as best they could.

During that first morning and afternoon there was no drinking water, no medical supplies, and no blankets. At one point, Shaukat Ali helped remove the mangled body of a girl named Sabina, who had treated him like an older brother and had promised to help find him a wife. He could not bring himself to look at Sabina's face — and years later, he would still find it impossible to recall the moment he covered her body with a shawl without weeping. By evening, they had barely made a dent in the remains of the building.

The darkness that descended over the southwestern rim of the Vale of Kashmir that night was absolute, unbroken by a single lightbulb or streetlamp in the entire Neelum Valley. Then it started to rain.

This was not a soft patter or an intermittent drizzle, but a full-on deluge. The torrent rendered what was left of Patika cold and drenched. It fell so hard and so relentlessly that the ruins were swiftly filled with small rivers. They sluiced through the wreckage of the town's buildings, and they threaded around the bodies of its dead.

Shaukat Ali spent that night caring for a girl named Sura. Although she had been horribly injured and was in terrible pain, the only comfort he could offer was to hold her head in his lap and try to keep the rain from her face with his jacket. Long after midnight, when the rain had finally stopped, the aftershocks continued. He tried to keep track of the number, but stopped counting when he got to one hundred. The most haunting thing he remembered from that first night, however, he told me later, was the stillness between the convulsions.

Packs of *gidhad* (jackals) and wild dogs roam throughout the foothills of those mountains after sunset, and on any given night — especially during the *azan* (the muezzin's call to evening prayer), their howls tend to create a mournful racket that resounds across the ridgetops and through the valleys.

That night, not a single animal made a sound.

There is a twelve-hour time difference between Pakistan and the Rocky Mountains, and on the night of October 7, I was in a hotel room in Salt Lake City, where my son and daughter had a tae kwon do tournament scheduled for the following morning. When my wife, Tara, called shortly after 9:30 P.M. with news of the first damage reports from Kashmir, the kids and I had just returned from dinner at T.G.I. Friday's. Tara had no details, and I couldn't raise anyone in Pakistan. I tried to call Suleman, Saidullah, Parvi, Nazir, and every other person I could think of but couldn't get through — not even to Sarfraz on his satellite phone.

I asked Tara to keep trying to reach Suleman and if she got through, to tell him to keep in touch whenever and however possible. The kids wanted to go swimming, but before they did I sat them down on a bed and told them what had happened.

"Dad, how can we do a tae kwon do tournament tomorrow," asked Amira, "when the kids in Pakistan are dying?"

"Are Apo and Suleman okay?" chimed in Khyber, before telling me that I should immediately head off to Pakistan to help.

"It's hard to understand why there has to be suffering and tragedy like this in the world — and it's going to get worse," I told them as they clung tightly to my hands. "But we will do everything we can to help our friends over there. For now, let's say a prayer to keep them in God's hands."

Later that night, I jumped online. Tremors had been felt throughout central and southern Asia, and most of the early reports seemed to focus on the two apartment towers in Islamabad that had fallen down. As for the villages deep in the mountains and the people who lived near the quake's epicenter, I knew that it would be another several hours before details even started to emerge.

For now, my immediate concern was for the welfare of our staff and their families, followed closely by that of our teachers, students, and schools. The CAI projects that were closest to the epicenter were our pair of artillery-deflecting schools in Gultori, some eighty miles away. Many others were a hundred miles distant, certainly within range of a major quake.

By working the phones through most of that night and a good portion of the following day, I was able to confirm that all members of our operation and their families were safe and that all of our schools in Pakistan were still standing. There had been no deaths, not even any injuries, and only a minor crack in the lower wall of the Al Abid Primary School in Skardu. By that time, however, it had also become clear that the damage inside Kashmir was catastrophic.

Reports indicated that numerous towns and villages throughout northern Pakistan were completely wiped out. On each street and in every neighborhood, there were extended families in which every member of the clan — dozens of men, women, and children — had been killed instantly and interred together beneath the rubble of their homes. In the capital city of Muzaffarabad, the main hospital was demolished, killing more than two hundred patients. The city's prison had also pancaked, burying fifteen prisoners and wounding forty others while sixty survivors ran to safety. (One of the only structures left standing was a special set of gallows in the courtyard that could accommodate three condemned criminals at the same time.) Somewhere amid the wreckage of Muzaffarabad University, hundreds of college students had been buried alive. Families wandered the streets, refusing to return to their homes. Children, women, and men sat or stood in the open and wailed. By nightfall, dogs roamed the streets, tearing at the bodies of the dead until patrolling soldiers shot them down.

During the previous half century, Pakistan had suffered through four wars, two military coups, and any number of floods, bombings, political assassinations, and other disruptions, but there had never been anything quite like this. The trembler registered a magnitude of 7.6, approximately the same as the 1906 San Francisco earthquake. Satellite photos would later reveal that the quake had triggered 2,252 landslides, according to two American seismologists. Within a ten-mile radius of the town of Patika, there wasn't a single hospital bed, working telephone, or drop of municipal drinking water. The death toll according to the U.S. Geological Survey would eventually exceed eighty-six thousand, qualifying it as the worst natural disaster in the history of Pakistan, and the twelfth most destructive earthquake of all time.

A quarter of those casualties — nearly eighteen thousand dead — were children, most of them students who were in school when the earthquake struck. Strangely, the vast majority of those dead schoolchildren were girls, and as the debris was cleared away and the bodies were recovered, the explanation for this imbalance slowly emerged. While the boys had tended to race to safety by bolting out the windows and doors, most of the girls had instinctively huddled together and perished. Also, thanks to the government's tendency to channel the best resources toward male students before seeing to the needs of the females, many of the girls did not have desks — which might have saved thousands of lives had the girls been able to crawl under them for safety.

According to Pakistan's Ministry of Education, 3,794 schools and colleges in Kashmir and 2,159 in the Northwest Frontier Province had been destroyed. Roughly half a million students had been cut off from their studies. The education infrastructure for the region — offices, records, payrolls, everything — was gone, and more than five hundred teachers were dead. In less than four minutes, an entire generation of literate children had been wiped out.

It would take months before the extent of

the destruction had been fully cataloged and analyzed. For the moment, the only thing the people of northern Pakistan really had was a name for what had befallen them.

In Urdu, the word for earthquake is *zalzala*. But throughout Kashmir, then and to this day, the event that took place on the morning of October 8 was simply known as the *Qayamat* — "the apocalypse."

Shaukat Ali spent all of Sunday, October 9, clawing at the rubble in search of injured girls, three of whom were pulled out alive. By now his hands were torn and his clothing was covered in blood. That night, the cries of girls who were trapped inside, which had been growing fainter, finally died out, leaving only silence. Just before noon on Monday, however, Shaukat Ali heard whimpers coming from the section of the wreckage where the fourth-grade classroom had been located. He and a group of men clawed feverishly at a hole in the rubble, dislodging a rain of stones and dirt.

"You idiot bastards, stop throwing rocks at us!" came a voice from within. "Can't you see that we are helpless and stuck?"

"This is your master Shaukat Ali," shouted Chaudry. "Are you okay?"

"We need water," came the response, "and

we don't like you throwing stones at us when we have done nothing wrong!"

An hour later, a dozen men had cleared away several stones weighing more than two hundred pounds and a maze of twisted rebar to expose a pair of fourth graders named Aanam and Anii. They were surrounded by a close circle of fifteen of their dead friends, whose bodies had protected them from falling debris and cushioned the worst of the impact. Although Aanam and Anii could not see each other in the darkness and the dust, they had been holding hands for seventy-five hours.

After the girls were safely extracted, each guzzled a bottle of mineral water, then ran straight home. Later that evening, Shaukat Ali decided it was finally time for him to do the same.

When he reached the village of Batangi, he found his mother, Sahera Begum, huddled shivering in the rain under a sheet of plastic next to the ruins of their house. Nothing was left, not even her shoes or the family Koran. From his mother he learned that one of his sisters had been killed and already buried, along with his brother-in-law and all of his closest childhood friends. Of the 165 houses in his community, only 2 had been partially spared.

The following day, Shaukat Ali walked back into the center of Patika to purchase a shovel, a pick, some kerosene, and a pair of shoes for his mother. Then he returned home and started to dig out her belongings. With the help of his brothers and sisters, he spent that day and the next excavating the remains of her household and rigging a temporary shelter. Then on the seventh day, he walked twelve miles into the city of Muzaffarabad and was amazed by what he found.

Amid the wreckage and the chaos was a completely new town: a chaotic bazaar filled with supplies flown in from the world outside, new neighborhoods fashioned from tents and plastic, and most striking of all, new faces. The Red Cross, the Pakistani army, and the American army were all there, along with a host of international relief organizations, and the media. They were handing out free clothing and food, which Shaukat Ali could not bring himself to accept. He also refused to accept a job: The Red Cross desperately needed to hire translators, and people with his skills were in high demand. They were offering one hundred dollars a day in pay, more than he could make in a month. Instead, he went back to Patika and met with Saida Shabir, the principal of the Gundi Piran Girls' School.

A diminutive figure with dark eyes, thick glasses, and a limp, Shabir was nevertheless a formidable woman. She had been an educator for nearly thirty years, rising from teacher to administrator on the basis of a ferocious work ethic, and when she opened her mouth to express her displeasure, even the men stopped talking. She was known — and feared — for her fierce temper, her ability to make things happen fast, and a willingness to dress down any student, teacher, or government official who failed to conform to the standards she had set.

Shabir and Shaukat Ali agreed that although rebuilding the region's educational infrastructure hardly qualified as a top priority in the minds of the military and government officials who were spearheading the relief efforts, schools — especially girls' schools — were a potent symbol of progress. Getting classes up and running as quickly as possible could offer a beacon of hope for the entire community.

"Shaukat," ordered the headmistress, "go back down to Muzaffarabad, speak to the army commander who is in charge, and find out what sort of assistance he can offer."

Upon returning to Muzaffarabad, he approached a Pakistani army colonel who had been tasked with distributing relief supplies and explained that he needed several canvas tents so that he and Shabir could reopen their girls' school and resume classes. When the colonel realized that Shaukat Ali was serious, he called him a fool.

"Yes, that may be the case," replied Shaukat Ali. "But if the Pakistani army refuses to provide shelter, then we will have to begin teaching in the open air — and as you know, winter is just around the corner."

When he left Muzaffarabad, he had four eight-by-twelve-foot canvas tents — enough to accommodate six hundred students.

Back in Patika, he and Shabir agreed that time was short. All across Pakistan, government-administered schools would conduct final exams the following March, and if the girls of the Gundi Piran school were to have any chance of passing those tests, classes needed to resume as quickly as possible. Word was sent out that the school would reopen on November 1.

That afternoon, October 13, the rain finally stopped and it started to snow.

In the meantime, having returned home to Bozeman, I was anxious to survey the damage and talk with people on the ground. I realized, however, that it was probably more important for me to stay in the States for now. Our supporters and donors, old and new alike, would be sending in checks and wanting to know how we were going to spend the money. The mountaineering and the outdoor communities would surely want to donate tents, sleeping bags, parkas — and many of these people would be looking to us for guidance on how to get those supplies to Pakistan. All of which put me in a rather awkward and uncomfortable position.

Providing aid in the midst of a natural disaster is an extraordinarily complex and expensive job that presents almost impossible difficulties, even for organizations that specialize in this kind of work. The infrastructure for delivering food, providing shelter, and ensuring sanitation — not only for the victims but also for the relief workers — often has to be created from scratch and set up on the fly. Restoring power, transportation, communication, and proper medical care requires professionals with enormous expertise. In the face of such challenges, the notion that a group as tiny as the Central Asia Institute — an NGO that by then had built fewer than fifty schools on a budget of less than a million dollars a year — might somehow reinvent itself overnight as an emergency relief provider was well meaning but supremely impractical.

We were not set up for emergency work, we knew almost nothing about the business of disaster relief, and with our new initiative in Afghanistan, our limited manpower and financial resources had already been stretched to the breaking point.

On the other hand, given what had just happened, a large chunk of northeastern Pakistan had just been cut off from the rest of the world and left to fend for itself. Whether we liked it or not, the residents of this region were now, quite literally, the people at the end of the road.

On October 10, Sarfraz finally called. He was already in the earthquake zone.

Sarfraz had felt the vibrations at his home in Zuudkhan, instantly grasped the significance of what had taken place, and hit the road. It had taken more than forty-eight hours for him to make his way to Islamabad and then head east, hitching rides in trucks, minivans, and jeeps and hiking over the sections that had been buried by landslides.

As soon as I heard his voice, I started grilling him about what was happening, but he told me to hold off with the questions. It would be several days, he explained, before he would be able to reach the most remote sections of the disaster area. Once there, he would take stock of the situation and report his findings back to me. Then we could decide together how the Central Asia Institute might be able to help. If we had a role to play, he suggested, it would depend heavily on what had happened to the local schools. For the moment, what we needed most was information.

His first destination was Balakot, a town on the eastern edge of Pakistan's Northwest Frontier Province. The scene that greeted him there was shocking. In some places, the road was lined with bodies waiting for relatives or friends to identify them for burial. In other places burials were already taking place, but thanks to a shortage of picks and shovels, people were digging graves with wooden boards or their bare hands. In one particular spot, he came upon a woman sitting by the debris from a collapsed school that her two daughters had attended. The rubble had already been pushed aside with a bulldozer, and the area had been combed by cadaver-sniffing dogs, who had failed to turn up any sign of her daughters, but the grieving mother refused to believe that her children's bodies were not inside. Sarfraz tried to console her, but she was refusing to eat, drink, or sleep.

From Balakot he continued working his way north up the Kaghan Valley, which is heavily populated by ethnic Pathans, a notoriously insular community. Many of these people seemed to react negatively to the idea that intruders from the outside were there to help. "Why are you coming here?" several locals demanded of Sarfraz. "We have no food or shelter for even ourselves — go away!"

Eventually Sarfraz managed to befriend an elderly Pathan named Mohammed Raza, who advised him that it would probably be best if he left the area for now. The residents would eventually begin turning their attention to the business of rebuilding schools, counseled Raza, but now was not the proper time. Should Sarfraz return in a year or two, he would probably meet with a better reception.

Based on the response he had received in the Kaghan, Sarfraz's conclusion was pessimistic. If people didn't exactly welcome *him,* a fellow Pakistani, how would they respond to the arrival of an American working for a foreign NGO like the Central Asia Institute? After returning to Islamabad and sharing his negative prognosis with me, he posed a difficult question.

If the Kaghan Valley would not work out, was it appropriate for us to start exploring the more remote areas that lay directly along the border between India and Pakistan — the places where outsiders had not ventured in years? In other words, should we consider venturing into the heart of Pakistan-administered Kashmir?

This made both of us pause to take a deep breath.

In addition to its notorious geological instability, Kashmir lies atop a web of political fault lines whose intractable complexity is matched only by the clash between the Israelis and the Palestinians. The origin of this conflict can be precisely dated to midnight on August 15, 1947, when Britain's Indian empire was officially partitioned into the new nations of India and Pakistan.

The upheaval of Partition produced one of the largest migrations of refugees in modern history (twenty-five million people) and the slaughter of nearly one million civilians, as Hindus and Sikhs fled south into India while Muslims raced in the opposite direction toward Pakistan. Another casualty was India's northernmost principality, the state of Jammu and Kashmir, which had a Muslim-majority population ruled by a Hindu maharaja named Hari Singh, whose great-grandfather had purchased Kashmir from the British in 1846 for 7.5 million rupees, or about 5 rupees per citizen — the cost of a cup of tea at an Indian roadside café.

Two months after Partition, Pakistan invaded Kashmir and rattled the composure of Hari Singh, a man whose interests up to that point had focused mostly on polo, late-night champagne parties, and shooting safaris. In the early hours of October 26, the maharaja fled the kingdom with his most exquisite jewels, his Webley & Scott shotguns, and his dog Tarzan. Meanwhile, the Indian government mobilized its entire fleet of passenger planes and airlifted three hundred Sikh troops into the capital city of Srinagar.

When the first round of fighting ended, two-thirds of Kashmir was in Indian hands, including Jammu, the Buddhist region of Ladakh, and the biggest prize of all, the legendary Vale of Kashmir. Pakistan controlled the regions of Gilgit and Baltistan, plus a sliver of southwestern Kashmir that India now refers to as Pakistan-Occupied Kashmir (POK) and Pakistan calls Azad Kashmir (Free Kashmir). On the map, Azad Kashmir is a narrow tongue of land, at some points only fifteen miles across, whose shape is similar to that of the Wakhan Corridor, but with a north-south orientation. The demarcation between the two Kashmirs corresponds almost exactly to the final position of the battle lines when the military ceasefire was declared in January 1949. This 450-mile border, which starts near the Indian city of Jammu and cuts a diagonal, northeastward swath toward China, is known as the Line of Control (LOC).

In 1965 and again in 1971, India and Pakistan fought wars in Kashmir, both of which Pakistan lost. Then during the summer of 1989, a civil uprising exploded among ordinary Kashmiris who wanted independence from both India *and* Pakistan. Within months, the revolt had turned into a violent war that would eventually pit some sixty separate Islamic guerrilla groups against half a million Indian army troops and result in the deaths of more than thirty-six thousand people. Atrocities were committed on both sides. While Indian security forces detained, tortured, and executed civilians, Islamic militants who had been trained in Pakistan slipped across the border to attack Indian soldiers and carry out an assassination campaign against Hindu poets, judges, and social workers. The situation was not helped by the fact that twelve months earlier, Pakistan had conducted its first successful nuclear-weapons test.

Repression and reprisal followed one another until April 1999, when eight hundred

Pakistan-supported militants launched a surprise attack across the Line of Control, seized a seventeen-thousand-foot ridge overlooking the cities of Kargil and Dras in India-controlled Kashmir, and began shelling a vital Indian military road that connects the cities of Srinagar and Leh. India responded with full force, and by early May there was heavy fighting along one hundred miles of the border. By July 4, when the Indian counterattack and pressure from the Clinton administration had forced Pakistani prime minister Nawaz Sharif to back down, both sides had reportedly put their nuclear strike forces on alert, provoking President Clinton to declare Kashmir "the most dangerous place on earth."

According to the United Nations, the final disposition of this disputed region — which has been pending for more than sixty years — is to be determined by a plebiscite among Kashmiri citizens, the majority of whom are still Muslim. Until that vote takes place and residents on both sides of the LOC are afforded the chance to exercise their UN-sanctioned right of self-determination, Kashmir is likely to remain inherently unstable and highly volatile.

By the time of the 2005 earthquake, Azad Kashmir had been closed to almost all foreigners for decades. As a result, despite having spent more than a dozen years living and working throughout Pakistan, I knew almost nothing about this place. The Central Asia Institute had no relationships, no connections, and no history in this part of the country. In short, we hadn't shared a single cup of tea in Azad Kashmir.

Given the magnitude of the disaster, however, the restrictions on foreign travel had been lifted overnight and NGOs from all over the world were now pouring into the area. So I suggested to Sarfraz that he should get back on the road and do his best to make his way into the eastern side of the damage zone, deep inside Azad Kashmir.

At this point, of course, neither Sarfraz nor I had ever heard of the Gundi Piran Girls' School — nor had we met Shaukat Ali Chaudry or Saida Shabir. But the events that would eventually draw all of us together had now been set in motion.

CHAPTER 8
NO IDEA WHAT TO DO

When your heart speaks, take good notes.
— SUSAN CAMPBELL

Distribution point after earthquake, Neelum Valley, Pakistan
PHOTO: © 2005 TERU KUWAYAMA

On October 15, Sarfraz again headed out of Islamabad, this time in the direction of Muzaffarabad, gateway to ground zero of the earthquake. The road he took proceeded east from Pakistan's capital and wound into the foothills past the idyllic summer resort of Murree, a former British hill station where lowlanders flee the Punjab's sweltering, humid heat in summer. From Murree, the road plunged down through a series of stunning canyons to the Kohala Bridge, which marks the entrance to the green hills of Azad Kashmir. Sarfraz was amazed to note that the Frontier Works Organization (FWO), Pakistan's military civil-engineering unit, had already managed to clear more than a dozen massive landslides and open the road. But upon rounding the bend into Muzaffarabad, which sits at the confluence of the Neelum and Jhelum rivers, he found himself confronted once again with the sort of carnage and suffering he had already witnessed in the Kaghan Valley.

Almost every structure in the city was cracked, leaning, or collapsed. Each street and alley was crowded with homeless, wandering, injured, or traumatized adults and children whose emotional stability was not helped by the numerous aftershocks. In every neighborhood, Pakistani army crews were sifting through wreckage searching for bodies and any possible survivors. People were milling everywhere, dazed and looking for food and water.

Sarfraz spent that first night in a sleeping bag on the sidewalk outside the Al-Abbas Hotel and Restaurant, which was perched on a cliff high above the Neelum River (and which the members of the Dirty Dozen would eventually dub the Crack Hotel on account of the massive vertical fissure that zigzagged down one side of the structure). The next day, as he moved about the city, he called me on his sat phone to report that there would be an inevitable bias toward concentrating most emergency supplies in Muzaffarabad in order to use the city as the staging area for the whole region. This, Sarfraz went on to explain, was good news to the residents of Muzaffarabad; but it would offer little comfort to the 2.5 million displaced people in the surrounding valleys and hillsides who were cut off from most contact with the outside world.

After laying this out, Sarfraz proposed that he head northeast in an effort to reach the most remote villages along the most distant reaches of the Neelum Valley, a 150-mile-long gorge carved by the Neelum River, which is named after the color of the rubies that can be mined at various points along its folds, and which once served as one of the world's most important centers of Buddhism. Thanks to its precipitous canyon walls and the fact that it had received some of the heaviest Indian artillery shelling during the past two decades, the Neelum qualified as perhaps the most underserved district in all of Azad Kashmir. By virtue of these attributes, argued Sarfraz, this was probably where we would want to target our work. (Although we didn't know this at the time, more than 10 percent of the valley's 140,000 residents had perished in the earthquake, and the majority of these victims were schoolchildren.)

I told him I agreed completely, and I wished him luck.

Sarfraz had hired a car to bring him this far, but when he saw the condition of the road beyond Muzaffarabad, he sent the driver back to Islamabad and continued on foot, carrying several bottles of water, his sleeping bag, and a package of salted crackers. The road up the Neelum Valley was blocked by dozens of landslides, and in some areas entire slabs of mountain had crashed into the river.

As he threaded his way through the mud and the debris, everyone whom he spoke to had a story, and every story was tragic. Without exception, each person he encountered had lost at least one close relative, usually more. Anyone who had been inside a building was lucky to be alive, although most of them had lost all of their worldly possessions. It seemed like nearly everyone was limping or had a field dressing that was matted with dried blood. Men and women either carried two or three children on their backs or pushed their families along in a wheelbarrow. With his sleeping bag and his package of biscuits, Sarfraz qualified as a man of enviable riches.

That night, while sleeping under a smashed truck, he called me on his sat phone. "The roads are filled with people: people walking, people looking for food, people crying," he reported. "It is very bad everywhere. When it is dark and when nobody is looking, even I start to cry."

Most natural disasters are followed by a high degree of chaos, and the first goal of the authorities is to try systematically to reduce that chaos. But in Azad Kashmir during the second week of October, things only seemed to become more confused and more disorganized with each passing day. Within forty-eight hours, the only two roads leading from Islamabad into the devastated valleys to the north were jammed with every kind of conveyance, including donkey, bicycles, and rickshaws, as relatives and friends poured into the province in the hope of finding loved ones. From all across Pakistan, well-intentioned volunteers were now rushing into the mountains to offer assistance. As a result, the few stretches of highway that had not already been blocked by landslides were now hopelessly gridlocked. At one point, the Pakistani army began bulldozing vehicles off the road in order to get the flow of traffic going.

Adding to the confusion was the flurry of international assistance that was converging on the stricken region. The international NGOs needed a plethora of ancillary support, including Land Cruisers, kitchens, generators, remote servers for their laptops, mineral water, and much more. In order to facilitate the flow of humanitarian and medical aid, five crossing points along the LOC between India and Pakistan had been opened — but these thoroughfares were soon bottlenecked as aid teams began arriving from around the world. Twelve days after the quake, the Pakistani government still had not reached 20 percent of the damaged areas. Two weeks after that, the U.N. World Food Program would estimate that five hundred thousand people still had not received any aid at all. By the middle of November, more than three million refugees would be huddling in the mountains without shelter or adequate food on the threshold of the winter.

As Sarfraz headed north, hiking first from Muzaffarabad to Patika and then proceeding for seventeen hours from Patika to the village of Nousada, he could see that in many places the landslides that had destroyed the roads had also obliterated entire communities. Ten miles north of Muzaffarabad, for example, lay the Kamsar refugee camp, home to about a thousand Muslim refugees from India-controlled Kashmir who had been living there since 1992. The camp had been situated on a narrow bench approximately two thousand feet above the Neelum River; during the quake, half of the settlement had broken off the hillside and plunged into the gorge, taking with it more than three hundred of the camp's residents. The buildings on the portion of the bench that remained intact had all been destroyed, rendering the seven hundred survivors refugees twice over.

Three days after leaving Muzaffarabad, Sarfraz reached the village of Nouseri, where every house had been obliterated and people were wandering the trail in rags, still unable to fathom what had taken place and having not the faintest notion of where or how to begin rebuilding their lives. Eight miles farther on, in the tiny hamlet of Pakrat, he met a woman named Alima whose husband and two children had perished in the quake. She was squatting atop a wooden bed outside the remains of her home, staring blankly at a sheaf of papers. These were the official documents that she was supposed to fill out in order to qualify for a government disbursement of cash. In addition to being immobilized by her despondency, Alima was illiterate.

"I asked the *fauji havildar* (army sargeant) for help," she said to Sarfraz, "and all he gave me was this piece of paper — and when I started to complain and ask for food, he told me to go away or he would beat me with his stick. This paper is not even food enough for a dog."

Alima's predicament struck Sarfraz as twisted and surreal, a kind of satire of cruelty. The forms that she was supposed to fill out featured a slew of questions to which she had no answer, including the place and date of her birth, her age, and her national identification number.

"How is a woman like this ever going to survive?" he exclaimed that night on the sat phone. "Everywhere I am looking, there are dead bodies, and the people who are not dead act like they are dead. This is too much. No one has any idea of what to do."

Sarfraz is a resilient man who has lived a challenging life, but the scenes he was encountering in Azad Kashmir were beginning to grind him down. Each night, his report to me was depressingly the same. In every direction, from every angle, the world seemed to be filled with chaos and despair.

One of the few bright spots to which Sarfraz could point during his reconnaissance trips involved Operation Lifeline, an internationally organized effort to transport emergency supplies via helicopter into isolated villages and towns all across Azad Kashmir. This mission included several choppers provided by the British and the Germans, along with a number of Pakistan's own Soviet-era Mi-17 helicopters. The heart and soul of the operation, however, involved fourteen American Chinooks flown by an Army Reserve unit from Olathe, Kansas. These machines, along with their two hundred pilots and support crew, were the unsung heroes of the early relief effort.

The Chinooks had flown in straight from the war in Afghanistan within two days of the quake, and their first mission involved ferrying bulldozers, trucks, and other heavy equipment necessary to rebuild the main roads, while using their return flights to evacuate the severely injured. Later, they hauled tents, roofing materials, medical supplies, flour, cement, baby formula, and anything else that might be needed — including a special consignment of sewing machines. The 6,000 tons of material that the helicopters delivered in the first three months following the earthquake — one of the most massive helicopter airlifts ever conducted — was eventually credited with keeping half a million people alive over the ensuing winter.

As the choppers penetrated ever deeper into the damage zone, their fame increased, and eventually the toys that were most coveted by the children of Azad Kashmir were little plastic helicopters. Everyone loved the Chinooks and their crews, who were invariably greeted with waves and cheers and, of course, hordes of kids. Sarfraz talked to some of the pilots and learned that those who had served in Iraq could not believe that the people of Pakistan actually *liked* them. In the coming years, many of these pilots and their crew members would look back upon those weeks as the highlight of their military careers.

As the Chinooks delivered their payloads of heavy equipment and as the traffic jams were sorted out, the roads gradually began to open up. By the middle of October, Sarfraz reported that Muzaffarabad had become command central for the entire relief effort as the big international aid organizations — UNICEF, Oxfam, the Red Cross, CARE, the Red Crescent Society, and more than a dozen others — erected satellite dishes, set up computer banks, and began stockpiling supplies. But "upside" in the more remote communities, there was little evidence of this progress, which created a troubling dichotomy. In downtown Muzaffarabad, for example, Sarfraz saw six large emergency field hospitals lined up in a row, each equipped with generators and surgical supplies. A village only ten miles away, however, might have received absolutely nothing. Six months after the earthquake — in some instances even a year later — Sarfraz was still hearing about villages that had not received a single ounce of aid.

Another problem was lack of coordination. In the earliest weeks of the catastrophe, the supplies that were flown in by helicopter were distributed almost randomly. Whenever a helicopter began heading up a valley, everyone could hear it coming, and the race was on. The supplies were distributed on a first-come-first-served basis, and many of the scenes that unfolded on the chopper landing zones were quite unpleasant. In some areas, a refugee camp stocked with tents, clothes, and food would simply materialize — courtesy of the Chinooks — and thousands of people would rush in to grab what they could. A week later, another camp might be set up four miles away, and everyone would rush *there*. Amid the "every man for himself" atmosphere, some people enjoyed a windfall while others wound up with nothing.

By the end of October, Sarfraz was also starting to notice an odd gap between what was being delivered and what people actually needed. A number of outdoor manufacturers from the United States, for example, had donated impressive quantities of high-tech mountaineering tents made with synthetic fabrics that are highly flammable. As the weather turned cold, these tents became crammed with families who relied on candles and kerosene lanterns for illumination and who prepared their meals on cooking fires directly outside the front flap. Many of these tents ended up catching fire, resulting in horrific burns and several deaths, especially among children. In retrospect, low-tech, heavy-duty canvas shelters would have been more effective and less dangerous.

A notable exception to this trend were the "home-rebuilding kits" donated by the Turkish government after significant consultation with refugees on the ground. The kits, which Turkish officials purchased in Pakistan, consisted of hammers, nails, shovels, saws, wire, corrugated sheet metal, and other essential building items so that people could fashion temporary shelters in their own villages instead of packing up and moving to a refugee camp. When I later asked people in Azad Kashmir what had benefited them the most during the aftermath of the earthquake, the reply was fairly consistent: getting the roads reopened and the Turkish home-construction kits.

By early November, Sarfraz was starting to

see groups of women who would bundle up huge bales of donated clothing — expensive waterproof parkas, pants, and bibs — and set them on fire to heat water or for cooking. It turned out that what these women really needed was an efficient source of cooking fuel, and without a steady supply of kerosene or propane, they were forced to prepare their families' meals over fires made from The North Face, Patagonia, and Mountain Hardwear gear.

This clothing was used for other purposes as well. Later that month, Sarfraz e-mailed me a photograph of a sheep grazing on a hillside with a puffy down jacket wrapped around its hind end. Clearly, what these refugees needed was building material with which to fabricate shelters to keep their livestock alive. Since no one had asked them, however, they were doing their best to improvise. The instinct to help was wonderful, but one can only imagine what the down jacket donor would have thought if he or she had seen what his or her gift eventually was used for. The sheep photo graphically illustrated the limitations of simply fire hosing relief supplies into an area without proper coordination.

Such chaotic methods sometimes provoked cynicism and exacerbated people's frustration. On one trip, Sarfraz met a police officer from Muzaffarabad named Qurban Ali Shah, whose father had been killed in the quake. This man was quick to pull out an impressive sheaf of calling cards collected from various individuals and aid groups who had arrived in the city over the preceding weeks. One was from a Chinese doctor, another from a German "emergency architect." Dozens of these people had passed their contact information along to Qurban Ali Shah, and not one of them had ever followed up. All he had to show was his collection of business cards.

In other instances, expressions of international concern that failed to result in concrete action provoked feelings of betrayal and anger. Such was the case at the Gundi Piran school, where the tragedy itself and the valiant rescue efforts became a focal point for the international broadcast media, whose representatives flew in on quick helicopter jaunts to obtain graphic visuals for their broadcasts. According to teachers at Gundi Piran, crews from major television networks based in Britain, France, the United States, Germany, Japan, and Italy all descended on the school, along with dozens of reporters from various radio stations, newspapers, and magazines. A number of these journalists apparently reacted angrily when headmistress Saida Shabir, in order to protect her staff and students' fragile emotional state, prevented the reporters from conducting intrusive interviews with them. Months later, Shabir regretted having given them any access to the school whatsoever. Despite the massive news coverage, she said, she had yet to receive a single substantive gesture of assistance — not one brick, not one pen — from an NGO or a member of the Pakistani government. No one had even helped to provide decent funerals or burials for the seven girls who had been pulled from the wreckage of the school and whose bodies had never been claimed — presumably because their entire families had been killed.

In the end, Shaukat Ali and several other members of the faculty were forced to dig a set of graves themselves and to lay the girls to rest in the courtyard of the ruined school.

Unfortunately, some of the smartest and most effective assistance was provided by groups of Islamic militants. Within seventy-two hours of the earthquake, Al Qaeda's number two leader, Ayman al-Zawahiri, issued a dramatic videotaped message urging Muslims around world to help the victims of this disaster. "I call on all Muslims in general, and I call on all Islamic humanitarian associations in particular, to move to Pakistan to provide help to their Pakistani brothers, and that they do it quickly," he declared. "All of us know the vicious American war on Muslim humanitarian work."

In response, resourceful and energetic young *jihadis* were often the first to show up during the earthquake's aftermath, in many cases appearing days or even weeks before the Pakistani army or the international aid organizations arrived. According to Ahmed Rashid, author of *Descent Into Chaos* and the foremost independent journalist reporting from Afghanistan and Pakistan, seventeen extremist groups that were either on the United Nations' list of terrorist organizations or banned by the Pakistani government were reactivated during this time as Islamic NGOs. They did an impressive job of putting together sophisticated relief operations, delivering supplies and medical care to victims with speed and efficiency when no one else could.

One of the first such groups on the scene was Jamaat-ud-Dawa, the political arm of the banned extremist militia Lashkar-e-Taiba, the pro-Taliban, Pakistan-based organization that would carry out the horrific terrorist attacks in Bombay in November 2008 that resulted in the deaths of 173 civilians. Another elaborate operation was run by the extremely conservative group Jamaat-e-Islami. After setting up base camps in several ravaged towns, Jamaat's Al-Khidmat Foundation began dispatching its operatives to remote areas where motorized vehicles could not penetrate. Not far from the Jamaat-e-Islami operation in Muzaffarabad was another camp sponsored by the Al Rashid Trust, which was created by Dr. Amir Aziz, a British-trained orthopedic surgeon who has admitted to treating Al Qaeda leaders, including Osama bin Laden.

Amid the rush to provide tents, food, and medical supplies, few of the western NGOs seemed to be giving much thought to schools. Based on past experience, however, the militant groups who were busy setting up their aid networks fully understood the power of education under such circumstances. Back in the winter of 1989, when the Soviets had pulled out of Afghanistan and the country was struggling to get back on its feet after ten years of war, the Saudi government had sponsored thousands of conservative madrassas, religious institutions open only to boys and designed to instill a fundamentalist interpretation of Islamic law. During the 1990s, about eighty thousand boys who had received hard-line religious instruction in these madrassas were fed directly into the ranks of the Taliban. Now, it seemed a similar dynamic was beginning to unfold in Azad Kashmir. Within a year, a number of these camps would become fertile recruiting grounds for Islamic militants looking for new followers.

Inside one refugee camp that I saw in Muzaffarabad, the mess tent where families came to receive their daily rations had been set up directly adjacent to an enormous tent that functioned as a madrassa where young boys were being tutored on the nuances of jihad. Many of the refugee parents were not happy about the fact that their children were attending these extremist schools, but because the *jihadis* were providing them with food, shelter, and medicine, they were reluctant to object.

Combining aid with ideology was a highly effective strategy — and this same formula would repeat itself four years later when two million Pakistani civilians were displaced by the Pakistani army's offensive against the Taliban in the Swat Valley. (By the summer of 2009, hard-line Islamist charities had established precisely the same kind of foothold and were pushing their antiwestern agenda among the residents of the Swat refugee camps.)

I have always been dismayed by the West's failure — or unwillingness — to recognize that establishing secular schools that offer children a balanced and nonextremist form of education is probably the cheapest and most effective way of combating this kind of indoctrination. Despite the fact that the American government has never grasped its importance, this calculus has been at the heart of what we do from the very beginning — and with Sarfraz in the lead, we continued to pursue this agenda in Azad Kashmir during the winter of 2005.

By January, Sarfraz had managed to commandeer several UNICEF tents from army depots in Balakot and Muzaffarabad. After transporting these tents to the most distant villages in the Neelum Valley, such as Nouseri, Pakrat, and Behdi, Sarfraz set about identifying the leaders — the most energetic people, who were the survivors in the broad sense of the word. With their help, he then located teachers, arranged for their salaries, and then started rounding up the parents and kids in order to get the schools going.

Within a couple of months, Sarfraz had set up more than a dozen of these little operations in places that lay beyond the reach of the most outstretched NGO or government authority. Needless to say, in a region where every school in every community had been completely destroyed, this was barely a drop in the bucket. But everyone who works with the Central Asia Institute believes in the value and the power of this little drop. On the grand scale of things, Sarfraz's tent schools were miniscule; but among the people at the end of the road, these projects offered a catalyst for hope.

Amid the devastation of Kashmir that autumn, this is what passed for sharing three cups of tea.

Meanwhile, back in Montana, I was not having an easy time of things. Within hours of the earthquake, the e-mails, phone calls, letters, and checks were pouring into our little two-room office in Bozeman. The people who were calling and writing were often quite insistent about the fact that as far as they were concerned we had the resources and the connections to help in this disaster — and they expected us to do something immediately.

Truth be told, however, I had no idea what the CAI could or should do at this point — and indeed, the entire purpose of Sarfraz's reconnaissance trips was to collect the information that would enable us to make wise decisions and distribute our resources intelligently. That was my message to the people who were contacting us, but at the time my methodical and pragmatic approach didn't seem to carry much weight. Throughout October, donors flooded our office with tents, clothing, and outdoor gear; and attached to each contribution was a request, implicit or otherwise, that we please do something — *anything* — to assist the stricken citizens of Pakistan during their bleakest hour of need.

Many of our supporters also sent money, and by the week before Thanksgiving, we were sitting on more than $160,000 that needed to be spent in behalf of education.

As I huddled in my basement office listening to Sarfraz report on the confusion and the despair, the madrassas, and all the other things he was witnessing, the most powerful reaction I experienced was a deep sense of guilt over my absence from the front lines. At night, I would wake up at about 2:00 A.M. with the refugees on my mind and find myself unable to get back to sleep. Then at 4:30, I would drive over to Gold's Gym to work out with Jeff McMillan, a trainer who is also a friend and who frequently stops by to assist Tara and the kids during my long absences. Nothing seemed to help, however, and I quickly became trapped in an obsession with the fact that I simply wasn't doing enough. It was finally Tara, who understands me better than any other human being, who decided to act.

"Let's go out to dinner tonight," she said. "We need to talk."

When we got to the restaurant, she got straight to the point.

"Sweetie, if you just stay here you are going to drive yourself and the rest of us crazy. So when we get home, I'm going to pull out your duffel bags, and I want you to start packing. It's time for you to go and do what you do best. This is your calling. And when you get home, we will be here waiting for you."

The timing was terrible — the holidays were just around the corner, and as Tara and I both knew, if I left now there was no way I could be back home for Christmas. This was a very difficult decision, and in the end, the person who made it on my behalf was my wife and best friend. She knew that although I was home, I was not really home — and in order to return home with full heart and mind, I needed to leave now.

On Thanksgiving morning, I was on my way.

The Mortenson family visits with Chagga tribal friends in Mamba Village, below Kilimanjaro, circa 1968. PHOTO © 1968 DEMPSEY MORTENSON

The Mortenson family visits the Hussein family. Sondus, Pakistan, 2007. PHOTO © 2007 MOHAMMED NAZIR

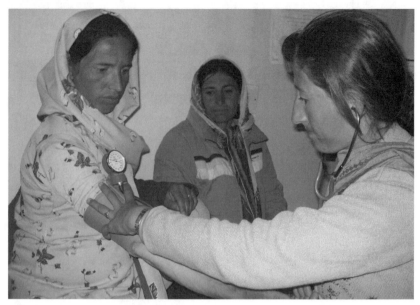

CAI maternal health scholarship student Nasreen takes blood pressure of Jamil, eight months pregnant. Charpurson Valley, Pakistan. Photo © 2009 Genevieve Chabot

Kirghiz family outside of their kirghoo (yurt), Bozai Gumbaz. Wakhan, Afghanistan. Photo © Sarfraz Khan 2009

Buzkashi horse game, Sheva valley, Badakshan province, Afghanistan. PHOTO © 2006 SARFRAZ KHAN

Faisal Baig hands flour bag to Sarfraz Khan for Kirghiz nomads, at the place where the Kirghiz first asked Greg in 1999 for help to build a school. Charpurson Valley, Pakistan. PHOTO © GREG MORTENSON 1999

Kirghiz herder and bactrian (double-humped) camel taking a load to Bozai Gumbaz. Little Pamir, Afghanistan. Photo © 2008 Sarfraz Khan

Central Asia Institute's Pakistan staff: Rear, left to right: Faisal Baig, Mohammed Nazir, Sarfraz Khan, Greg Mortenson, CAI's executive director. Front, left to right: Apo Razak, Suleman Minhas, Haji Ghulam Parvi, Saidullah Baig. Photo: © courtesy 2008 Central Asia Institute

Afghan widows Hatija (left) and her sister with their children in the Schamshatoo refugee camp. Pakistan, 1998. Photo © 1998 Greg Mortenson

Sarfraz Khan and his horse Kazil at Bozai Gumbaz, Afghanistan. Kazil died after crossing the difficult Irshad pass in late fall 2006. Photo: 2005 Greg Mortenson

Waziri tribesmen who abducted Greg Mortenson near Razmak, North Waziristan, Pakistan. Greg was detained there for eight days in July 1996. PHOTO © 1996 GREG MORTENSON (TAKEN AFTER HIS RELEASE).

Farzana (far right) and students of the Nouseri Girls' School after Pakistan's October 2005 earthquake. PHOTO © 2005 GREG MORTENSON

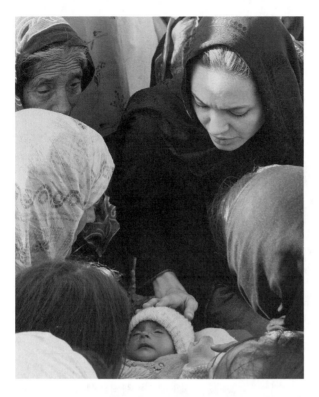

UNHCR Goodwill Ambassador Angelina Jolie with a two-month-old baby at Gari Habibullah refugee camp after Pakistan earthquake. PHOTO © 2005 COURTESY UNHCR/J. REDDEN

Fozia trains at Mr. Cunningham's Tae Kwan Do Academy in Bozeman, Montana. From a hamlet in Neelum Valley, Pakistan, she is the first local female to pass her bar exam and become an attorney, which she did in 2008. PHOTO: GREG MORTENSON

Abdul, a young orphan and mechanic, covered in grease and working only for food and shelter. Pul-e-Khumri, Afghanistan. PHOTO © 2003 GREG MORTENSON

Gundi Piran schoolgirls study outdoors after the 2005 earthquake, which killed one hundred and eight of their fellow students. Azad Kashmir, Pakistan. PHOTO © 2006 GREG MORTENSON

The Neelum Valley's Nouseri Girls' School, built after the 2005 earthquake. Azad Kashmir, Pakistan. PHOTO © 2007 GREG MORTENSON

Haji Ghulam Parvi (left) with Shaukat Ali, former Taliban and CAI teacher. PHOTO © 2009 SARFRAZ KHAN

CAI scholarship students from Azad Kashmir who are studying in Rawalpindi read CAI's Journey of Hope. PHOTO © 2008 GENEVIEVE CHABOT

Outdoor school in the village of Saw, Kunar Province, on the Pakistan-Afghanistan border, 2007. PHOTO © 2008 WAKIL KARIMI

Parveen—the first female high school graduate in Wakhan, now in a maternal health training program. Wargeant village, Afghanistan. PHOTO © 2004 GREG MORTENSON

Rubina, a widow in Wakhan corridor, Afghanistan. PHOTO © 2007 GREG MORTENSON

Sitara (Star) school, opened in 2008 with 1,600 students. The school is in Ishkoshim, near the Afghanistan-Tajikistan border.
PHOTO © 2009 GREG MORTENSON

Greg Mortenson with Sardhar Khan (left of Greg) and Wohid Khan (right of Greg). Badakshan, Afghanistan. PHOTO © 2008
PHOTO SARFRAZ KHAN

Mullah Mohammed, former Taliban and now CAI accountant for Wakhan corridor, with his family. Khundud, Afghanistan.
PHOTO © 2008 SARFRAZ KHAN

Sarfraz Khan (left) and Wakil Karimi with U.S. Army Lieutenant Colonel Christopher Kolenda, Commander, FOB Naray. Kunar Province, Afghanistan. PHOTO © 2008 COURTESY CHRISTOPHER KOLENDA

Captain John Kirby (left), Admiral Mike Mullen, chairman— Joint Chiefs of Staff (right), and Greg Mortenson at Pushgur Girls' School inauguration. Panjshir Valley, Afghanistan, 2009 PHOTO © 2009 SARFRAZ KHAN

Najeeba teaching at a CAI's women's literacy center in Kabul.
PHOTO © 2009 GENEVIEVE CHABOT

Greg, Khyber, and Amira Mortenson (left to right), with Gultori war refugee schoolgirls. Skardu, Pakistan. PHOTO © 2007 TARA BISHOP

Greg Mortenson leaves President Zardari's house after receiving the Sitara-i-Pakistan (Star of Pakistan), one of Pakistan's highest civil awards, on March 23, 2009. PHOTO © 2009 TERU KUWAYAMA

CHAPTER 9
FARZANA'S DESKS

But once the ruins fluttered with voices and we came upon an improvised school. . . . In the sunlight falling through the fractured walls, the children turned to stare at us, clear-faced and smiling.
— COLIN THUBRON,
Shadow of the Silk Road

House destroyed in earthquake, Azad Kashmir, Pakistan PHOTO:
© 2005 TERU KUWAYAMA

291

Over the next six weeks, shifting combinations of Sarfraz, myself, and the Pakistani members of the Dirty Dozen penetrated into the furthest corners of the Neelum Valley. Occasionally we hitchhiked, once or twice we rode donkeys, but mostly we just walked. We subsisted on crackers and ramen noodles, we drank river water treated with iodine tablets, and we slept beneath wrecked vehicles on the road or under a tarp. When Sarfraz and I were alone, we moved even further into what we referred to as our lean-and-mean mode, dozing for three hours a night and keeping ourselves going by swallowing handfuls of ibuprofen and guzzling endless cups of tea. I called Tara every now and then, but the horror that surrounded us robbed me of the energy to think much about home.

I quickly discovered that Sarfraz had not exaggerated the extent of the destruction and the misery. Even now, nearly two months after the quake, thousands of people were still missing. Were they dead, injured, in a refugee camp, or staying with relatives somewhere else? No one knew, partly because the search crews were still uncovering bodies from the wreckage, and partly because everyone seemed to be on the move.

The roads were filled with little groups of men, almost always from the same community, who had ventured forth together in search of a distribution point where they could obtain food and shelter for their relatives and neighbors. Once they discovered a camp that was stocked with these supplies, these men would join up and then send word back to their home village for more people to come down. Soon enough, almost all of the survivors of a destroyed village would have relocated en masse. The camps in which they congregated reminded me of the Afghan refugee settlements I had often visited on the opposite side of Pakistan — overwhelmed by the stench of human waste and lacking sanitation, sewage treatment, and adequate drinking water. At night, people struggled to sleep in close-packed tents. During the day, they milled around with nothing to do.

Over time, some of these camps broke up as the supplies evaporated, forcing the residents to disperse and move on. In other cases, the camp might emerge as a semipermanent supply hub and begin transforming into something that resembled an actual community. Under such circumstances, the refugees would begin finding menial jobs and replacing their plastic-tarp shelters with shacks cobbled together from construction scraps.

This changing human dynamic drew us into the refugee camps, too. Once inside, we'd ask what village the people were from, how many children were in their community, and whether their schools had survived the quake. The answer to this last question, we discovered, was always no. In the fifty or sixty villages of the upper Neelum Valley, every single school had been completely destroyed. We thought there might be an exception somewhere, but if there was, we never found it.

Each of the schools in this region had hosted anywhere from 150 to 600 students, and in almost every case, between a third and half of the children had perished. Shoddy construction was often the main culprit. In many instances, the government subcontractors who had put up these buildings had cut corners by placing their roof beams forty or more inches apart (the spacing should be no more than twenty-eight inches). Others had also used a sand-to-cement ratio of ten to one (as opposed to six to one) or had failed to employ rebar or double-cast steel for reinforcement.

The resulting structural failures tended to conform to one of two patterns: Either the roof had come apart and the pieces had fallen directly onto the children's heads, or the walls had disintegrated and the roof had crashed down as a solid unit. In the latter situation, it was not unusual for every single student to have died. In the tiny village of Nousada, 198 students were buried alive in this manner. Three years later, in the summer of 2009, the cement roof slab was still splayed across the side of the hill where the school had once stood. To this day, it continues to serve as a memorial stone marking the mass grave of the children of Nousada.

Within these remote villages, there was often very little government or NGO activity for the purpose of providing food or medical care and no effort whatsoever to address education needs. In a few places, the Pakistani army had erected a large tent and announced that it was now the local school, but this was rarely adequate. In such traumatized communities, it was necessary to find someone who was capable of teaching — or to bring in a teacher from the surrounding area — and then to support that person with books, teaching materials, and a salary. In the area where we were focusing most of our efforts, Sarfraz's tent schools were often the only institutions that seemed to have any staying power.

Throughout December and the first part of January, we paid visits to each of the communities where Sarfraz had started a tent school in order to find out what kind of support was needed to keep them going. In the communities Sarfraz had not yet visited, we started this process from scratch. The initial results were often chaotic and confusing.

The key was to find one or two dedicated teachers around whom we could establish the school. If we had over one hundred students per teacher, we set up two shifts of three or four hours each, one shift for the boys, another shift for the girls, with the older students helping the younger ones. Given the extent to which people were moving around, a certain school might have two hundred students one day and four hundred students the next. The teachers came and went with equal unpredictability as they tried to put their lives back together.

Obviously, this was less than ideal, but often it was the best we — or anyone —

could do. Given our limited manpower and resources in these mountains, our follow-up work during the first months after the catastrophe wasn't as tight as it needed to be. Nevertheless, during the winter of 2005–6, someone from our local staff visited each of these tent schools every week or two in order to pay the teachers, monitor the progress of the students, and make arrangements for supplies to be delivered. In the absence of assistance from the government or the big international aid organizations, this was the only help that these communities would get for now — and often the impact was significant. Despite the fact that classes were supposed to be in recess during the coldest months of winter, heroic teachers labored to keep the schools running so that their students would not get behind. This became a point of pride in many of the devastated communities. Parents would bring tea and chapattis for the students' lunch, then sit in the back of the class, listening to the lessons and ready to step in and help if asked.

During this time, the manner in which people responded to us changed, too. Slowly but surely, word began to spread about the odd couple of Azad Kashmir: the broken-handed Ismaili from the Charpurson Valley and his lumbering, bear-shaped American sidekick dressed in a mud-colored *shalwar kamiz*. And gradually, relationships began to take root.

Sarfraz and I never presented ourselves as emergency-relief workers, but people knew that we wanted to help. This counted for a lot, especially in places where no one else from the outside world, except for the Chinook crews, had managed to pay a visit. But what counted even more, I think, was the fact that in each community we made a point of consulting with the elders and the parents in order to find out what *they* thought they needed. In a way, even though we had come into this stricken valley in order to build schools and to promote education, we were inviting the people of the area to become *our* teachers. And in so doing, Sarfraz and I wound up relearning the lesson that had originally been imparted to me, all those years ago, by the silver-bearded Haji Ali in the village of Korphe.

When you take the time to actually listen, with humility, to what people have to say, it's amazing what you can learn. Especially if the people who are doing the talking also happen to be children.

Farzana was a beautiful ninth grader with deep brown eyes and dense black eyebrows who lived in the village of Nouseri. Her story bore the same dimensions of tragedy and loss that had marked the lives of all the surviving children of Nouseri, where more than a third of the community's 1,500-odd residents had been killed and only a handful of homes were still standing.

Farzana's mother, Jamila Khattoon, and her twelve year-old brother, Nabil, had been killed inside their house when the roof collapsed. Two miles down the road lay the ruins of the local girls' school where Farzana's thirteen-year-old sister, Sidra, was one of forty-seven students killed. Aside from Farzana herself, the surviving members of her family included her father, Nur Hussein, a veteran of the Pakistani army, and her three-year-old sister, Kurat.

The weeks following the earthquake left little time for grieving. Nouseri's water system had been completely destroyed, which meant that every day, Farzana and the other women of the village were obliged to hike two miles and descend three thousand feet to the river and climb back up carrying fifty-pound jugs filled with water. Meanwhile, Nur Hussein had to leave the village each morning for a six-hour round-trip hike to the nearest Pakistani army camp, where he collected the family's daily allotment of flour, plus some cooking oil, salt, and tea.

When Sarfraz and I made it to Nouseri, the surviving students were supposed to be studying their lessons in one of the tent schools that Sarfraz had set up on an earlier visit. Attendance at this school, however, was extremely spotty. The kids were around — we could see them moving about the village — but most of them were avoiding the school and did not even seem to want to come near it. No one could tell us why, until one day when I was sitting on the floor of the tent school with the teacher and the handful of kids who were willing to attend class, including Farzana.

Before I left Bozeman, my wife, who is a psychotherapist and often works with traumatized women, had advised me to encourage the children who had survived the earthquake to talk, draw, write, or even sing about their experience — anything that might enable them to get their feelings out in the open would start the healing process, she said. So during a lull in the class, I cleared my throat and posed a question.

"Would anyone like to talk about the earthquake today?"

There was dead silence. Several of the children glared. One of the girls ran out of the tent, sat down by the door, and started to cry, wiping her eyes with her *dupatta* (head scarf).

Well, now you've really gone and done it, Greg, I thought to myself.

Then a quiet, low voice came from the back corner of the tent. It was Farzana, whose little sister, Kurat, was clinging to her back.

"Let me tell you for all of us," she began.

There was a long pause and some reshuffling. The girl who had been sitting outside in tears padded softly back into the tent.

"*Bismillah ir-Rahman Rakham ir-Rahim,*" Farzana spoke. "In the name of Allah, the Merciful, the Beneficent."

"This is very difficult for all of us," she continued. "The day of the Qayamat is like a black night that we want to forget, so please forgive us for being so sad."

In painstaking detail, she went on to describe the quake itself — pausing often to keep herself from breaking down, allowing time for her fellow students to insert a murmured comment.

"We were just starting school when a strange roar came up the valley, like a lion, and then there was a quiet few seconds, which was followed by a violent ruffling, like an old man shaking the base of a young apricot tree as hard as he could. Then after a minute, it was quiet again. And then there was a ripple in the whole mountain — like a wave on the water."

Everyone nodded.

At that point, explained Farzana, the buildings started to collapse. The walls disintegrated first, then the roofs came down in an explosive shower of concrete and wood. As the buildings shattered, clouds of dust rose from the debris and the sky turned dark. Then the screaming began, and over the screams you could hear the shouts of the parents who were running down the hill from the village to find their children. Within minutes, the clatter of picks and shovels arose as the men started attacking the rubble. There were fewer screams now — it was mostly moans and crying. And the air was still thick with dust.

Farzana's description of the events of that morning was very vivid and exceptionally detailed, and something about not only the precision of her words but also the manner in which her thoughts and emotions seemed to play across her face as she spoke led me to wonder if she might be able to clear up the confusion surrounding the school's attendance problem.

When she was finished, I asked her why so few kids were coming to class.

"Because there are no desks in the tents," she said matter-of-factly.

This was interesting, but also odd. In this part of the world, many homes lack chairs and people are much more comfortable sitting on the floor. In many of our schools across Pakistan and Afghanistan, it is not unusual for an entire class to sit cross-legged on the floor while the teacher stands. The lack of desks seemed like a strange reason not to go to school.

"Why are desks so important?" I asked.

"They make children feel safe," she explained. "And with desks, the tents feel more like a real school."

This seemed to make sense, and I nodded, but she wasn't finished.

"But even if the classes are held outside, you should have desks outside, too," she said. "Only then will the children come to class."

This seemed rather mysterious, but something about Farzana's earnest directness made me want to trust her. So the next day Sarfraz and I began rummaging around a pile of rubble in the remains of the girls' school and scavenged the shattered remains of several dozen desks. That afternoon, we rounded up a few men and paid them to start refurbishing. Word of this activity spread quickly, and within an hour or two of our installing the desks in the tent, dozens of kids were filing into class.

What Farzana had understood was that in the minds of the children, desks provided concrete evidence that at least within the confines of their classroom, a degree of order, stability, and normalcy had returned to their lives. In a traumatized world where everything had been turned upside down and the ground itself had given way, a desk offered certitude. It was something you could trust.

That marked the beginning of "Operation School Desk."

Armed with Farzana's insight, we started retrieving the remains of broken furniture from every possible source, and over the next week, our team of amateur carpenters knocked together about eight hundred desks for every tent school in the area. But it didn't end there. Other organizations in Balakot and Muzaffarabad got wind of Farzana's insight, and soon schools up and down the Neelum Valley were filling up with desks. From that time forward, desks became a requirement for all of the tent schools we established in Azad Kashmir.

In terms of solving the staggering crisis besetting Azad Kashmir, this desk business barely merited notice. It did, however, represent a small step forward during a moment when almost nothing seemed to be going well. And more important, perhaps, it was something that had been initiated by the children themselves.

As I was about to discover, however, it wasn't simply the children of Kashmir who had something to say to us.

In the middle of January, I was forced once again to say farewell to Sarfraz and return home to Montana. I was loath to leave the earthquake zone, but the run-up to the publication of *Three Cups of Tea* was in full swing, and this would offer a chance to raise some much-needed funds for our work in Pakistan and Afghanistan.

Back in Bozeman, as I struggled to immerse myself in the endless rounds of phone calls and e-mails, all I could really think about were the survivors whom I'd left behind in Azad Kashmir. I found myself dwelling on the disparity between the urgent work that needed doing over there and what struck me as the rather mundane office tasks that I was performing in the United States. Within a week of getting home, I was depressed, disengaged, and already plotting how to return to Pakistan.

That's where things stood one evening in late January as I was reading a bedtime story to Khyber, who was five years old at the time. *He* was happy I was home, and that made me happy, too. Moreover, reading to him and Amira had always been one of Tara's and my favorite things to do. But as I read the words to *Where the Wild Things Are* by Maurice Sendak, tracing each sentence with my finger, my mind was preoccupied with issues on the opposite end of the planet.

What time was it in Kashmir, and where was Sarfraz right now, and when would he be calling? How many teachers were on our payroll in the Neelum Valley at the moment, and did I need to wire funds to Islamabad in order to cover their salaries for this month?

Oh my goodness!

My reverie was derailed by the realization that my son had stopped listening to my voice and begun to enunciate the words on the page for himself. He was not reciting these words from memory. Khyber was reading for the first time in his life.

When you are a parent, the instant your child first begins to read is a moment of the purest magic. It doesn't matter whether you happen to live in Kashmir or Montana or Tanzania or Manhattan — witnessing the fire of literacy ignite in the mind of a child is something transcendent. To me, it felt exactly like releasing the string on a helium-filled balloon and watching it ascend into the sky all by itself.

But there was another feeling, too. Mixed with the intoxicating sense of buoyancy was an awareness of the many other milestones in the lives of my children that I had irrevocably missed. Their first steps. Their first spoken words. Their first bike rides. Their first day of school.

These developments, which are the delight of so many parents, had all unfolded while I was at work on the far side of the world, attending to the needs and the dreams of other people's children. And yet right now, I was permitted to be lying next to my own son for this one precious moment. The piercing combination of joy and loss was too much to bear, and the tears began rolling down my face.

This was deeply puzzling to Khyber, who had no way of grasping the enormity of this moment for his father.

"Daddy, what's the matter? Are you okay?" he asked, comforting me with a pat on the shoulder.

"Yes, Khyber, I'm okay, and I'm so proud of you today," I responded. "You know how to read!"

Khyber then called out to Tara, who was in another room with Amira, and they dashed into the bedroom and tumbled onto the bed with us. For the next hour we stayed up past the children's bedtime, snuggled together as a family while Khyber continued to read, with some help from his big sister. Tara and I proudly celebrated the precious time together.

That evening offered one of the most succinct encapsulations of the blessings and the burdens that come out of the work I do to promote literacy and education for young readers in central Asia. It also helped sustain me through the challenges that were to unfold in the weeks ahead.

By February, Sarfraz had come to the conclusion that regardless of how eager we might be to use some of our earthquake-relief money to begin converting our tent schools into permanent structures, circumstances required that we wait. Back in December, we had been able to catch a few flights on the Chinooks, and from above it was easy to see how radically the landscape had been changed. Alluvial fans had been altered, drainage channels had changed, and hillsides that had taken centuries to terrace into arable fields had been eliminated. Thanks to those changes, entire villages would need to relocate, which meant that no one could be sure exactly where hundreds of thousands of people would ultimately end up.

Given this uncertainty, Sarfraz counseled, it was too early to start putting up actual buildings. Instead, he declared, what we needed to concentrate on was figuring out how to provide clean, dependable water sources. In the communities where we were working this was a top priority because, among other reasons, a good source of water is a prerequisite for a school.

In the villages of Baltistan, most of the water systems relied on glacial melt. In the villages of Azad Kashmir, however, there was an almost total reliance on springs, many of which had now been permanently plugged or rerouted. Taking everything into account, Sarfraz thought it was necessary for us to put in small water-collection tanks and delivery pipes for five villages, including Nouseri. With my approval, he paid modest sums to two water engineers to design these systems. He also managed to finagle quite a bit of free PVC piping from the Public Works Department in Rawalpindi, including twenty thousand feet for Nouseri alone.

So far, so good. Who could possibly be

opposed to such a project? As it turned out, a Pakistani subcontractor who was working for an American contractor who, in turn, was receiving funding from the USAID objected on the grounds that the Central Asia Institute did not have an official permit to distribute water in Azad Kashmir.

You are an education NGO, he argued, whereas I have prepaid contracts to distribute hundreds of thousands of plastic bottles of mineral water, by truck and by helicopter, from warehouses in Muzaffarabad to the villages of Azad Kashmir.

When Sarfraz reported this to me, I initially thought he was kidding. By any yardstick one might care to use, the prohibitively expensive bottled-water delivery contract was a ridiculous boondoggle. Nevertheless, we were forced to spend several weeks wrangling with various government ministries in Azad Kashmir before the mess was sorted out and we were granted retroactive approval for the water-delivery systems that Sarfraz, exasperated by the unnecessary red tape, had already begun constructing.

At home in Montana, these and many other challenges formed the grist for my family's dinner-table conversations throughout February and March. Sarfraz's phone updates and the photos that he e-mailed provided Khyber and Amira with a sense of the challenges we were up against, and I was pleased by the interest that my son and daughter appeared to take in these matters. Then one evening, Amira posed a question that seemed to leapfrog over the tangled talk of PVC piping and the politics of sweetheart government deals for American contractors.

"Hey, Dad," she asked, "what kinds of games do the children in your Kashmir schools play?"

Amid the devastation and the despair of the earthquake zone, I didn't recall seeing much in the way of games. But then again, it was possible that Sarfraz and I had been so focused on the mechanics of getting our water-delivery systems and our tent schools up and running that we simply hadn't been paying attention.

"Um . . . I'm not sure," I replied. "I honestly have no idea."

"Well," declared Amira, "you should get those kids some jump ropes."

Then she threw me a sharp look, as if a switch had just been flipped in her mind.

"Dad, you don't have any playgrounds *at all* in your schools, do you?"

"No," I admitted. Playgrounds had not exactly been at the top of the priority list for

Sarfraz and me.

"You really need to put them in," she declared. "All children need to play, especially ones that are suffering and hurting like the kids in Pakistan."

In truth, some of our schools did feature dirt fields where the kids were able to play soccer. But we had no real playgrounds with swings and slides and seesaws. How had we not thought about this earlier?

The next day, Amira phoned two of my friends, Jeff McMillan and Keith Hamburg, at Gold's Gym in Bozeman and told them that she needed their help in rounding up jump ropes. Word spread quickly, and before we knew it, Amira had more than two thousand jump ropes in our living room. We shipped them off to Suleman in Islamabad, and later that spring — along with an additional seven thousand jump ropes that we purchased in Rawalpindi — they were distributed throughout our tent schools and beyond.

The kids responded in a manner that mirrored their reaction to Farzana's desks. The play and exercise brought joy and delight to them, and their enthusiasm spread like wildfire into the depressed communities. Before long, we were fielding requests to supplement the jump ropes with cricket bats and soccer balls. And like Farzana's desks, Amira's jump ropes provoked a revision of the Central Asia Institute's operations policy.

Since the spring of 2006, we've incorporated playgrounds into most of our new schools, and we have also been working to retrofit a few of our existing schools with swings, seesaws, and slides. Our loyal donors love this idea and have been more than happy to chip in. The playgrounds have also won fans in some unexpected quarters. In the summer of 2009, for example, a group of elders who sympathized with the Taliban paid a visit to one of our schools in Afghanistan with a request to tour the facility. As they walked into the compound and put down their weapons, the leader of this delegation, a man named Haji Mohammad Ibrahim, spotted the playground and broke into a big smile. For the next half hour, he and his companions gleefully sampled the swings, the slide, and the seesaw. When they finally quit playing, Haji Mohammad Ibrahim announced that they did not need to see the inside of the school.

"But don't you want to take a look at the classrooms?" asked the principal.

"No, we have seen enough," replied Haji Mohammad Ibrahim. "We would like to formally request you to come to our village in order to start building schools. But if you do, they absolutely must have playgrounds."

CHAPTER 10
SARFRAZ'S PROMISE

*Nobody ever lives their life all the way up
except bull-fighters.*
  — ERNEST HEMINGWAY,
    The Sun Also Rises

Two sisters in UNHCR earthquake refugee camp, Pakistan
PHOTO: © 2005 TERU KUWAYAMA

317

While we continued moving forward with our tent-school projects in the upper Neelum Valley, down in Patika the teachers at the Gundi Piran Girls' School were dealing with their own set of challenges. On November 1, the school had reopened for business in the tents that Shaukat Ali had requisitioned from the Pakistani army. On the first day of class, only seven girls made an appearance, along with a handful of teachers. One of those teachers was Saima Khan, who continued to show up every day despite the fact that she was still recovering from a severe leg fracture.

Because most of the girls were still in mourning and all of them had lost their textbooks, notebooks, even pencils and pens, Shaukat Ali began the first classes by reading to them from poetry and religious texts. "Reading, literature, and spirituality are good for the soul," he told them. "So we will start with these studies."

As the weeks rolled by, word spread that the school had reopened, and girls slowly began trickling back. By the middle of December, there were 145 students — a remarkable number, given that only 195 of them had survived the earthquake.

They spent the winter of 2006 huddled in the tents without electricity or running water, trying to keep warm with blankets and several boxes of clothing donated by a nearby Red Cross compound. Some of the students wore black leather aviator jackets or blue blazers from American businessmen; others wrapped themselves in silk scarves or high-tech Nordic ski gear. One girl in the fifth grade wound up with a bright bubble-gum pink coat that would have done justice to the wardrobe of a Miley Cyrus groupie.

Adding to the physical hardship was a general anxiety over the upcoming exams, which would serve as a prerequisite for entry to the region's upper-division schools. After the trauma of the earthquake and the many weeks of missed classes, teachers and students alike began to worry that many of the girls might fail. During the evenings, scores of them stayed beyond normal school hours to get caught up.

In March, they held the exams. When the

results arrived, it turned out that 82 percent of the girls had passed.

Saida Shabir considered the performance truly remarkable, given the odds that her teachers and students were up against. At the same time, though, the results — which would have been acceptable under normal circumstances — seemed to underscore the enormity of the problems that Gundi Piran continued to confront. Six months after the earthquake, the school still lacked a building, basic services, and teaching supplies — and given the doleful state of reconstruction in Azad Kashmir, it was doubtful that any of these issues would be redressed anytime soon. Despite the progress they had made, the future looked bleak.

What Ms. Shabir had no way of knowing at the time, however, was that help was on its way — although the emissary who had been dispatched by fate with the mission of untangling her troubles had quite a distance to travel, and he was about to confront some major obstacles of his own along the way.

Despite the nearly impossible demands associated with managing the tent-school projects in Azad Kashmir, Sarfraz was still also responsible for ramrodding our initiative in the Wakhan Corridor. By May 2006, his duties in Afghanistan and Pakistan had expanded to the point of absurdity. He was now managing eighteen tent schools and five water-delivery systems within Azad Kashmir's earthquake zone while simultaneously supervising the construction of seven new schools in the Wakhan.

In addition to the challenges of keeping all of this on track at the same time, there was the fact that these thirty projects were spread between two different countries and separated by the densest, most rugged concentrations of high peaks on earth. Each two-hundred-mile trip from Azad Kashmir to the Wakhan required him to cross four separate mountain ranges — the Pir Panjal, the Karakoram, the Hindu Kush, and the Pamirs. Moreover, the logistical hassles Sarfraz faced inside the Wakhan were every bit as demanding as those of working inside the earthquake zone. One of his biggest headaches, for example, stemmed from our discovery that after nearly thirty years of war in Afghanistan, there was an insufficient number of skilled masons and carpenters inside the Wakhan.

The solution to this particular problem, Sarfraz decided, was to import teams of skilled craftsmen from Pakistan who could build the first schools inside the Corridor while training their Afghan counterparts. So he began escorting parties of up to twenty construction workers at a time over the Irshad Pass and inserting them directly into the Wakhan. None of these workers had visas or passports, but Sarfraz was able to negotiate special permission from Wohid Khan's Border Security Force. Each trip took three days. The masons and carpenters would start off at 4:30 A.M. and trudge for fourteen hours before stopping for the night. They carried almost no food because the tools in their backpacks weighed more than eighty pounds.

Once the masons were set up on a job site, Sarfraz would whip back over the pass on his horse, jump into his Land Cruiser, and make a beeline down the Karakoram Highway for Azad Kashmir. After a week or two of madly dashing around the Neelum Valley, the Land Cruiser would again race north along the Karakoram Highway to the Charpurson Valley. There Sarfraz would transfer to his horse and scuttle back over the Irshad to monitor the masons' progress, order up new supplies of cement and rebar, and settle accounts with Mullah Mohammed, our ex-Taliban bookkeeper, balancing the debit side of the ledgers with the bricks of cash that Sarfraz had stuffed into his saddlebags.

(He often hauled tens of thousands of dollars at a time, wrapping the money in his dirty clothes and hiding it under cartons of the K2 cigarettes that he incessantly chain-smoked as part of what he called his "high-altitude program.")

These round-trip journeys over the Hindu Kush could be brutal. Sarfraz rigged a special rope that enabled him to sleep in the saddle, and he set such a relentless pace that on one occasion upon reaching the village of Sarhad on the far side of the pass, his horse, Turuk, dropped to the ground and died. (Upon hearing the news of Turuk's passing, one of our board members donated four hundred dollars for the purchase of a replacement, a sturdy white pony whom Sarfraz named Kazil, who continues to this day to perform heroically on behalf of education in the Wakhan.)

This was grueling, relentless, burnout-inducing work that involved constant motion, little sleep, and no time off whatsoever. And yet Sarfraz seemed to thrive on all of it. Listening to his progress reports every third or fourth night as I moved across the United States on my own mad dash to raise the money that would pay for what we were doing in Pakistan and Afghanistan, I pictured Sarfraz less as a man with a crippled right hand and more as an unstoppable force of nature: a whirling gyre of pigheaded determination quite unlike anything that had ever blown itself across the hinterlands of the western Himalayas.

That summer, however, he gave me one of the biggest scares of my life.

June marked the high point of the Wakhan's summer construction season, so Sarfraz was going full steam on all seven of his projects inside the Corridor when, on June 12, I received an emergency phone call from Ted Callahan, a part-time mountain guide who was conducting an extensive study of the Kirghiz nomads of the eastern Wakhan as part of his Ph.D. research in anthropology at Stanford University. Ted, who had hooked up with Sarfraz in the hope of getting an introduction to the Kirghiz, reported that forty-eight hours earlier Sarfraz had begun experiencing sharp pains on the right side of his abdomen. As the pain worsened, Sarfraz had grown weaker and developed a pasty, feverish complexion. It was nighttime, and they were now in Babu Tengi, a village in the central Wakhan, effectively the middle of nowhere. Ted, a certified EMT, feared that Sarfraz was in danger of dying.

Ted and I agreed that the next move involved getting Sarfraz to Qala-e Panj, less than twenty miles west. Unfortunately, there wasn't a single vehicle in Babu Tengi, so they had no choice but to start walking. Sarfraz was stumbling badly, so Ted and two masons kept him braced from both sides. Meanwhile, I started working the phones from Bozeman to figure out how we could extract our man from the Wakhan. I placed calls to Wohid Khan and to some contacts at the State Department, as well as phoning some friends at the U.S. military headquarters in Bagram, thirty miles north of Kabul.

Two hours later, a decrepit Soviet-era jeep came chugging down the trail — word had spread that Sarfraz was in trouble and needed help. Deep into the night the jeep crept along, skirting the washouts and the crater-size holes that dot the trail between Babu Tengi and Qala-e Panj. Having little suspension and no shock absorbers, the vehicle bounced hard on the horrendous road. Sarfraz had no pain medication except for his jumbo-size bottle of ibuprofen, which was of no use because by now he was unable to swallow. The pain he endured on that four-hour drive must have been excruciating.

When the jeep ambulance arrived in Qala-e Panj, Sarfraz begged Ted to let him stop.

"Just leave me here to die," he pleaded. "It is not possible for me to go any further." Ted was determined to push on, however, and asked the driver to keep moving toward the village of Khundud, where he hoped they might find a better vehicle and perhaps some medical assistance at the local dispensary. When they reached Khundud, several men in the village scoured the dispensary and all the local shops, but there was no medicine to be found. At this point, Sarfraz had curled into a fetal position and was nearly unconscious from the pain. Ted decided to let him spend a day recuperating before they proceeded further.

The following day, after another horrific ride in a minivan, they reached the town of Ishkoshem, which sits along the Tajikistan border. Ted rounded up a doctor, who took one look at Sarfraz and advised an immediate helicopter evacuation to Pakistan. Even a delirious Sarfraz, however, understood that a private, cross-border flight between Afghanistan and Pakistan would be extremely difficult to set up on such short notice — and even if it were possible, the chopper would wind up delivering him directly over the Hindu Kush to Chitral, a two-day drive from the hospitals in Peshawar. Perhaps it would be better, Sarfraz suggested, to keep

moving west in the hope of reaching Faizabad and its airport.

Unbeknownst to Sarfraz or Ted, our friends
at Bagram had by now called to inform me
that the U.S. military was ready to dispatch
a chopper into Ishkoshem and fly Sarfraz to
Kabul. There were some concerns about the
weather, however, and before we could set
up the rendezvous, a pair of Ford Ranger
pickup trucks dispatched by Wohid Khan
roared in, scooped up Sarfraz and Ted, and
raced off in the direction of Faizabad.

Even while teetering on the edge of catastrophic organ failure, Sarfraz was impossible to keep up with.

When they reached Faizabad, Ted had Sarfraz rushed directly to the hospital, where a
doctor told him he had developed a massive
septic infection and needed an operation.
Sarfraz, who had zero interest in undergoing
surgery anywhere inside Afghanistan, told
the doctor to pump him full of antibiotics,
and the next morning he and Ted caught a
Red Cross plane into Kabul. When they arrived, a special flight arranged by our good
friend Colonel Ilyas Mirza, a retired Pakistani military aviator who managed Askari
Aviation charter service, was waiting to fly
him to Islamabad. Within minutes of arriving at the Combined Military Hospital in

Rawalpindi, Sarfraz was rushed directly into surgery. His entire extraction had taken four days.

On the operating table, the surgeons discovered an enormous abscess in Sarfraz's gall bladder and also determined that the infection had spread to his liver. They removed his gall bladder during that first surgery, then put him back under the knife three days later to deal with the liver. Between operations, he was under the continuous supervision of Suleman and Apo, who tag teamed the duties of meeting with his doctors, obtaining his prescriptions, seeing to his bills, making sure he was fed, and keeping me constantly informed.

At some point during his five-day stay in the hospital, Sarfraz casually mentioned to his colleagues that his stomach pains had actually surfaced *before* his trip into Afghanistan and that the pain had been severe enough that he'd consulted a physician in Gilgit, who had urged him not to leave for the Wakhan before getting an operation. Sarfraz's response to this news had been to declare that the school projects in Afghanistan were too important to be postponed and that his operation would simply have to wait until he got home.

Suleman and Apo decided it was best to

keep silent for several months before sharing this information with me.

When Sarfraz was finally dismissed from the hospital, I told him to rest for a few days in Islamabad and then to head home to Zuudkhan, where he was to be given a special set of protocols designed personally by me. By this point, I had calculated that Sarfraz had been on the move almost continuously since the early spring of 2005, nearly sixteen straight months without a break.

"You are to spend a minimum of one month, but preferably two, sitting in Zuudkhan doing absolutely nothing," I barked at him over the phone a few days later. "You are permitted to tend to your goats, gently brush Kazil, and look after your wife. Other than that, any form of work or activity is strictly forbidden."

"Those are your orders, sir?" Sarfraz asked.

"Yes, Sarfraz, those are my orders, and they are not negotiable. Now go home and get some rest!"

"Okay, sir. No problem."

Several months later, when I finally pieced together the story of what happened next, I learned that Sarfraz had begun plotting his return to the Neelum Valley before he was discharged from the hospital in Rawalpindi.

Within forty-eight hours of arriving back in Zuudkhan, he was hunched behind the wheel of his red Land Cruiser, clutching the still-healing incisions in his abdomen, roaring down the Karakoram Highway in the direction of Azad Kashmir.

When he arrived in Muzaffarabad, he was struck by how little progress had been made during the month that had passed since his last visit to the earthquake zone. North of the city, despite all the relief efforts, women still carried water in plastic grocery bags. In the upper reaches of the Neelum, bodies were still being discovered in the wreckage. Bulldozers were everywhere.

Sarfraz spent most of the next four weeks supervising the tent schools and the water-delivery projects in the upper Neelum. Then one day in late July, he noticed that there was a new footbridge across the Neelum River to Patika and he decided to do a little exploring. When he got to the Patika bazaar, he heard for the first time about the plight of the Gundi Piran girls' school and figured it couldn't hurt to drop by and pay a visit to Saida Shabir.

To his surprise, she was not at all pleased to see him. All spring and summer, Saida had been wrestling with a burgeoning sense of frustration and outrage over the fact that despite the dozens of visits from journalists, relief workers, and concerned government officials, still no one had made the slightest effort to rebuild her ruined school. By the time Sarfraz showed up, the headmistress's patience was finished.

"What are you doing here and what do you want?" she demanded, pointedly declining to offer him a cup of tea.

Sarfraz politely explained that he would appreciate being given the chance to tour the school.

"You don't seem to understand," she replied. "I am the headmistress, and I am asking you to leave now. Go away!"

Sarfraz has an uncanny way of winning people over, and as she proceeded into a barrage of comments about the unwanted guests she had received week after week, he listened without saying a word.

"As-Salaam Alaaikum," he said when she had finished, invoking the Islamic greeting that is traditionally offered *before* a conversation begins. "Honorable Madam, my name is Sarfraz Khan. I am a village man, a former teacher, and a representative of the Central Asia Institute, which specializes in helping to promote girls' education."

With that, the headmistress reluctantly

agreed to give him ten minutes to tour the school — but she warned him that he did *not* have permission to take photographs, take notes, or speak to the teachers or the students. After they had walked past the tents and observed the classes, Sabir sat him down on some rocks out of view of the students.

"Okay, now you are here, and I'm sorry we do not even have a chair or carpet for you to sit on," she sighed. "What exactly do you want?"

"Madam, the Central Asia Institute is not a typical NGO," he assured her. "It's true that we do tend to talk an awful lot, but we *also* build schools." If she would permit him to take some photographs and assess the damage that had been done, he promised her that he would find the money, return, and build her a new school.

"I'll believe it when I see it," replied Shabir, still suspicious but ready to be convinced.

In addition to the fact that Sarfraz had absolutely no authorization to be making such a promise, he now found himself confronting another problem. As a rule, the CAI's schools are more solidly built than the norm in Pakistan or Afghanistan — although our buildings are constructed cheaply and efficiently, we don't cut corners when it comes to design, materials, or adherence to code. But even so, nothing we had built so far was capable of withstanding a direct hit from a major quake — and in Azad Kashmir, earthquake-proof construction was clearly going to be a prerequisite for getting kids back into school on a long-term basis.

Having spent the last several months talking to students and their parents up and down the Neelum Valley, Sarfraz and I had both realized that most parents would not permit their children to resume classes inside buildings resembling the ones that had suffered such catastrophic collapse the previous October. If we eventually wanted to move away from temporary tent projects and start putting up permanent schools in these devastated villages, we would have to do something different. And it turned out that several years earlier, Sarfraz had heard a rumor about something that might work.

China's Xinjiang Province, which shares a border with northern Pakistan, suffers from almost as many earthquakes as Kashmir, and over the years, western Chinese architects and engineers had developed a keen interest in earthquake-proof construction techniques. More than two decades ago, Sarfraz had heard about this during conversations with several of the Chinese engineers who had helped build the Karakoram Highway (which passes just to the east of the Char- purson Valley). More recently, he had heard rumors that the Chinese had been trying to expand their earthquake-proof techniques into Pakistan. If so, might they have some- thing that would work in Kashmir?

The search for an answer took him to a densely packed commercial district in Is- lamabad known as G9 and into the local offices of a Chinese company called CAC, which was based in the city of Urumqi, in Xinjiang Province. Three days after having bid farewell to the dubious headmistress of Gundi Piran, he dropped by the CAC of- fices and asked to see a sample of the firm's work.

At first glance, the Chinese design was a bit disappointing, especially compared with the kind of schools Sarfraz was used to con- structing. Almost all of the CAI buildings feature impressive stonework and some aes- thetic touches of design and color. By con- trast, the Chinese earthquake-proof build- ings appeared ugly and utilitarian. They also had a prefab look that made them seem, on the surface, rather flimsy. Even Sarfraz had to concede, however, that the science behind the design was impressive. The buildings were put together on principles that western Chinese designers had identified more than fifty years earlier, working with wooden structures whose pieces fit together like a loosely jointed log cabin. The detached fittings gave the frames a built-in "play," which enabled them to disperse seismic forces by shaking and rattling without collapsing. They were engineered to withstand magnitude-8.2 earthquakes, and the Chinese were prepared to offer a twenty-year guarantee.

Impressed, Sarfraz concluded that the design would have met with my approval had he bothered to pick up the sat phone and pass this information along to me — which, of course, it was impossible to do without revealing that he had gone "off protocol" and was no longer home in Zuudkhan. So instead, he gulped and moved on to the next stage.

Did the Chinese think that the school yard in Gundi Piran offered a suitable building site?

Perhaps, replied the Chinese engineers, but they would need to see some photographs.

No way, retorted Sarfraz. The safety of the people who would be using these buildings could not be entrusted to photographs. If the Chinese were serious about wanting to do business, they would need to get into the red Land Cruiser — right now — and make the trip to Azad Kashmir.

During the following three days, Sarfraz and a trio of Chinese engineers toured three possible building sites in the Neelum Valley, including Nouseri, Pakrat, and Gundi Piran — where, despite the fact that Sarfraz had brought along tea and biscuits, the visitors failed to make a dent in Saida Shabir's skepticism.

"Don't worry, I will have the firm commitment shortly!" he assured her as they left.

"*Inshallah,*" she replied. "But if you want to come back here again, you better have some building materials with you."

As they toured the sites, the Chinese engineers explained to Sarfraz that the aluminum frames for the school buildings would need to be prefabricated to the required dimensions in Urumqi, then hauled in trucks over the 15,397-foot Khunjarab Pass, then down to Islamabad and over to Azad Kashmir. There, the company's own crew would bolt the structure into place on a special concrete foundation that floated on a bed of crushed rock and Styrofoam, which would help to dampen the seismic shock waves. Fair enough, replied Sarfraz.

Back in Islamabad, Sarfraz told the Chinese he'd be in touch, then set about confirming everything he'd been told. He checked in with several engineers serving in the Pakistani army who were familiar with earthquake-proof construction techniques and then ran those findings past another set of engineers working with the American military in Azad Kashmir. He also hauled out his laptop and pored over several Web sites with dense reports on earthquake-resistant design. When it all checked out, he returned to the Chinese.

"Okay, we are ready to start," announced Sarfraz.

"We don't start anything without money," replied Yanjing, the head engineer, as he handed over an estimate of the total cost for three schools.

Now it was time for Sarfraz to sit down and put together a memo addressed to me.

Even though August 13 was a Sunday, I was, as usual, sitting down at my desk in the basement to start my day at 5:00 A.M., when the fax machine bleated and a document started scrolling through:

I am very sorry sir, but I need a wire transfer of $54,000 for three schools in Azad Kashmir — Pakrat, Nouseri, and Patika. . . .

The memo, which was three pages long, included sample drawings and a budget for bolts, rebar, sheet metal, and hammers.

It ended with a typically direct suggestion from Sarfraz.

Please discuss with CAI board and send funds immediately.

This was the moment I first became aware that the Central Asia Institute was apparently ready to leap into the business of building earthquake-proof school buildings.

My first reaction, it must be said, was one of surprise and some annoyance. Given Sarfraz's previous recommendations about the wisdom of holding back on constructing permanent buildings until the population of Azad Kashmir had stopped moving around and the situation had stabilized somewhat, I had assumed that we would be running our tent schools for quite some time, perhaps even years. I had also assumed that we would wait for the provincial government of Azad Kashmir to take the lead on developing a new earthquake-resistant building code and then follow suit. The idea that we might decide to spearhead this initiative on our own during a time when our personnel and our resources were already sorely overtaxed had, quite frankly, never occurred to me. So what in the world was Sarfraz talking about in this memo?

I was about to pick up the phone and put

this question to him, but it was already ringing.

"Did you get my fax?" he demanded.

"Yes," I replied. "Let's start with the fact
that you're not in Zuudkhan sitting under a
tree tending your goats."

Sarfraz had no interest in exploring that
topic and steamrollered directly into the
issue at hand. Nearly a year had passed since
the earthquake occurred, he declared, and
the people of Azad Kashmir — especially
those who lived in the Neelum Valley —
needed to see something real happening,
not just a couple dozen tent schools. Moreover, the few permanent government school
buildings that had been reconstructed were
inappropriate, having been raised directly
over the footprints of the old schools, and
with the same techniques that were responsible for the structural failures that had
killed so many children. This was no way
to proceed because the next time an earthquake occurred, even more kids would die.
What was needed — immediately — was for
someone to demonstrate to the government
that safer schools could be built for the right
cost. Since no one else had stepped up, we
had no choice but to take on this responsibility ourselves.

"That may all be true, Sarfraz, but you

know that the board of the Central Asia Institute has to approve all of our expenditures, and the budget for 2006 has already been allocated."

"Yes. That is why you must convince them to make a special exception. This is a problem you can solve."

"But Sarfraz, the board doesn't even meet again for another two months. Even if I could convince them, this can't happen until October."

"We cannot wait until October. Winter will be here soon. Please call them now and get approval over the phone."

"Sarfraz, let me explain something —"

"Sir!" he interjected. "I made a *promise* to a madam who is principal of a *school*. You always tell us that we must listen to find out what people truly want. Well, okay. I listened, I found out, and then I made a promise. If we don't keep our word, she will never believe us again."

Sigh.

"So you will send the goat today?"

Sarfraz and the rest of the Dirty Dozen have a habit of referring to any funds that are wired from the United States as "the goat" — a nod to Haji Ali, the chief of Korphe, who had been forced in 1996 to give a dozen of his prized rams to a rival tribal chief in exchange for Korphe being accorded the honor of having the first school at the upper end of the Braldu Valley.

As it happened, we still had $75,000 left in our special $160,000 earthquake-relief fund, and all we needed was the board's approval. Even so, the idea of committing the bulk of what we had left to some fancy technology brought into Pakistan from western China seemed risky. The Red Cross had by now set up a big base right across the Neelum River from Patika, so everybody up and down the river would be watching. If this project backfired in some way, not only our finances but also our credibility would suffer. And finally, there was the calendar.

"It's already *September,* Sarfraz," I moaned. "You know as well as I do that nobody starts building anything in the mountains in September."

"No problem, sir. It is not too late."

(In fact, he went on to point out, his calculations indicated that we could finish all three projects within one month.)

"Well, okay, what about customs and everything having to come in from China? Have you thought about that?"

"No problem, sir. Everything has been arranged."

(He had already confirmed that the Chinese had their customs paperwork in perfect order. The trucks from China would be off-loaded at the customs station about an hour inside the border, where the Pakistani truckers would take over. Six or seven truckloads would be sufficient for all three schools.)

"Start to finish, one month, sir," declared Sarfraz. "I promise."

Still I was reluctant. The whole scheme seemed to be unfolding much too quickly. Maybe Sarfraz's energy and enthusiasm had finally gotten the best of him and affected his judgment.

"Sarfraz, for me to even consider agreeing to this, first I'd have to research this technology for myself, and then I'd have to talk to the board, and then . . ."

"No problem, sir," he interrupted. "Call me when you have made your decision. I am waiting by the phone."

Then he hung up.

Five minutes later, he sent me another fax, this one a sheaf of pages with budgets, contracts, and engineering specifications. I peeled off the schematics and drove over to Montana State University, just a few blocks away, to run them past Brett Gunnink, the head of the civil engineering department. Brett was impressed and confirmed that the design was sound. Then I began calling the board members and walked each of them through the arguments: The people needed hope; we had the money; a new standard of safe school construction needed to be set.

Fair enough, said the board members. *Let's do it.*

Time to call Sarfraz.

"Sarfraz, you realize that if this doesn't work out, we'll lose credibility and our reputation will be *hatam* (finished) in Azad Kashmir?" I told him when I phoned back with the news. "You understand how important this is, don't you?"

"No problem, sir, the U.S. Army Chinooks are ready to fly the loads into the Neelum Valley tomorrow. So you will send the goat today?"

"*Inshallah,* Sarfraz, I will send the goat today."

The last of the many aspects of this enterprise on which Sarfraz had kept me in the dark was the fact that he had already set his machinery in motion on the assumption that I would say yes to the proposal. Word had been sent to the Wakhan, and a squadron of his most trusted masons from the Charpurson Valley had dashed back across the Irshad Pass, raced down the Karakoram Highway, and were now in Muzaffarabad waiting to assist the Chinese, who had been put on standby.

I wired the money to Pakistan, and work started immediately. I learned later that the atmosphere at each job site was cheery to the point of being almost jubilant. This was one of the first enterprises in the region that conveyed the feeling that what was being raised up might actually be better than what had been destroyed. As a result, the mood among the men who built those schools, Pakistani and Chinese alike, was unlike anything the Neelum Valley had seen in more than a year. They laughed, they joked, they sang at night — and to a man, they worked like demons.

Nineteen days later, all three schools — Pakrat, Nouseri, and Patika — were finished.

The pictures Sarfraz took of the new structures were uploaded a day or two later and e-mailed to my account. I looked them over with Tara, Khyber, and Amira. The school in Pakrat was tucked into the side of a steep hill, and a beaming girl in a colorful *dupatta* stood by the door. In Nouseri, they had created a six-room structure, and each of the photographs offered proof of Farzana's desks. It was the pictures from Gundi Piran, however, that we found most arresting.

At Saida Shabir's school, the structure that Sarfraz had created was a 162-foot-long, one-story building containing twelve classrooms that was painted white and neatly highlighted with red trim. About fifty feet away and facing the school was an open-air veranda, supported by steel posts and covered by a metal roof. Here, girls who were still too traumatized by the morning of October 8, 2005, could sit at their desks and attend classes without fear of being trapped inside.

Directly in the center of the veranda's cement floor, the construction team had left a rectangular patch of open ground. This was where the seven girls whose bodies were never claimed had been buried. Separated from their families and their loved ones, they now lay together in a neat row. Each grave was marked by a modest stone, and all of them rested with their heads toward the blackboard.

The reason for this design was beautifully clear to anyone who might step into the open-air classroom. If any grace or redemption can be said to reside in the words of a teacher who is imparting the gift of literacy, then that benediction will now pass directly over the graves of those lost little girls every day that the Gundi Piran school is in session.

Later that night, after my wife and children had fallen asleep, I went back down to the basement and pulled the photos up on my computer to marvel again at what had been achieved. As I scrolled through the images, I couldn't help thinking back to my father and the fulfillment of the prediction he'd made in the summer of 1971 when he inaugurated the Kilimanjaro Christian Medical Centre with the declaration that within a decade, the head of every department in that hospital would be a local from Tanzania.

It was then that it occurred to me that without quite intending to follow in my dad's footsteps, I was now watching something no less marvelous unfold in Kashmir.

CHAPTER 11
THE CHANCE THAT MUST
BE TAKEN

History is a race between education and catastrophe.
— H. G. WELLS

Refugees leaving Pakrat village after Pakistan earthquake PHOTO:
© 2005 TERU KUWAYAMA

On November 1, 2006, just five weeks after the new earthquake-proof schools were completed, Prince Charles and his wife, the Duchess of Cornwall, arrived in Islamabad for a five-day goodwill tour. During this trip, their first visit to Pakistan, the royal couple was scheduled to spend about three hours conducting a review of several reconstruction projects in Patika. Part of the purpose behind the stopover was to return global media attention to the continuing plight of the earthquake victims in Azad Kashmir and to underscore how much work remained to be done. The plan called for the royal couple to drop by a health-care facility built by the International Committee of the Red Cross, a German veterinary center that had given away nearly 1,500 milk cows to local residents, and the brand-new Gundi Piran girls' school.

Prior to the event, Shaukat Ali, who had

helped to spearhead the effort to reopen classes at the school the previous November, was interviewed and vetted by personnel from the British embassy, then prepped on greeting the royal couple when they arrived at the Gundi Piran school. For the occasion he wore a snow white *shalwar kamiz* and polished black shoes. With his round gold-rimmed glasses and his *mujahadeen*-style beard, he cut quite a figure.

Security was tight throughout the royal visit, with British bodyguards shadowing the couple's every move. Each major road within Patika was closed down early in the morning, and around 10:00 A.M. a Royal Navy helicopter, accompanied by a pair of Pakistani Mi-17 military choppers, touched down at the supply depot near the center of town. The prince and the duchess stepped out in matching cream outfits, and after walking through Patika's bazaar, where children welcomed them with Union Jack flags, applause, and waves, they walked to the Red Cross hospital and then proceeded to the Gundi Piran school.

Shaukat Ali presented the duchess with a pashmina Kashmiri shawl, which he placed around her shoulders. Saida Shabir greeted the royal couple with tea and biscuits, and two girls handed them bouquets. After greeting the teachers, the prince and the duchess paid visits to several different classrooms and spent a few minutes at the graves of the girls whose bodies had never been claimed. Then something odd happened.

Turning to Shaukat Ali, the prince asked who was responsible for rebuilding the school. Without missing a beat, Shaukat Ali declared that credit went to two organizations: the Aga Khan Foundation — an Ismaili NGO that does excellent work in Muslim communities throughout Asia — and a construction company from China. The Central Asia Institute was never mentioned.

This struck the CAI staff as rather strange, and after the royal couple had departed, several of them approached Shaukat Ali and demanded that he explain himself. Flustered by the anger and the hurt he had caused, he protested that he had been confused about the CAI's role in the reconstruction of the school — confusion that was exacerbated by the fact that, unlike most NGOs, we had failed to advertise our accomplishment by putting up a large billboard with our name in front of the building when it was completed.

He had a point about the billboard — a detail that had somehow slipped through the cracks during the rush to finish the building. Moreover, the remorse he expressed over his faux pas seemed genuine and quite sincere. What struck me most forcefully, however, was a comment that Shaukat Ali later made to a visiting American journalist, who shared the remarks with me.

"You know, I think that what the Central Asia Institute has done here is a small kind of miracle," he said. "Without help from anybody else, and without differentiating on the basis of religion, tribe, or politics, this organization has changed the minds of the people who live in this area, 70 to 80 percent of whom are conservative Muslims. Before the earthquake occurred, many of these people were thinking that the American people are not good. But the CAI has proved that this is not true — and now the people here are paying much respect, much honor, to this organization."

Unfortunately, this failed to carry much weight with Sarfraz, who was incensed when he heard the news that our role in rebuilding the Gundi Piran school had gone unrecognized. After apologizing to me for five minutes on the phone, he laid into Shaukat Ali with a vengeance, offering several colorful options for what sort of punishment would be most fitting.

"Sarfraz, Sarfraz — please *relax*," I pleaded. "None of this matters. The kids have their school, and in the end, that's all that counts. Why don't you and I try to find something else to get mad about?"

And sure enough, we did.

One of the survivors of the collapse of the Gundi Piran school was an eleven-year-old girl in the fifth grade named Ghosia Mughal, who, as it happened, was filling a teapot with water from the outdoor water spigot when the earthquake struck. Ghosia's escape carried with it a cruel twist. The 108 victims at Gundi Paran included her mother, Kosar Parveen, who taught Urdu and Arabic to the eighth grade. The roster of those who perished also included two of Ghosia's sisters, Saba and Rosia, along with many of her closest friends.

Ghosia's family's home on the mountainside above the school was also destroyed, so a distant uncle took in the surviving members of the household, who included Ghosia, her older sister, her younger brother, and her father, Sabir, who had been paralyzed by a stroke ten years earlier. Since October 2005, they had been living in a metal shed next to the uncle's house, which was located on a hillside at the edge of Patika. In summer, the interior temperature of the shed would climb to 120 degrees; during winter, a bucket of water would freeze solid overnight.

Ghosia came to our attention several months after the royal visit to Gundi Piran, and she quickly emerged as one of the first test cases in a new initiative that my staff and I had devised in response to an interesting problem.

Providing girls with a basic education that includes literacy and math skills is, of course, fundamental to what we do — and the benefits of that basic education package, in Pakistan and Afghanistan alike, are indisputable. But starting around 2003, when the first generation of CAI-educated girls began graduating, we found ourselves confronting the blunt fact that in the remote and impoverished villages where we do the bulk of our work, a girl with a grade-school education faces extremely limited opportunities in terms of what she can do with her skills. Her schooling will eventually correlate with improved health standards and lower birth rates in her village, which will enhance her community's quality of life. And her education will, of course, also serve as a springboard for her own children's education. But unless that girl can land a job outside her home, it is unlikely that her skills will translate into a substantial boost in her family's income — and in the isolated villages of rural Pakistan and Afghanistan, these opportunities are almost nonexistent. Women cannot work as shopkeepers because in conservative Islamic culture, interaction with men outside their family is forbidden; and for similar reasons, they cannot move to a city to find a job. Aside from becoming a teacher, there are almost no jobs available for rural women outside the home.

This, we discovered, has several consequences. First, it gives rise to a cycle of students becoming teachers who educate their own students to become teachers, and so on. Second, the first wave of educated women to emerge in a community have no role models or support network whatsoever to help them pursue higher education and eventually move into the workforce as doctors, lawyers, engineers, and a range of other professions through which women can, if they wish, build wealth and attain greater control of their lives. In short, we began to realize that not only the institutions we built, but also the people passing through them, would require intensive follow-up, broad support, and long-term commitment in order to eventually become self-sustaining. For poor people in poor countries, very little simply falls into place.

As we observed these issues emerging, we

began asking ourselves how we might break this cycle and widen the options of the girls who were graduating from our schools. The answer we came up with was to start a program in which we identified the best students and financed their advanced studies beyond the high-school level. The idea was that these scholarship girls would serve as trailblazers who would open the doors for those who followed. We would channel a portion of our resources into this cadre of elite girls, and they would serve as a vanguard for others. Slowly but surely, we would prepare our young graduates for careers of all sorts.

That, at least, was the theory. In practice, it turned out to be quite a bit more complicated.

When we first started wrestling with this idea, we soon realized that any scholarship program would be complicated by the problem of providing security and supervision for girls who were studying away from their homes. This is a paramount concern for almost all rural families, who are deeply anxious about the liberalizing, westernizing effects of living in a big city. To address this, we would need to provide conditions under which the girls could live and study under the eyes of trusted female chaperones and be guarded 24-7 by an armed man at the door. We also needed the spiritual blessings of local mullahs.

With this in mind, in early 2007 we began funding the construction of our first girls' hostel. In Skardu, Haji Ghulam Parvi, the former accountant from Radio Pakistan who had quit his job to become our Baltistan manager, oversaw the construction of a large building designed to house five dozen of the brightest girls from our schools in villages in the surrounding area. These were girls who had won scholarships either to supplement their studies with additional work at the local high school or junior college or to help them undertake two-year programs in areas such as maternal health care. That same spring, we started a similar program for eight girls in the Charpurson Valley and began sending them to Gilgit for their studies, where they were supervised by Saidullah Baig, our Hunza manager.

Around the same time, we also turned our attention to Azad Kashmir, where the scholarship program would have to be set up in tandem with our school-building efforts. Our first task was research. I wanted to know how many potential scholarship students were out there in the Neelum Valley; how many of these girls were in our schools; and what sorts of challenges these students faced with respect to their families. To answer these questions, I turned to Genevieve Chabot, an energetic woman from Bozeman. It turned out that Genevieve was completing her Ed.D. in education at Montana State University. I proposed that we place her in charge of launching our Azad Kashmir scholarship program. Her first mission would be to canvass the Neelum Valley in order to search out the most promising young girls for scholarship consideration. And this is how she came to meet Ghosia Mughal.

In the spring of 2007, on her first visit to Pakistan to begin assembling her dossier of nominees, Genevieve paid a visit to the Gundi Piran school, where several students urged her to speak with a twelve-year-old girl sitting in the front row of her class. Ghosia was by now in the seventh grade and had scored the highest marks in her class. Despite the fact that her family had no money aside from her stricken father's meager twelve-dollar-per-month pension, she was brimming with confidence and ambition, and she had set her sights on attending medical school in Islamabad and returning to Patika as a doctor. Saida Shabir confirmed that Ghosia was the school's "top student."

Based on Genevieve's report, I decided that she should be one of the first CAI scholarship recipients in the Neelum Valley.

There was only one problem: Her father, who had initially agreed to give permission for her to accept the award, had now changed his mind and withdrawn his consent.

This, it turns out, is not an uncommon response to the prospect of a young girl receiving funding for higher education. After expressing their delight at the chance to pursue an advanced degree, many of our scholarship candidates will then go on to explain that a grandfather or grandmother or aunt is from the "old times" and does not support them.

"They will have to pass away," we often hear, "before I am permitted to continue any further in school."

Another major obstacle involves local community leaders and religious authorities who, for a variety of reasons, have their own set of objections. As a result, we tend to see many tears during these interviews. It can be painful and deeply frustrating to watch as the ambitions of a talented girl are thwarted or unnecessarily delayed. In this manner, Nasreen Baig, the green-eyed woman from the Charpurson, was forced to wait a full ten years before she was allowed to take up her maternal-health-care scholarship in Rawal-pindi. Similarly, Jahan Ali, the granddaughter of Korphe's headman and my mentor, Haji Ali, faced strident objections from her father, Twaha, who was more interested in fetching a high bride-price for his daughter than in seeing Jahan go to our hostel in Skardu for advanced training in public health. (Twaha later relented, and Jahan is now studying at the Government Degree College in Skardu.)

The true reasons behind these objections can often be difficult to ferret out, and when they eventually reveal themselves, they sometimes have a powerful logic. Such proved to be the case with Ghosia.

When Genevieve, Sarfraz, and Saidullah Baig paid their initial visit to the family, Ghosia's father, Sabir, and both of her uncles were skeptical, and a number of issues were raised. They were concerned that Ghosia was too young. They were worried that it was unfair to give her a scholarship while ignoring the desires of her older siblings. And they didn't want to see her leave home. After several follow-up visits, however, another issue emerged. As the youngest surviving daughter, it turned out that Ghosia was her father's primary caregiver. Without her services, he would be completely incapacitated.

Sabir's fears were entirely understandable, and when they finally became clear, we decided to tackle the problem in two directions at once. First, we proposed that paying for a nurse who could attend to her father should be part of Ghosia's scholarship. And second, we invoked the most powerful argument we have at our disposal, which I sometimes think of as the "carpe diem appeal." In this case, it was delivered by Saidullah Baig.

"In the life of a person," Saidullah reminded Ghosia's father one evening, "there may come along the one opportunity that *must be taken*. When this opportunity arrives, you cannot let your concerns about yourself be a burden to your daughter, whom you love and for whom you want the best. We will try to help everyone in your family, but you must recognize that this is *Ghosia's* opportunity. Many people in our country never get this opportunity at all. Ghosia may never get another one. If you allow it to pass by without seizing it, you may not have another chance."

Saidullah was too modest to mention as part of his argument that years earlier and at considerable personal sacrifice, he had put his own wife through both high school and college, one of the few men in northern Pakistan ever to have done such a thing — and that as a result of this commitment, she now has an excellent job in a private school in Gilgit. Nevertheless, Saidullah's exhortation had a powerful effect on Ghosia's father.

"Yes," he nodded after deliberating for several minutes. "We will do whatever is best for my daughter."

Since that conversation, Sabir has continued to waver. We are very hopeful that with time and patience, he will eventually see the wisdom of allowing Ghosia to accept her scholarship and give his consent. In the meantime, however, we found ourselves confronting another situation in which it has been almost impossible to remain optimistic.

During the same period when we were negotiating with Ghosia's family, I received word about a man named Dr. Mohammad Hassan, a relatively prosperous dentist who lived in a village called Bhedi, high up in the Neelum Valley, and who was hoping we might consider giving his daughter Siddre a scholarship. Although we usually try to target the poorest families, who need our help the most, I passed this man's contact information along to Genevieve and suggested she might want to follow up. In addition to the fact that Dr. Hassan had provided some valuable assistance by steering us in the direction of other qualified scholarship applicants, he was an important man with influence in his part of the Neelum Valley — someone with whom we would do well to maintain friendly relations.

So one evening, Genevieve, Sarfraz, and Mohammed Nazir drove up the mountainside in Bhedi to meet with Dr. Hassan and the other members of his family, who besides Siddre included his wife, his four other daughters and two sons, and a son-in-law named Miraftab, who was visiting that evening from Muzaffarabad. Siddre proved to be a bright and articulate young woman who was finishing the twelfth grade at the Gundi Piran school and whose ambition was to attend college, become a doctor, and then return to Bhedi to put her skills to use. After her mother greeted the three guests in the common room, the women of the household ushered Genevieve into the kitchen, leaving Sarfraz and Nazir to talk with Dr. Hassan and Miraftab about Siddre's future.

Sitting on the concrete floor in the firelit kitchen, Genevieve learned that the women of the family were absolutely giddy about the prospect of Siddre pursuing her medical degree, but her brother-in-law, Miraftab, stood in opposition. Inside the common room, Sarfraz and Nazir quickly came to the same conclusion. Dr. Hassan was halfheartedly concerned that this American NGO wanted to convert his daughter to Christianity, but Sarfraz was successful in explaining that the CAI was a secular organization and had no interest in religious conversion. Miraftab, however, objected fiercely to the idea of a scholarship for his sister-in-law, and when the men had finished their discussion in the living room, he moved into the kitchen, took up a post on a bench with the women sitting on the floor below him, and directed his remarks to Genevieve in English.

Why, he wanted to know, did she think she could come into this culture from the West and propose to send "our girls" off to school? What did she think had given her the right to even dare to suggest a scholarship for a girl?

Miraftab then went on to ask what Siddre could possibly do with her education that would be of benefit to her family and to the people in Bhedi. And finally he got around to the heart of the matter. What the CAI *really* needed to be offering to this family — the only kind of sponsorship that made any sense and that would have actual value — was a scholarship not for Siddre, but for *him*.

The CAI staff spent that night with Dr. Hassan's family, and Genevieve slept in the same room with the daughters, who were weeping and distraught over Miraftab's behavior. The following morning, Siddre reiterated her dream of attending medical school. (Like so many of the girls we interview in these situations, she used the word for "dream" in Urdu — *khawab*.) Before they bid farewell and left, however, Miraftab made it clear that his position had not changed, thereby ensuring that Siddre's *khawab* would never be realized.

Driving down the mountainside that morning, Sarfraz turned to Genevieve and asked what she thought of Miraftab. She replied that he didn't seem to understand how important the education of just one girl could be for the entire village. Sarfraz and Nazir both agreed and went on to vent their frustration over the manner in which a son-in-law had been permitted to sabotage a talented young woman's chance of pursuing higher education.

It is always difficult to witness the end of a girl's *khawab,* but it's especially hard to swallow when such a thing has been undermined by a male member of her own family who has failed to overcome his envy and resentment over the opportunity she is being presented with. In many ways, Sarfraz, Genevieve, and Nazir agreed, building schools was proving to be easier than dealing with the obstacles thrown up by the extended families of our scholarship candidates.

Later, Genevieve wrote up a report that concluded that although Siddre would have made an excellent scholarship candidate, Miraftab had rendered the situation impossible. After reading what she had written, I reluctantly agreed that as long as Dr. Hassan was willing to permit his son-in-law to have a veto over his daughter's future, we would not be able to fund her medical-school expenses.

That is where matters have stood — and will continue to stand — until Miraftab changes his mind. If and when he relents, Siddre's scholarship will be waiting for her.

In the meantime, however, I was about to confront some new and unexpected challenges of my own back in the United States.

In February 2007, the just-published softcover edition of *Three Cups of Tea* surged onto the *New York Times* paperback nonfiction best-seller list. Driven by a grassroots interest from local bookstores, women's book clubs, and community organizations all across America, the book as of this writing has spent more than 140 weeks on that list, forty-three of them in the number one position.

This exposure and publicity, week after week and month after month, seemed to offer an unparalleled chance to spread the word about the importance of girls' education in Pakistan and Afghanistan while raising money for new schools. So on behalf of the thousands of young girls who were still waiting to attend classes, I set out to turn the CAI into a promotion-and-fund-raising machine.

With word spreading about the story behind *Three Cups of Tea,* the invitations started pouring in. As the campaign accelerated, several experts on marketing and promotion strongly advised me to concentrate mainly on addressing adults, for the obvious reason that they were the ones who would be purchasing copies of the book and donating money to the CAI. This strategy struck me as shortsighted and narrow. Plus, I simply prefer hanging out with kids. So I did my best to combine "official" events — the lectures and the book signings with adults in the evenings — with more informal appearances with children in the mornings and afternoons, many of them at libraries and schools.

As the bookings were made, my schedule quickly ballooned to the point where it was out of control. Back in 2005, I had traveled to eight different cities to give presentations on the work that we do in the western Himalayas. During 2007, I made a total of 107 appearances in eighty-one American cities. The results were impressive: Between 2005 and 2007, the CAI's gross intake tripled. The emotional and physical toll, however, was enormous. In January of 2007 alone, I made eighteen appearances in fourteen cities at venues ranging from the Harvard Travellers Club in Boston and the Rochester Public Library to the Blue Heron Coffeehouse in Winona, Minnesota. In April, there were fifteen events in thirteen cities. By September, my calendar called for speeches in Rosemont, Illinois; Charlotte, North Carolina; Helena, Montana; Bainbridge Island, Washington; and eighteen other places, all of which merged into a muddled blur in my mind.

On November 20, I crashed.

The venue was West Chester University in Pennsylvania. I had flown into Philadelphia from California, having made eleven appearances during the previous seven days in San Francisco, Palo Alto, San Jose, Colorado Springs, and Carbondale. I rented a car and punched in the address on the GPS system, and as I made my way toward yet another hotel, I was overcome by the sudden sensation of being wiped out and utterly overwhelmed. I also had no idea what I was going to say to all those people in five or six hours and found myself starting to panic. I called my wife from the car and told her that I was in trouble.

Upon hearing my voice, Tara feared that I might be experiencing a full-on panic attack. Nevertheless, after settling me down and talking me through my anxieties, she asked me to eat some food, get a little sleep, and give the speech.

I got to the hotel, took a shower, ironed my shirt, and slept for two or three hours. The next day I made it to the university on time and gave my presentation. But after it was over, with hundreds of people coming up to say hello, I found myself confronting one of the things I find most daunting.

Following my presentations, it is not uncommon to be greeted by a line of up to one thousand people who hope to purchase a signed copy of *Three Cups of Tea,* shake my hand, and share a few words about their own experiences in the third world or express their interest in volunteering their services overseas. In such situations, I understand that it's important for me to maintain speed and avoid getting into a long discussion with each and every person. My instinct, however, is to hang on to each exchange rather than letting it go to move along to the next one. Slowing down, making eye contact, and trying to establish a connection is important to me. The pace is draining and time-consuming. (Some of these book signings have gone on for five hours until 2:00 A.M.) But balancing out that scale is the value to the Central Asia Institute of having people walk away with a positive feeling of acknowledgment. There is also an element of basic respect and gratitude: After all, these are the people who pay for our schools. Without their support, it would be impossible to do what we do.

In West Chester on that day, however, I lost the desire and the ability to connect with others. Instead of reaching out to the people in front of me, all I wanted was to pull back inside myself. I felt as if I were standing inside a tunnel with the walls squeezing in. Overtaken by a sense of dismay over how disjointed and profoundly exhausting my outreach campaign had become, I was seized by the impulse to run out of there. Toward the end of the line, however, was a third-grade girl who had been waiting patiently to hand me a letter to take to one of our students in Pakistan — a letter that started: "To my best friend in Pakistan, you are my hero. I have a bucket of pennies at home that I collected so you can go to school. . . ."

Thus was I reminded, even in this moment of personal extremis, of one of the main reasons why I do what I do.

I was scheduled to attend a dinner on campus later that evening, but there was no way I could have pulled that off. Instead I returned to the hotel, fell onto the bed, and passed out. Several hours later, I phoned Tara and told her I didn't know where I was or what was going on. She calmed me down again, then told me to get on a plane and come home.

When I reached Bozeman, she and the kids met me late at night at the airport and gave me a big hug, and then we returned to the house and snuggled up for story time. Later, my wife told me she had already arranged with our board of directors and with Jennifer Sipes, our amazing operations director in Bozeman, to cancel my next appearance. Both of my cell phones would be turned off, and at the peril of arousing my wife's displeasure, I was now under orders to ignore all e-mails and remain at home for the next week.

Mulling over what had happened, I found myself frightened and a bit confused. Up to this point, the idea of "crashing" was something I had never even considered. When I'm working with Sarfraz and the other members of the staff in Pakistan and Afghanistan, I often labor at an intense pace for weeks on end with almost no sleep and little nutrition. As I was beginning to realize, however, there was a big difference between being in Asia working directly with communities and with our teachers and students (which is a form of interaction that I find energizing and inspiring) and being in the United States engaged in nonstop promotion, salesmanship, and fund-raising — which leaves me feeling drained and debilitated.

Tara puts it simply: "Some people need to charge up by getting plugged in to others, while Greg needs to charge up by getting unplugged from others."

What was equally clear to me, however, was that the unexpected success of *Three Cups of Tea* had created a unique moment for the Central Asia Institute, one that might not occur again. In short, this was one of those opportunities that *must be taken*. Personally, I would prefer to spend my time rattling along the dirt roads of Baltistan and

Badakshan with Sarfraz, but what I wanted and needed didn't really matter. If the Central Asia Institute was urging the parents of our scholarship nominees to set aside their personal concerns and desires in the service of something larger, how could I not hold myself to the same obligation?

The conclusion was unavoidable. Like it or not, I was now the fund-raising engine of the Central Asia Institute, and as such, my duty was to remain mostly in the United States pulling in the donations that would fuel the work that Sarfraz and his colleagues were handling so superbly on their own. So in 2008, I hurled myself into yet another 169 appearances in 114 cities, traveling almost nonstop, and every few weeks experiencing yet another "crash" that would force me to hole up in a hotel room or make a beeline back home to Bozeman.

During this time, I barely made it overseas, which meant that I was now all but cut off from the people and the landscapes that I loved and that had drawn me into this work in the first place. This was unbearably difficult and painful. But as Sarfraz's phone calls and e-mails continued to remind me, it was also the only way to complete what we had started in Afghanistan — a place where we still had business to finish and a committment to keep with Abdul Rashid Khan's Kirghiz horsemen. A committment, it turned out, that was about to draw us into a new relationship with a group of individuals who had dedicated their lives not to the mission of peace, but to the enterprise of war.

PART III
THE SCHOOL ON THE ROOF
OF THE WORLD

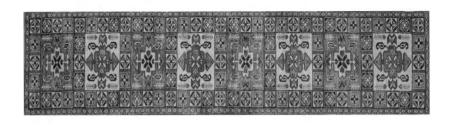

CHAPTER 12
AN E-MAIL FROM THE
AMERICAN COLONEL

Education is the long-term solution to fanaticism.
— COLONEL CHRISTOPHER KOLENDA, U.S. ARMY December 26, 2008, *The Wall Street Journal*

Captain Nathan Springer (left), Ghulam Sahki, and Colonel Christopher Kolenda, Kunar Province, Afghanistan PHOTO: © 2008 COLONEL CHRISTOPHER KOLENDA

As a veteran who enlisted in the U.S. army four days after graduating from high school and spent two years on active duty in Germany between 1975 and 1977, I have the utmost respect and admiration for the men and women who have chosen to serve in the American armed forces. As a humanitarian and an advocate of literacy, however, I have also had my share of disagreements with the military over the years.

In 2001, my initial support for the U.S. decision to go war in Afghanistan quickly faded after I began hearing about the high level of civilian casualties inflicted by the American bombing campaign — an estimated 2,700 to 3,400 deaths between October 7 and December 10 according to Marc Herold, an economist at the University of New Hampshire. What disturbed me was not only the level of suffering inflicted by the Department of Defense on the Afghan population but also the manner in which these tragedies were described. In his daily press briefings, Donald Rumsfeld triumphantly cataloged the losses inflicted on Taliban and Al Qaeda forces by American bombs and cruise missiles that were dropped into heavily populated areas. But only when pressured by reporters — and even then, resentfully and as an afterthought — did he bother to mention the "collateral damage."

In my view, Rumsfeld's rhetoric and his demeanor conveyed the impression that America's army of laptop warriors was largely indifferent to the pain and misery that were being inflicted on innocent women and children. This impression was reinforced by the Bush administration's complete disinterest in acknowledging, much less compensating, those civilian victims. In the end, the signal that this wound up sending — both to me and to the Central Asia Institute's staff and friends in Afghanistan — was that the United States placed little or no value on the lives of noncombatants in one of the poorest and most desperate countries on earth.

Toward the end of 2002, I was given the opportunity to express these views when a marine general who had donated a thousand dollars to the CAI invited me to the Pentagon to address a small gathering of uniformed officers and civilian officials. In the course of my talk, I devoted a few minutes to explaining the tribal traditions that governed conflict in that part of the world — including the manner in which warring parties hold a *jirga* before joining a battle in order to discuss how many losses each side is willing to accept in light of the fact that the victors will be obligated to care for the widows and orphans of the rivals they have vanquished.

"People in that part of the world are used to death and violence," I said. "And if you tell them, 'We're sorry your father died, but he died a martyr so that Afghanistan could be free,' and if you offer them compensation and honor their sacrifice, I think that people will support us even now. But the worst thing that you can do is what we're doing — ignoring the victims by calling them 'collateral damage' and not even trying to count the numbers of the dead. Because to ignore them is to deny they ever existed, and there is no greater insult in the Islamic world. For that, we will not be forgiven."

I concluded that speech with an idea that had come to me while touring the wreckage of a home I had seen at the site of a cruise-missile strike in Kabul.

"I'm no military expert, and these figures

might not be exactly right," I said. "But as best I can tell, we've launched 114 Tomahawk cruise missiles into Afghanistan so far. Now take the cost of one of those missiles, tipped with a Raytheon guidance system, which I think is about $840,000. For that much money, you could build dozens of schools that could provide tens of thousands of students with a balanced, nonextremist education over the course of a generation. Which do you think will make us more secure?"

It was a harsh message, and although my host and the other members of the audience were unimpeachably gracious and polite, I could not help but imagine that my words were met with a dismissive response. And so it came as something of a surprise when, during the months that followed, members of the U.S. military continued reaching out to ask questions, exchange ideas, and express their thanks for the work that we were doing.

The watershed moment came with the publication of the *Parade* article in April 2003 and the massive influx of donations that resulted, which placed us on a stable financial footing in Pakistan while funding our expansion into Afghanistan. During the next ten months, we were inundated with mail (the initial letters we received had to be carted out of the Bozeman post office in canvas sacks), and some of the most moving correspondence we received came from American servicemen and servicewomen, such as Jason B. Nicholson from Fayetteville, North Carolina.

"As a captain in the U.S. Army and a veteran of the war in Afghanistan with the Eighty-second Airborne Division," Nicholson wrote, "I have had a very unique and up-close perspective on life in the rural portions of Central Asia. The war in Afghanistan was, and continues to be, bloody and destructive; most of all on those who deserve it the least — the innocent civilians who only wish to make a wage and live a decent life with their families. CAI's projects provide a good alternative to the education offered in many of the radicalized *madrassas* from where the Taliban sprung forth with their so-called 'fundamental Islamacism [sic].' What can be better than a future world made safe for us all by education? The Central Asia Institute is now my charity of choice."

This marked a new beginning in my relationship with the American military. The story of how that process unfolded — the opportunities it created, the lessons it imparted, and the rather dramatic role it came to play in the final push that Sarfraz and I made to fulfill our promise to the Kirghiz of the Wakhan — is one of the more remarkable wonders that befell us during our time in Afghanistan.

As it turned out, Captain Nicholson's overture coincided with the start of an immensely challenging transition for members of the U.S. armed forces, who found themselves confronting two massive insurgency movements, the first in Iraq and the second in Afghanistan. As the violence escalated in both countries, a growing number of American officers became convinced that the military needed to transform itself from an organization focused exclusively on destroying its enemies to one that combined lethal operations with the promotion of security, reconstruction, and development. "Nation building," a phrase that had provoked immense derision following the Clinton administration's involvement in Bosnia, Kosovo, and Somalia, reemerged as an integral part of a new doctrine framed by General David Petraeus, who jointly oversaw the publication of the U.S. Army Marine Corps *Counterinsurgency Field Manual*. The key idea — the notion that when it comes to long-term security, stabilizing war-torn countries can be as important as defeating the enemy — was most succintly expressed by Admiral Mike Mullen, chairman of the Joint Chiefs of Staff, who told the House Armed Services Committee in September 2008, "We can't kill our way to victory."

At the center of this approach to warfare is a skill set that extends considerably beyond the traditional duties of soldiering. In part, it includes tasks that have typically fallen under the umbrella of civil affairs and engineering: rebuilding water-treatment plants, schools, electrical power grids, and other municipal services that are vital for a stable society. Equally important, however, is the effort on the part of soldiers — especially officers — to master the cultural nuances of the countries in which they are deployed by embracing fields of study that include anthropology, history, sociology, language, and politics. The aim is to enhance security by fostering relationships and building a sense of trust at the grassroots level with community leaders, village elders, and tribal authorities.

Among the proponents of this approach to counterinsurgency were a number of officers who had stumbled across *Three Cups of Tea,* which was never intended to appeal to a military audience. In some cases, the book had been recommended by the officers' spouses, who had been exposed to it in neighborhood book clubs or churches, where it garnered quite a following shortly after its publication in 2006. In other cases, children in military families heard about the book in school as a result of Pennies for Peace, a program designed to raise money for children in Pakistan and Afghanistan that we started up in 1996 and that is currently running in more than 4500 elementary schools across the United States and abroad. Finally, hundreds of servicemen and servicewomen encountered the book when it was adopted as part of a required reading list for officers enrolled in graduate-level counterinsurgency courses at the Pentagon.

Before long, we were receiving hundreds of e-mails, letters, and donations from people who had served in Afghanistan or Iraq and who were writing to let us know that they had returned from their tours of duty firmly convinced that providing young men and women with a moderate education was the most potent and cost-effective way to combat the growth of Islamic extremism. Around the same time, Christiane Leitinger, who runs Pennies for Peace, noticed that the program was becoming enormously popular in school districts dominated by families whose parents served in the military — places like Camp Lejeune, North Carolina (the largest Marine Corps base on the East Coast), San Antonio, Texas (where army medics train at Fort Sam Houston), and Coronado, California (headquarters of the Naval Air Forces Command and a major training site for Navy SEALs).

By early 2007, Jennifer Sipes, our office manager in Bozeman, had begun fielding invitations asking me to come and speak at a number of gatherings of active and retired members of the military. The first of these came from Dr. Steve Recca, a retired naval officer who at that time served as the director of the Center for Homeland Security at the University of Colorado in Colorado Springs. When I returned Dr. Recca's phone call, he explained that his organization was hoping to gain a better understanding of "how homeland defense can be promoted through education" and "the exent to which ignorance is the real enemy." I flew out to Colorado on a bitterly cold evening in January and was ushered across campus to a chapel that seated an audience of two thousand people, which meant that more than half of the five thousand people who showed up wound up standing outside in the snow. At the end of my presentation, a man walked up and handed his card to me. He was a general at the North American Aerospace Defense Command and asked if I might be interested in giving a similar presentation at NORAD.

From that point, invitations began pouring in from all over the country: service academies and war colleges, veterans' organizations, and more than two dozen military bases. I was asked to return to Washington and give another briefing to the Pentagon, then later flew to Florida to talk to senior officers from CENTCOM (U.S. Central Command, which manages all American military operations in the Middle East and central Asia) and SOCOM (Special Operations Command, which directs elite units like the army's Delta Force.)

As I responded to these overtures, I began to glimpse the earnestness with which the American military was incorporating cultural education into its strategic doctrines. As I spent time at places like West Point in New York, the Air Force Academy in Colorado, or the Marine Expeditionary Force headquarters at California's Camp Pendleton, I was struck by the sheer amount of effort and energy that soldiers were pouring into understanding Islamic history and civilization. At the U.S. Naval Academy in Annapolis, for example — where I was invited by Matthew Morse, a midshipman who had joined up after 9/11 and later read *Three Cups of Tea* — I was able to sit in on a religion class in which the students analyzed a section of Leviticus in the Old Testament and then compared it to related passages in the Koran. Later that same day, a sociology class featured a spirited discussion involving the manner in which the former shah of Iran and the Ayatollah Khomeini based two speeches on radically different interpretations of the same sentence in the Koran.

During these encounters, I was struck by the realization that some of the values held by cadets, officers, and enlisted personnel seemed to mirror my own. For example, many of these people displayed genuine humility, as well as a deep respect for other cultures. After spending time with them, it was also clear to me that their patriotism was rooted in, among other ideals, a reverence for tolerance and diversity. But perhaps what impressed me the most was their emotional sincerity and their moral honesty. More than almost any other profession I have encountered, members of the military seem willing to acknowledge their failures and mistakes and to recognize that this is the first step toward learning and growth.

Eventually, I came to understand that a group of people who wield enormous power happen, oddly enough, to espouse some of the very same ideals imparted to me by people in Africa and central Asia who have no power at all. The reason for this, in my view, is that members of the armed forces have worked on the ground — in many cases, during three or four tours of duty — on a level that very few diplomats, academicians, journalists, or policy makers can match. And among other things, this experience has imbued soldiers with the gift of empathy.

In April 2009, I paid a visit to the Marines' Memorial Association in downtown San Francisco, where Major General Mike Myatt, the former commanding general of the First Marine Expeditionary Force who led the invasion into Kuwait, gave me a tour of two L-shaped, ash gray walls engraved with the names of every marine who has died in Iraq and Afghanistan since 2001. What struck me as forcefully as the litany of names on those walls was a comment that General Myatt dropped.

"There were thousands of civilians killed," he remarked. "I wish we could have built a wall for all of them, too."

In addition to the enhanced feelings of admiration and respect that were, for me, invariably a by-product of these encounters, I was also struck by an unexpected reciprocity of vision when it came to what, in my view, may be the most important insight of all.

Of the hundreds of soldiers I have spoken with during the past six years who have been deployed in Afghanistan, almost every one of them firmly believes that the best way to augment our security is by truly being of service to the Afghan people — and moreover, that the capacity to render this service meaningfully and well is predicated upon listening, understanding, and building relationships. In this respect, the goal of enhancing our own security is best achieved by enhancing theirs. And the most critical building block to accomplishing both is education.

Prior to these meetings, my judgment of the American military's conduct in Afghanistan was harsh and rather uncompromising — and even after these encounters, I still have my objections. Between June and November 2006, for example, the U.S. Air Force according to a Defense Department briefing, dropped roughly 987 bombs on Afghanistan, exceeding the 848 bombs that were dropped between 2001 and 2004. The resulting civilian casualties generated deep revulsion among the Afghan public.

Nevertheless, as I experienced the equivalent of sharing three cups of tea with the U.S. military, my perspective began to change. In a way, each side had something to teach the other, and we both wound up emerging wiser and enriched by the encounter. In the end, I also came away with the conclusion that the military is probably doing a better job than any other institution in the United States government — including the State Department, Congress, and the White House — of developing a meaningful understanding of the complex dynamics on the ground in Pakistan and Afghanistan.

My encounters with American soldiers have been extremely gratifying for me on a personal level, but they have also influenced the manner in which we do our work at the Central Asia Institute. Nothing illustrates this better than the set of events that began to unfold on September 15, 2007, when I opened my e-mail in-box and clicked on the following message:

Dear Central Asia Institute,
    I am the Commander of Task Force Saber which serves the 190,000 people in northern Kunar and eastern Nuristan Provinces in Afghanistan. Our primary goal in this counterinsurgency is to provide hope

for the good people of Afghanistan, particularly the children. Building schools is one of my top development priorities.

I am convinced that the long-term solution to terrorism in general and Afghanistan specifically is education. The conflict here will not be won with bombs but with books and ideas that excite the imagination toward peace, tolerance, and prosperity. The thirst for education here is palpable. People are tired of war after 30 years and want a better future. Education will make the difference whether the next generation grows up to be educated patriots or illiterate fighters. The stakes could not be higher.

As you know, Kunar and Nuristan are among the most impoverished areas in this war-torn country. Well over 90% of the schools in the area are "open-air" schools; some have tarps, others simply try to hold class under a tree. We have begun a school partnership campaign to connect American with Afghan schools to help build grass-roots connections between our children and our countries. We have delivered a wealth of school supplies, but there is never enough.

Reading *Three Cups of Tea* has inspired me even further to pursue the development of Afghan schools and education. I am not sure if the CAI can help these schools in any way. I do want to let you know how inspirational your work is for the people of Afghanistan and Pakistan.

Best regards,
LTC Chris Kolenda, U.S. Army

I was, of course, gratified to be hearing from an officer whose respect for education mirrored my own. But what really caught my attention was the place from which this colonel was writing.

Northern Kunar and eastern Nuristan is a storied landscape of soaring mountains and steep-walled gorges embedded in the heart of the Hindu Kush. The region, which defines Afghanistan's northeastern border with Pakistan, is steeped in a web of myths surrounding the origin of its inhabitants — a race of fierce pagans who bore the features of southern Europeans, were fond of imbibing wine, furnished their homes with tables and chairs, and spoke a language unintelligible to any of the Muslim neighbors who surrounded them. Known since ancient times as Kafiristan, "the country of the unbelievers," it qualifies as one of the most isolated, mysterious, and least-known places on earth, even as late as the second half of the twentieth century.

As Eric Newby relates in his marvelous travelogue, *A Short Walk in the Hindu Kush,* the inhabitants of this area descended from stragglers of the army of Alexander the Great, who passed along the edges of what is now Nuristan Province on his way to India in 326 B.C. and fought a battle against residents of the Kunar Valley. Since then, visitors to the area have been few and far between. Chinese Buddhist monks made scattered reference to it during their travels to India in the sixth century, Tamerlane's forces invaded one of its valleys in the fourteenth, and the Emperor Babur sampled some of its wine in the fifteenth. Other than that, the inhabitants of Kafiristan were largely left to their own devices until 1895, when Abdur Rahman, the emir of Afghanistan, invaded with a trio of armies that attacked simultaneously from three separate directions. The main force, which consisted of eight infantry regiments, one cavalry regiment, and a battery of artillery, marched through the Kunar Valley and defeated the Kafirs in a single decisive battle — although holdouts fought house to house with spears and bows and arrows and set fire to their own villages before surrendering — at which point the entire population was converted by sword to Islam.

Thanks to their impenetrable terrain, their extensive cave networks, and the border they share with Pakistan's lawless Tribal Areas, northern Kunar and eastern Nuristan emerged as a favored sanctuary for several mujahadeen groups during the 1979–89 occupation of Afghanistan by the Soviets. In the 1990s, several thousand Arab militants established a number of bases throughout Kunar and Nuristan with the help of Osama bin Laden. Following 2001, the region served as a safe haven for Taliban and Al Qaeda fighters, who used it as a conduit for moving weapons and fighters from Pakistan into Afghanistan. In the summer of 2005, after insurgents shot down an American Chinook helicopter in the Korengal Valley, killing sixteen Special Forces soldiers and the crew, Kunar became known among U.S. soldiers as "enemy central." By the summer of 2006, not a single NGO was operating anywhere inside the region.

Thanks to all of this, it was hard to conceive of a part of Afghanistan that offered a more potent combination of danger, remoteness, and hostility toward outsiders. And yet here was a U.S. commander who was asking for help because he considered building schools to be one of his top priorities?

Clearly, this was someone worth getting to know.

Christopher Kolenda grew up in Omaha, Nebraska, the son of a JAG lawyer in the Army, which perhaps was what led to his joining the United States Military Academy at West Point. He was an excellent student who loved history and read everything he could about the Romans, the Greeks, and the rise and fall of empires. As a captain, he attended graduate school at the University of Wisconsin, where he completed a degree in modern European history, and where he also began to collect the writings of military leaders, which he eventually compiled into a book called *Leadership: The Warriors' Art,* which is now read my many aspiring military commanders. He became an Airborne Ranger and later the Commander of the 1st Squadron, 91st Cavalry of the 173rd Airborne Division, which in 2005 was notified that it would be deploying for Iraq. As they continued training and organized Arabic language classes, they received mandatory orders instead to deploy to Afghanistan — which they did in May 2007. Their headquarters was at Forward Operating Base (FOB) Naray in northern Kunar.

Task Force Saber's five main forward operating bases had initially been set up in 2006 when the U.S. Army put in a string of posts extending along Afghanistan's eastern border with Pakistan. The primary mission for the seven hundred plus U.S. soldiers under Kolenda's command and the six hundred Afghan soldiers partnered with them was to conduct counterinsurgency operations and bring stability to the area. A major part of that mission, as they saw it, involved building relationships with hundreds of village elders, tribal leaders, and mullahs in the surrounding communities. Kolenda's headquarters, located just outside the village of Naray, was poised along the border between Kunar and Nuristan, an area with 190,000 residents where U.S. forces had undergone some of their most ferocious fighting against the Taliban and Al Qaeda in 2007.

In a classic army command outpost, an officer like Kolenda would keep a detailed set of maps cataloging the most vital pieces of military intelligence about the opposing force: an outline of the enemy's resources that included troop deployments, supply and transportation networks, patterns of movement, and level of firepower. Colonel Kolenda's information certainly included a similar layout of the Taliban and Al Qaeda units operating in the surrounding area. But his data extended far beyond the usual inventory of the insurgents' manpower and their range of weaponry. After six months of drinking tea and listening to speeches at tribal *jirgas,* he and his soldiers had established a connection with almost every major and minor community leader and religious authority in the civilian population. In addition to knowing their names, faces, and tribal affiliations, the Americans understood exactly where each of them fit into the region's political and economic hierarchy. In short, Kolenda and his men had a grasp of the complex network of kinship ties, blood feuds, economic disputes, and ethnic rivalries that shaped every aspect of life in the rural communities of the surrounding region.

During the course of their deployment, Kolenda and his soldiers had scrambled to assemble an accurate assessment of the inner workings of tribal society in northern Kunar and eastern Nuristan. This body of knowledge wasn't perfect, but the information these men had gathered was impressive — and when they rotated to their next postings, the information would be passed along to their replacements, who would continue the process. In the meantime, however, the colonel's connections had developed to the point where he was beginning to get a handle on the problems that the surrounding communities were struggling with and how he might be able to help — which brings us back to the reason why he had e-mailed me.

After responding to Kolenda's first message, we corresponded several more times, and during one of these exchanges he told me about a village called Saw, which was located across the Kunar River seventeen kilometers from his Naray headquarters, and which presented an unusual opportunity.

Several times each month, the Naray outpost had been subjected to rocket attacks launched from mountain ridge lines near the village. Having received a number of credible reports about insurgent activity in and around Saw, the colonel had good reason to suspect that people from Saw might have had something to do with these attacks. Instead of conducting a cordon and search operation through the village, Kolenda and his team developed a more creative approach: They decided to convene a *jirga* with the village in order to find out what grievances might be motivating them to conduct rocket attacks.

Kolenda's counterpart in the Afghan National Army (ANA), Lieutenant Colonel Sher Ahmad, submitted the request for the *jirga.* In the meeting, the elders explained that a previous cordon and search had been conducted in the village several years earlier, and during the course of this operation, a number of belongings had allegedly been stolen. As a result, the villagers felt that their honor had been violated, and some among them were keen on seeking revenge. During this same meeting, several of the elders also happened to mention that education was extremely important to the community, but that because they lacked a school, their eight hundred children were forced to study outside, and winter was approaching quickly.

Many of the American soldiers, it turned out, had been receiving school supplies donated by their families and neighbors back in the states. So after the *jirga,* these supplies were gathered together — they amounted to three truckloads — and the following week, a second *jirga* was convened for the purpose of handing these materials over to the village. The very next day, the elders of Saw showed up outside the Narray outpost asking to see Colonel Kolenda and Colonel Ahmad. They had brought with them more than one hundred thank-you notes, written in Pashto, by the children of the village.

The elders and the two colonels wound up talking for more than two hours, and during this conversation, it became clear that residents of Saw were desperate to find a way of building a school. Kolenda was convinced that this shared passion for education offered a basis for building a solid, long-term relationship. Unfortunately, however, the colonel did not have the resources to give the villagers what they wanted — which is why he had turned to me.

Could the CAI possibly help?

At first, I wasn't exactly sure that we could. The Central Asia Institute is not affiliated with the U.S. military, and in order for us to maintain credibility with the communities in which we work, we bend over backward to keep this distinction clear. (For that reason, I will not even permit people who visit our schools to wear military-type camouflage fatigues.) There were also a number of practical concerns, starting with the fact that Kunar and Nuristan are extremely dangerous, and extending into the same issue that we confronted in Kashmir: Having never worked in this area before, we had no relationships, no network of contacts, and no friends.

Those concerns were substantial. Offsetting them, however, was the simple fact that I admired what this American commander stood for and what he was trying to accomplish. If there was a way for us to help without compromising our reputation as an organization that had no connection, financial or political, with the U.S. government, it might be worth exploring.

But first, we'd need to find a person who could pull this off. And as it turned out, I had someone in mind.

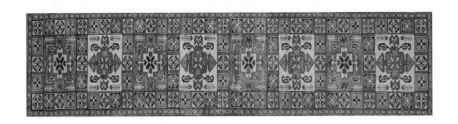

CHAPTER 13
THE MAN FROM THE JALOZAI REFUGEE CAMP

It is only with the heart that one can see rightly;
What is essential is invisible to the eye.
— The Little Prince, ANTOINE DE SAINT-EXUPÉRY

Urozgan elders with Wakil Karimi (lower right), Haji Ibrahim (upper right), and Greg Mortenson PHOTO: © 2009 TERU KUWAYAMA

Wakil Karimi and I met in the spring of 2002 when I checked into the Peace Guest House on Kabul's Bagh-e-Bala Road during one of my early trips into Afghanistan. A bearded Pashtun with rounded facial features and kind brown eyes who dressed in a neatly pressed *shalwar kamiz* and vest, Wakil was no different from any of the thousands of ambitious young Afghan men who were tentatively venturing back to their homeland in the wake of the Taliban's defeat. And like many of his compatriots, his story — which I learned shortly after getting to know him — was the tale of a man who had spent the bulk of his life in a crowded refugee camp.

Wakil's boyhood memories of Afghanistan ended in December of 1979 when, at the age of seven, he and his entire family were forced to flee from their home following the Russian invasion. For two weeks, Soviet MiG fighters had pummeled their village with bombs, flattening nearly all the houses and killing many of the inhabitants.

The Karimis traveled by foot, horse, and donkey for four days and nights until they crossed the border into Pakistan on precipitous mountain trails and settled into Jalozai Refugee Camp, about twenty miles southeast of Peshawar. One of the largest of the 150 camps that Pakistan was hastily assembling to house some of the 4.5 million Afghan *muhajir* (refugees) who would eventually pour into Pakistan following the Soviet occupation, Jalozai was a barren area where seventy thousand people huddled in ramshackle tents and makeshift tarpaulin shelters without running water, electricity, plumbing, transportation, or the ability to feed themselves. The guards were cruel, some of the administrators stole much of the food and supplies for themselves, and entire sections of the camp were controlled by thugs. It was not the sort of place where one would want to spend more than a week, much less several months.

Although Wakil did not know it then, this would be his home for most of the next twenty-three years.

A week after settling his wife, his father, his sister, and his six children in the camp, Wakil's father, Abdul Ghani, did what most of the men of Jalozai were doing at the time. He bade farewell to his family, made his way back to Afghanistan to rejoin the mujahadeen, and disappeared into the fires of the jihad. Wakil's last memory of Abdul Ghani consists of a hug and a promise that they would see each other in a month. To this day, Wakil has no idea how his father was killed, when it happened, or where he is buried.

Wakil and his younger brother, Mateen, set out to make the best of the situation. At the direction of their mother, a woman who had never learned to read or write but who revered education, they studied in one of the makeshift classrooms in the camp for half of each day. The other half of the day, they worked to support their mother, grandfather, and four younger siblings. They sold water, they worked in a kiln that baked bricks, and eventually, after they learned English, they started the their own after-hours *maktab,* the Washington English Language Center, which taught English vocabulary and grammar to some of the camp's most ambitious language students. Then in the summer of 2002, word reached Wakil that the owner of the Peace Guest House in Kabul was looking for a manager who could speak English. The salary was two hundred dollars a month plus

411

gratuities. Intrigued, he made his way alone back to Afghanistan, interviewed for the job, and was sitting behind the desk of the guesthouse on the evening that I arrived.

When Wakil learned that I was hoping to set up girls' schools in his country, he approved in the strongest possible terms. "Oh, Afghanistan is the *perfect* place for your work," he exclaimed, "and girls' education is a must!" He also confided that he happened to know the ideal spot where we should begin: a little village thirty miles southwest of Kabul called Lalander, where the school had been destroyed by the Soviets and where — incidentally — Wakil's family happened to be from.

When I explained that we specialized in building schools in exceptionally remote areas, he listened politely, nodded, and proceeded to stay "on message" with the kind of unwavering discipline and blatant disregard of the facts that Karl Rove would admire. Over the next eighteen months, as Sarfraz and I flitted back and forth through the Peace Guest House on our way to and from the Wakhan, Wakil presented himself as a Pashtun version of an exceptionally gifted used car salesman. He never stopped smiling, he never raised his voice, and he never once abandoned his conviction that if he kept pressing, gently and earnestly, he would eventually persuade us to adopt Lalander as a "special exception" to our end-of-the-road policy.

Eventually, Wakil augmented his relentless persistence with a subtler and more devious strategy that involved arousing our sympathy by invoking an elaborate catalog of Lalander's miseries and misfortunes. Each time we arrived at the Peace Guest House, Sarfraz and I were treated to a litany of Lalander's liabilities that included the poor state of the road, the miserable quality of the water, the straitened circumstances of the inhabitants, and the level of apathy lavished upon the village by the Afghan government.

After more than a year of this, Wakil finally wore Sarfraz and me down to the point where one of us made the mistake of asking him to elaborate on something he'd said about Lalander — if memory serves, it had to do with the revelation that the Taliban had recently begun using the valley in which the village was located as a conduit for running heroin. Our request for more information provided the opening he'd been waiting for so patiently.

"Please, let us go and have tea with the *shura* elders," he replied, "and you will be able to see for yourselves."

How could we possibly say no?

It takes two hours to drive from Kabul to Lalander, which lies in the heart of the Char Asiab Valley, a river-carved canyon whose walls of bare orange and black rock soar nearly two thousand feet into the sky and whose narrow bottom is quilted with a patchwork of orchards that include peach, apricot, cherry, and mulberry trees. They also grow a lot of garlic around Lalander, so the air is anointed with a scent that is sweet and faintly cloying.

For all his salesmanship, Wakil had not misrepresented the place or exaggerated its misfortunes. The dirt road was so awful that a good runner could easily have outpaced us during the fifty minutes required to cover the last ten miles. Thanks to the extensive Soviet strafing and bombing, many of the mud-walled buildings in the village looked like decaying Mesopotamian ruins. With the exception of the rusted carcasses of Russian tanks and armored personnel carriers littering the riverbed, it felt as if we had stepped out of the twenty-first century and back into the Middle Ages.

When we arrived and convened with the elders in a *jirga* that Wakil had arranged in advance, it also became clear that the place desperately needed a school. The only form of education, it turned out, was informal religious classes taught in a mosque by one of the three local mullahs. One of these mullahs was resistant, but the community's 160 families and the other two mullahs were keen on building something better.

It was during this *jirga* that an unusual idea first occurred to us. Although Lalander looked and felt as remote as many of the places in which we normally work, its proximity to Kabul might make it accessible to the increasing number of journalists, donors, and officials from the Afghan government who were expressing interest in seeing the kind of work we do but could not afford to commit to an arduous six-day journey north to Badakshan and into the Wakhan. Thus, the question arose, might it not make sense for us to build a demonstration school in Lalander that could serve as a showcase for the kind of work we do?

In early 2004, I ran this query past the CAI board and was given a green light to move forward. Later that spring, with the help of thirty thousand dollars raised by the community of Lafayette, California, with the help of an attorney who was interested in funding a single school, construction started under the enthusiastic supervision of Wakil, who volunteered to act as the project's unpaid manager. Every Thursday and Friday — his days off at the Peace Guest House — Wakil made the drive from Kabul to the jobsite in order to monitor progress, order up new supplies, and keep things moving forward. And it was during these visits that he struck up a friendship with the boy named Gulmarjan.

Gulmarjan, who was fourteen years old and lived with his five sisters in Lalander, had never had the chance to attend school and could barely contain his excitement over the prospect of learning to read and write — an opportunity that, as far as Gulmarjan was concerned, could not arrive fast enough. As the weeks slipped past, his agitation burgeoned to the point where he was convinced that the pace of construction was not up to acceptable standards and, in an effort to prod things along, made a special point of badgering Wakil and reminding him how important it was to get things finished quickly. Whenever Wakil was in Kabul, Gulmarjan also developed a habit of grazing his goats as close as possible to the construction site so that he could monitor progress as he watched over his animals, then report his observations during Wakil's next visit. It was during the course of this surveillance, one afternoon in early June, that everyone in the village heard the sharp crack of an explosion from the direction of Gulmarjan's herd of goats.

Afghanistan is one of the most heavily mined countries in the world — during the Soviet occupation and the civil war that followed, virtually every corner the country was seeded with land mines — and according to the best estimates, the country still has somewhere between 1.5 and 3 million of these devices buried in its soil. They continue to kill or maim roughly sixty-five civilians each month, and as in so many other aspects of war, the people who bear the brunt of the suffering are children.

The device that Gulmarjan had stepped on was a Soviet antipersonnel land mine that had been placed in the ground more than twenty years earlier, and when he triggered the detonator, the explosion blew apart the lower half of his torso. When his distraught father reached him, he put the boy on a donkey (no one in Lalander has a car), then transferred him to a bicycle and frantically raced toward the nearest medical center, in Kabul.

Five hours later and barely a quarter of the

way to Kabul, Gulmarjan died in his father's arms.

In July 2004, I paid my first visit to Lalander and was impressed by how much progress Wakil's construction crew had made. The tragedy of Gulmarjan's death, however, had dampened everyone's spirits, especially when his father, Faisal Mohammed, dropped by to pay his respects.

A handsome man in his early forties with a salt-and-pepper beard and aquamarine eyes, Faisal Mohammed wanted to show me where his son was buried. It took less than five minutes to walk from the construction site to the spot where Gulmarjan had set off the land mine. His grave was a simple rectangular cairn of stones piled roughly two feet high, and at the head of the grave was a green metal cylinder — a Soviet-era artillery canister — supporting several wooden poles to which were affixed the green and white flags that flutter above graves all over Afghanistan. Scattered among the surrounding rocks we could spot fragments of metal — jagged pieces of copper and steel — that were parts of the mine that had killed him.

As Wakil, Sarfraz, and I stood in silence, Faisal cupped his hands in front of his chest and offered up a *dua* for the boy whose body lay at his feet. For many Muslim men, the birth of a son is life's greatest event, and thus the death of a son is surely one of the most devastating. But Faisal's sorrow penetrated to a level that the rest of us found difficult to fathom. In addition to his five daughters, he had also had two other sons — Gulmarjan's older brothers — and both of these boys were also dead. Faisal Haq, the oldest, had been claimed by diphtheria; and Zia Ullah, the middle boy, had been killed in a car accident. Now the third and last son had been taken, and the agony etched in Faisal Mohammed's face was beyond anything to which Sarfraz, Wakil, or I could do justice with words.

As we stood beside the grave and bore the weight of these thoughts, we could hear the sounds of men at work. The rattle of gravel flung from the end of a shovel and the wet slaps of fresh mortar troweled onto stone carried clearly from the jobsite, less than a hundred yards away. Perhaps it was our awareness of the proximity of this labor — and the manner in which the noise of the tools overlapped with the words of Faisal's *dua* — that drove home just how closely the birth of our school and the death of this boy had been enjoined. In any case, after a moment or two of silence I turned to Faisal and suggested that, with his permission, we would he honored to construct a concrete memorial pathway linking the school to Gulmarjan's grave that would serve as a memorial to his son.

When Faisal nodded his agreement and thanks, Wakil set about making the arrangements.

The school that Wakil saw through to completion is a real beauty. The green and white, single-story building sits on a slope just before the end of the road, perched above a grove of cherry and apple trees. There are six classrooms, plus a teacher's office and a playground. Just beyond the north side of the courtyard, a set of twenty steps leads to a concrete path, and at the end of the path is Gulmarjan's grave. He never had a chance to sit in a classroom and learn from one of the teachers, but we all believe that he is connected — symbolically, to be sure, but also in spirit — to the school he dreamed of one day attending.

Shortly after this project was completed, three things happened.

With the approval of her father, Gulmarjan's energetic sister, Saida, was enrolled in first grade. She has proven to be an exceptional student — her dream is to become the first female doctor in the history of Lalander. And in the eyes of her father — a man who until recently believed that all five of his daughters needed to remain at home — Saida now carries the unfulfilled promise of her three missing brothers in the palm of her hand.

Meanwhile, Faisal himself decided to go to school. Several months after his son's death, he enrolled in an eighteen-month training program to qualify as a professional de-miner, at the end of which he joined a company called RONCO, which removes land mines all over Afghanistan. The money was good (he earned about five hundred dollars a month, more than four times what he normally made), but the work deprived him of time with his family, so eventually he quit, sold a portion of his land, and voluntarily began cleaning the area around his village of land mines. By September 2009, he had discovered and removed thirty land mines around Lalander and its school.

And finally, Sarfraz and I decided to hire Wakil as the Central Asia Institute's Afghanistan director. By accepting this offer, he became the only Pashtun and *muhajir* member of the Dirty Dozen. Which is how the man from the Jalozai Refugee Camp became the first person I called in connection with Colonel Chris Kolenda's request for assistance in setting up a school directly across the river from the American firebase in Kunar Province.

In late 2007, I phoned Wakil and asked if he thought he could safely undertake a week-long scouting trip to the village of Saw. The safety part of my question was key, because as we both understood, this request could not have come at a more dangerous time.

Since late 2005, the Taliban insurgency had been steadily escalating as wave after wave of hardened and fanatical foreign fighters from Uzbekistan, Chechnya, western China, Saudi Arabia, and Yemen poured into Afghanistan. Having already spent time in Iraq, a number of these insurgents were well versed in the latest techniques for constructing improvised explosive devices (IEDs), conducting ambushes, and carrying out suicide attacks. The results showed almost immediately. According to the United Kingdom's Foreign & Commonwealth Office, from 2005 to 2006, the number of Taliban and Al Qaeda suicide bombings shot from twenty-one to 141, and the number of IEDs they detonated soared from 530 to 1,297.

The rising violence spilled into nonmilitary areas as well. In 2007, according to the

UNHCR, the Taliban killed thirty-four aid workers and abducted another seventy-six. They also stepped up their attacks on girls' education by executing teachers and students as well as burning schools. In 2006, Malim Abdul Habib, the headmaster of Shaik Mathi Baba Girls High School in Zabul Province, was pulled from bed at night, dragged into the courtyard of his home, and shot in front of his family. The following year, *Time* magazine reported, the Taliban shot dead three female students coming out of a high school in Logar Province. In several school districts around Kandahar, attackers tossed hand grenades through school windows and threw acid into the faces of girls attending classes. In neighboring Helmand Province, a teacher was shot and killed by gunmen on motorbikes, half a dozen girls' schools were burned to the ground by arsonists, and a high-school principal was beheaded. By 2007, according to *The Guardian* (U.K.), nearly half of the 748 schools in Afghanistan's four southern provinces, which were under the most serious assault by Taliban forces, had closed.

These were the conditions under which, one morning in the autumn of 2007, Wakil said good-bye to his wife, climbed into a battered Toyota Corolla, and headed east in the direction of Kunar.

His first stop was Jalalabad, a six-hour drive, where he met up with a friend named Gul Mohammed, who had several relatives in Kunar and planned to accompany Wakil the rest of the way. They spent the night at a hotel in town, and during dinner they quizzed several of the other guests about the situation in Kunar. One of the men Wakil approached, it turned out, worked for a de-mining crew and had spent quite a bit of time in Kunar. His report was chilling.

"The situation is okay for locals, but for foreigners and for anyone who is working with the foreigners, it is extremely danger-ous," the man declared. "If you go into Kunar, I do not think you will come back alive."

After Wakil and Gul Mohammed retired to their room, Wakil wrestled with the idea of turning around in the morning and re-turning to Kabul. He had a wife, six chil-dren, a mother, and more than a dozen other relatives who were completely dependent on him. How could he justify taking such risks? But then he fell asleep and had a dream.

In the dream, Wakil was typing at a key-board in front of a computer screen. When-ever he pressed the Enter key, the screen turned bright green. When he pressed the

Backspace key, however, the color of the screen changed to brown.

Enter — green. Backspace — brown.
Green. Brown.
Green. Brown.

When Wakil awoke the following morning, the dream was vividly etched in his mind, and its meaning was equally clear to him. As soon as he and Gul Mohammed had finished their breakfast, he pushed his chair back from the table and announced, "Okay, it is time to go."

"So you are going back to Kabul?" asked Gul Mohammed.

"No," replied Wakil, "you and I are going to Kunar."

"But I was thinking that you had decided we shouldn't continue because it's so dangerous."

"I know," replied Wakil. "But last night I had a dream that told me to keep going."

"What was the dream?" asked Gul Mohammed.

"My computer screen turned green whenever I pushed Enter, but when I hit the Backspace key, it turned brown. I think the dream means that if we don't keep moving forward and help the people of Saw village with their school, the whole area may become dry and brown. The elders, women, and children need our help, so we have to go. If I wind up dying, that's too bad, but I cannot just ignore a dream that reveals what Allah wants me to do."

"That makes sense," nodded Gul Mohammed. "*Allah Akbhar* — let's go."

The road out of Jalalabad headed straight north into the Hindu Kush, and ten hours later, as they passed from Nangarhar Province into Kunar itself, the two men were struck by the beauty of one of Afghanistan's least known regions. The road meandered through the heavily forested valley of the Kunar River past tiny mud-walled villages, each surrounded by a network of neatly terraced fields whose borders fit together like a jigsaw puzzle. The water-filled irrigation canals were lined with tall poplar trees whose pale green leaves shimmered when the wind played among them, while the tops of the mountains in the distance were capped with a mantle of snow. Every few miles, the road would pass through a cluster of tea *khanas,* stalls that sold cheap clothing and plastic sandals, and butcher shops where legs of fresh mutton were suspended from metal hooks. The scene had a pastoral somnolence that lulled Wakil into momentarily forgetting that this was also a theater of war.

Wakil knew no one in Kunar, but he was carrying several letters of introduction from Sahil Muhammad, a politician who represented the province in Parliament, as well as a list of local leaders supplied to us by Colonel Kolenda. Upon reaching the village of Naray, a few miles from Kolenda's post, he made contact with Haji Youssef, an imposing man with a carefully trimmed beard and copper-colored skin who served as the chief of police. Like Wakil, Haji Youssef had spent much of his boyhood in a refugee camp in Pakistan. Unlike Wakil, he had joined the Taliban shortly after returning home, then broke off his affiliation six months later, having realized that he wanted nothing to do with them — a move that earned him a spot on a Taliban hit list and provoked several attempts on his life.

To Wakil's surprise, there was no evidence of the sort of reception he had been warned about by the demining expert back in Jalalabad. In fact, quite the opposite. Haji Youssef was delighted to make his acquaintance and appreciated the letter of introduction from his member of Parliament. The chief of police also had no problem with Wakil's association with an American NGO, and he knew the American army commander personally, having attended a number of *jirgas* with

Kolenda. When Wakil explained about the school-building project in Saw, Haji Youssef promptly dispatched a trusted bodyguard to guide Wakil and Gul Mohammed up the road to the village.

After crossing the Kunar River on a wooden bridge that had been built by the Americans, Wakil drove into Saw and politely introduced himself to a group of elders as a fellow Afghan from the village of Lalander who was working with an American NGO that hoped to build a school for the children of the village. He requested a *jirga* that would include the elders and mullahs from Saw itself and the three surrounding villages that would also be served by the school.

When the *jirga* convened the following morning, the leaders of all four communities explained that they were so eager for a school that they had already decided on a suitable location and were prepared to sign a contract on the spot. Pleased and a bit taken aback, Wakil found himself in the odd position of having to apply the brakes and slow the process down. Before a contract was signed, he would need to inspect the location and then draw up a budget. There was also the question of final approval from Mr. Mortenson and his board of directors. But this is an excellent beginning, he assured the *jirga*. We will all work together, and you will have your school.

That was our first cup of tea in the heart of Taliban country.

A month later, Wakil returned with Sarfraz. The purpose of this second trip was twofold: In addition to finalizing arrangements with the village leaders of Saw, the two men felt that it was now time to formally make the acquaintance of the American military commander who had launched this initiative. So after making their way to Naray and paying their respects to the friendly police chief, they drove up to the heavily guarded entrance to Forward Operating Base (FOB) Naray and explained to a rather confused Afghan National Army soldier that on the instructions of their boss from Montana, who had been corresponding with the commanding officer, they were hoping to pay a call on Colonel Kolenda.

Like all foreign military bases in Afghanistan, FOB Naray boasted multiple layers of security, and threading through them normally requires a substantial dossier of letters, authorizations, and security-clearance badges. Wakil and Sarfraz had nothing beyond their identification cards and a copy of one of Kolenda's e-mails. Haji Youssef, who was with them at the outer perimeter, offered to help things along by firing several rounds into the air to draw the attention of the American soldiers inside — an offer that was politely declined. After an hour of extensive searches, Wakil and Sarfraz were finally permitted to proceed to the last gate, which was guarded by American soldiers.

"You must be Wakil and Sarfraz, here for three cups of tea," exclaimed one of the soldiers. "The colonel has been talking about you for days — welcome aboard!"

A minute or two later, a trim, clean-shaven officer with the black cluster-leaf insignia of a lieutenant colonel on his camouflage uniform came walking up and greeted both men with a warm hug and *"As-Salaam Alaaikum."*

As they walked in the direction of a Quonset hut that served as Kolenda's HQ office, Wakil spotted the minaret of a small but elegant mosque. Pleasantly surprised to discover a mosque sitting in the middle of a frontline American military base, he asked Kolenda if it would be permissible for him make up for several prayers that he had missed while they were on the road to Kunar. "We have come a long way and we are still alive," explained Wakil, "so I would like to express my thanks to Allah for the blessings we have had on this trip."

"Be my guest, Wakil, and we will have tea waiting for you when you are finished," replied Kolenda. "I also insist that you do us the honor of accepting our hospitality by staying for dinner and spending the night."

Later that afternoon, Sarfraz and Wakil were introduced to several of Kolenda's junior officers and enlisted men. Later still, a simple meal was served, after which the three men talked deep into the night about every aspect of the surrounding community and the importance of promoting education.

Sarfraz was fascinated and intrigued to be making the acquaintance of an American soldier who had developed such a keen interest in Afghanistan. "You know many things about the religion, the politics, and the culture of this place — what I call 'style,'" he said to Kolenda at one point. "What is the word that you soldiers use for style?"

"COIN," replied Kolenda without missing a beat. "It's an acronym that stands for 'Counterinsurgency Operations.'"

"Aha, 'coin,' like money, yes?" exclaimed Sarfraz. "This is a good word to remember. 'Coin' and 'style' are like brothers."

Wakil and Sarfraz spent a total of seven days in Kunar during that trip. They toured all four villages. They met with every one of the local elders, the mullahs, and the *com-mandhans*. They each drank several gallons of tea, and by the time they were back on the road and headed toward Kabul, the location and size of the Saw school had been agreed upon; a committee had been appointed to monitor the progress of the work and keep the books; and a thousand-dollar down payment had been handed over to get the project started.

Construction kicked off in May 2008 and extended through that summer, a period when Afghanistan witnessed the heaviest bout of fighting and the highest death toll for U.S. and NATO troops since 2001. On July 13, 2008, at a patrol base outside the Nuristan village of Wanat, a day's travel from Naray, *Stars and Stripes* reported that nine American soldiers were killed and fifteen were wounded during an all-day battle with Taliban forces — the highest single battlefield loss for the United States since the war had begun.

The school in Saw, our first undertaking within the confines of an active Taliban combat zone, was finished shortly before the seventh anniversary of 9/11. Several days later, the number of U.S. troops that had been killed in Afghanistan in 2008 surpassed the number of U.S. military casualties in Iraq for the same year — the first time that the death toll exacted by Afghanistan exceeded Iraq's. It was a grim milestone, and as if to underscore its implications, a week after the school was finished, the elders received one of the infamous "night letters" from the Taliban.

The one-page note, written in Urdu, was nailed to the door of the school under cover of darkness. It warned that if any girl over the age of fourteen was permitted to attend class, the entire building would be burned to the ground and any family that had sent its daughters to school would be targeted for reprisal.

The community was outraged by the threat, and after another *jirga* was convened, the elders decided to continue moving forward as planned. A few nights later, a second warning was delivered when the door of a house that Wakil had rented as a makeshift classroom during the construction phase was set on fire. Again, the elders convened, and this time they decided to fight back. But instead of reaching for their guns, they got creative. They appointed a local mullah named Maulvi Matiullah to be the headmaster of the school. As one of the most respected religious leaders in the community, Matiullah had a firm understanding of the

Koran and Islam. But he was also a strong proponent of secular education, including for girls, that embraced math, science, and geography, as well as reading and writing in Dari, Pashto, English, and Arabic.

Matiullah immediately set up a meeting with a group of the local Taliban fighters and informed them that his school was off limits, and that if they dared to harm a single student or teacher, they would be committing an offense against Islam. Shortly after the meeting, the mysterious night letter was removed from the door. To this day, the school has not been attacked or threatened once.

Meanwhile, Wakil found himself so inspired by the success of our venture in Saw that he put his head together with Colonel Kolenda and the two men identified a second Kunar project.

About twenty miles away from Saw was a village called Samarak, where the community had been clamoring for education. Samarak is perched high on the side of a mountain, and from its vantage point, one can see the northern reaches of the Hindu Kush that loom above our schools in the Wakhan and eastern Badakshan. Thanks to its isolation, Samarak also serves as a refueling stop for itinerant Taliban militants, who often extort mutton, bread, and other supplies from the residents. With the support of the community, however, Wakil supervised the construction of a five-classroom school, and by the end of 2008, 195 children were busy at their lessons.

Through a quirk of local demographics that must surely have enraged the insurgents in the surrounding hills, two-thirds of those students were girls.

As it turned out, our venture into Kunar at the behest of Colonel Kolenda had several consequences we could not have foreseen when Wakil made that first drive into the mountains from Jalalabad. By the autumn of 2009, we had constructed nine schools in Kunar's Naray district and had started another girls' school in Barg-e Matal, a village located in a part of neighboring Nuristan where there is such a dense concentration of Taliban operatives that a local police chief describes the place as being surrounded by "a ring of Kalashnikovs."

As remarkable as those developments were, however, what surprised me even more was an idea that was somehow hatched, during the course of these ventures, in the minds of Wakil and Sarfraz — an idea that they deigned to share with me one hot summer evening in the courtyard of Kabul's Peace

Guest House when they asked if I had any interest in hearing about their "grand plan for the future of the CAI."

"Well, sure," I said, "that might be something good for me to know about."

"Okay, so here is our idea," said Sarfraz, unfurling a map of Afghanistan and spreading his fingers across the northeastern part of the country.

"These are the schools we have built in the Wakhan, yes?"

I nodded.

"And these," said Wakil, pointing to an area directly to the south, "are the schools we have completed in Kunar and Nuristan — which, as you can see from the map, is basically connected to Badakshan, no?"

I nodded again.

"And here," continued Sarfraz, sweeping his finger south and west toward Kabul, "is the school that Wakil put together in Lalander. Do you see how these areas are all linked together and form a sort of arc?"

"Well, I guess so," I said.

"And now do you see where this arc is *pointed?*" asked Wakil, the excitement creeping into his voice. "Can you see where the *momentum* is heading?"

"Um . . . not really."

"Right *here!*" cried Sarfraz, mashing his

index finger into a town in the middle of Uruzgan, a dusty and impoverished province just north of Kandahar, the birthplace of the Taliban.

I took hold of Sarfraz's spectacles, peered closely at the map, and saw that he was pointing to a village called Deh Rawod.

"One of the homes of Mullah Omar?" I asked, referring to the reclusive, one-eyed supreme leader of the Taliban.

"Exactly!" exclaimed Wakil. "So what Sarfraz and I are thinking is that maybe fifteen or twenty years from now, just before the three of us are ready to retire, we are going to build a school in the village of Mullah Omar."

"And not just *any* school," added Sarfraz.

"Oh, no!" continued Wakil. "It will be a girls' *high school.*"

"— and if Mullah Omar happens to have a *daughter,*" interjected Sarfraz.

"— then we are going take and put her *directly* into that school!" yelled Wakil in triumph.

So now I understood what they had in mind: a picket line of girls' schools, a kind of Great Chinese Wall of women's literacy, stretching from one end of Afghanistan to the other, that would literally surround the Taliban and Al Qaeda with outposts of female education.

As I shook my head in disbelief, Sarfraz grinned, seized hold of the front of his *shalwar kamiz,* and yanked it up to reveal a T-shirt whose front had been inscribed in black Magic Marker with the Dari words *Ya Deh Rawod ya Heech!*

Rough translation: "Deh Rawod or Bust."

"Do you guys have even the faintest idea how crazy this is?" I asked.

With that, the man with the broken hand and the man from the Jalozai Refugee Camp looked at each other, nodded, and then did something I will remember forever.

They started to laugh.

Ha-ha-ha-ha-ha-ha-ha-ha-ha-ha-ha-ha-ha-ha-ha-ha-ha-ha!

Then they both shut up, sobered into silence by the sheer preposterousness of the vision they had just laid out — and by the realization that chasing such a dream could easily occupy the rest of our lives.

In that moment, the three of us lacked even the faintest understanding of just how swiftly the future was hurtling down upon our heads.

CHAPTER 14
BARNSTORMING THROUGH BADAKSHAN

Now I shall go far and far into the North playing the Great Game.
— RUDYARD KIPLING, *Kim*

End of the jeep trail in the Wakhan, Afghanistan PHOTO: © 2005
TERU KUWAYAMA

439

The Habib Bank was tucked away on the second floor of a four-story building in downtown Kabul's Shahr-i-Nau district, a colorful neighborhood that boasted several foreigner-friendly Internet cafés (one of which had recently reopened after having been blown up by a suicide bomber in May 2005) and a small park where a photographer was staging an exhibit featuring grisly images of land-mine amputees. Standing next to the entrance to the park was a man holding a length of chain attached to the neck of a trained monkey. At five minutes to nine on a Saturday morning in August 2008, the monkey's eyes darted up toward the bank's entrance as Sarfraz and I burst through the front doors. In his good hand, Sarfraz was clutching a plastic shopping bag that had just been handed to him by the woman who brings freshly baked bread to the bank's employees each morning. The bag now contained twenty-three bricks of cash totaling one hundred thousand dollars, each brick bound with a blue rubber band. The cash was coated in flour, and Sarfraz and I were running as if the devil himself were after us.

We dashed down the steps and across the sidewalk and hurled ourselves into a dented taxicab, whose driver swiftly shouldered his way into the morning traffic without bothering to glance in the rearview mirror. We sped past the Khyber Restaurant, past the cluster of young boys selling phone cards in the middle of the street, past the tea shops, the beauty salon, the Indian video store, and into the Wazir Akbar Khan Chowk — where the driver unwisely opted for a shortcut that involved entering the roundabout in the wrong direction.

Oops.

The taxi was brought to a halt by a member of Kabul's notoriously corrupt police force who stepped in front of the vehicle and slammed both fists down on the hood. Then he dashed around to the door, reached through the open window, and shook the driver by his lapels while unleashing a blast of enraged Dari into the man's face. From the backseat, Sarfraz calmly placed his hand around the scruff of the driver's neck and applied a viselike squeeze while barking a one-word command: *Burro!* "Move it."

The driver briefly weighed his options, then rammed his foot to the accelerator, leaving the cop kicking impotently against the side of the vehicle and enabling us to resume our race to the Kabul International Airport, where our plane was scheduled to begin boarding at 8:40 A.M.

"Getting hauled off to the police station with a hundred thousand dollars — no thanks," I muttered as Sarfraz extracted the money from the plastic bag and we began stuffing the bricks of cash into the pockets of our vests. "Hey, what time is it?"

"Five minutes after nine," grunted Sarfraz, glaring at the clock on his cell phone. "Too bad we cannot ring up Mr. Siddiqi."

Too bad, indeed — Mr. Siddiqi would have been a big help right then. A small, elegant man who dressed in gray woolen pants with Russian-style business shirts and a slim gray ties, Mr. Siddiqi had been the boss of the Kabul airport's control tower for over three decades, and during this time anyone who happened to have his cell phone number — which is to say, anyone who had taken the trouble to pay a visit to the control tower and have a cup of tea with Mr. Siddiqi — only needed to give him a ring if they were running late and he would make every effort to hold their plane. The fact that Mr. Siddiqi was now taking an extended vacation was creating all sorts of problems for people like me and Sarfraz, who insist on doing everything at the last minute.

"You know, we're about to miss this plane," I said. "Maybe we should call and find out —"

"—what Wakil is up to?" interjected Sarfraz, completing the thought. He was already dialing Wakil's cell phone to demand an update on his whereabouts. Several seconds into our Pashtun colleague's report, Sarfraz's face darkened with anger.

"Chai? *Chai?!*"

He listened for another beat, and then the yelling started.

"What are you doing sitting down sipping chai?! This is not the place for *Three Cups of Tea* right now! Get outside the airport — *immediately!*"

The taxi was now swerving between a clutch of donkey carts and a line of battered minivans that were clogging the road through a high-rent diplomatic district where the Indian government was hoping to build a new embassy to replace its old facility, which had

444

been destroyed by a suicide bomber only six weeks earlier. Meanwhile, the yelling continued.

"Have our tickets ready! Have a porter standing by for the bags! Tell security to let us through!"

We braced as the taxi whipped in a half circle around the Afghan Air Force MiG fighter jet mounted to a concrete pedestal that marks the entrance to the airport, and seconds later the driver screeched to a halt before the front stairs, where Wakil found himself subjected to the double-barreled misery of being excoriated simultaneously on the phone and in person by Sarfraz.

"Make sure this guy counts our bags! Pay the taxi driver! And when you're done with that —" Sarfraz was already disappearing through the entrance, so his final instruction was flung over his shoulder like a handful of loose change "— start making a *dua* for us!"

I snapped a quick salute to Wakil, who had cupped his hands in front of his chest and was offering a prayer to Allah to keep us safe in our travels, and shuffled off behind Sarfraz, who had been stopped by a security guard.

"What is your destination?" demanded the man.

"Dubai," replied Sarfraz and kept moving.

We raced down a hallway, out a door, and across an open-air courtyard, where another group of guards stopped us with the same question.

"We are going to Herat," declared Sarfraz as we swept past them and entered a second building.

"Wakil is coming along nicely in his training, no?" I asked as we flung our bags onto a conveyor belt feeding into the first of several scanning machines.

"I am much angry with him right now," replied Sarfraz before adding, grudgingly, "but he is improving, day by day."

Behind the scanning machine stood a pleasant man wearing a short-sleeved white shirt and tie. "And where are you two gentlemen flying to this morning?" he inquired.

"Kandahar!" said Sarfraz as he patted his vest pockets and stole a backward glance to confirm that we had not accidentally dropped a stray wad of cash worth the combined annual salaries of fifty Afghan schoolteachers.

Finally we reached the airline desk, where I handed our tickets over to a young woman wearing a black head scarf. Glancing at the slips of paper, she smiled apologetically.

"I am sorry to inform you that the flight to Faizabad has been delayed and will not depart until this afternoon."

Shortly after Sarfraz and Wakil had conceived the idea of laying down a line of girls' schools through the heart of Taliban country, the CAI's most-remote-area project director had decided to take Wakil under his wing and put him through an aggressive training regimen in the finer points of being Sarfraz Khan. Unlike the patient mentoring of the "style school" that I had undergone with Sarfraz for many years, the boot-camp tutelage to which Wakil was subjected mostly consisted of Sarfraz waving his arms in the air and shouting at him over a seemingly endless litany of infractions that included, among other offenses, failing to keep his cell phone on at all hours; tipping strangers off to his travel plans; neglecting to switch cars and drivers with sufficient frequency; and the worst category of sin — sitting down, sleeping, eating lunch, or any other form of unproductive activity that met Sarfraz's definition of loafing.

Although these methods appeared harsh, beneath all the yelling and the abuse resided a keen awareness of the dangers to which Wakil was exposing himself as the point person for our work in the Pashtun-dominated parts of Afghanistan. In his heart, Sarfraz knew that Wakil was taking greater risks than any of us, and he was terrified by the possibility that Wakil's activities on behalf of girls' education might eventually get him kidnapped or killed.

Although Sarfraz would never have told Wakil this directly, his protégé had been making marvelous progress. In addition to monitoring the school at Lalander and keeping his string of projects moving along in Kunar and Nuristan, Wakil had kicked off a host of other CAI initiatives. By the fall of 2008, he had started up a women's computer-training center outside Kabul — which within a year boasted more than a thousand students — and had put together a land mine–awareness program designed to be incorporated in all of our Afghanistan schools. His most astonishing achievement of all, however, took the form of a single piece of paper.

Thanks to the fact that Sarfraz and I had been unable to make any headway with the federal bureaucrats of Kabul, the CAI still did not have an Afghanistan NGO registration. This had not presented a problem during the early phase of our involvement because we enjoyed the full support and permission of the local authorities in the communities where we worked. But as our operations expanded, the costs of not being official were becoming more apparent. Without a license, for example, we could not keep a post-office box or open a bank account anywhere in the country, which made it extremely difficult to move money from one place to another. (For several years, Suleman Minhas had to drive from Islamabad to Peshawar and hand over a bag containing anywhere between twenty thousand and fifty thousand dollars in cash to Wakil or Sarfraz, who would then drive it through the Khyber Pass to Kabul.) Without the proper registration, we were also prohibited — except during emergencies — from flying between Kabul and Faizabad with the Red Cross, the United Nations, or PACTEC (a volunteer outfit that specializes in flying humanitarian workers around Afghanistan). As the intensity of the Taliban insurgency increased from 2004 to 2008, the drive from the capital to Badakshan was becoming riskier with every passing month.

In short, it was time for us to get our paperwork in order, and that summer Wakil had resolved to succeed where Sarfraz and I had failed.

With the help our friend of Doug Chabot, Wakil put together a sixty-page NGO application in English, and Dari and flung himself into the mission of pushing this document through the required channels at the Ministry of Economy, the Ministry of Interior, the Ministry of Education, and the Ministry of Foreign Affairs. During the course of almost seventy meetings, he was subjected to a host of petty humiliations and absurdities. The several dozen officials who reviewed his packet discerned many problems that included failing to submit separate applications for permission to build new schools and to rebuild damaged schools; failing to sign each form with a signature that exactly matched the signature on his passport; failing to include the word "Afghanistan" at the bottom of his local address in Kabul; failing to clearly state in the CAI's bylaws that our Afghan employees do not have to report for work on government holidays; failing to obtain a proper letter of authorization from a bank attesting that he had paid the one-thousand-dollar NGO registration fee; failing, once the proper letter of authorization had been obtained from the bank, to complete an additional form specifying that day's international exchange rate; and so on.

These requests were not impossible, but the solution to each problem cost Wakil several hours or days. As he threaded his way from the office of one bureaucrat to the next, he often found himself dashing across town to get a signature from someone in a different ministry or popping into the street to have photocopies made by one of the men who had a photocopy machine on the sidewalk, then running back to discover that the office that had sent him on the errand was now closed. The entire ordeal took almost a month, and he kept his cool throughout the whole process, until the final day, when he was informed that the license could not be handed over until it had received one final seal — the stamp for which had been locked in a cabinet, and the man with the key had already gone home.

"Come back tomorrow and you will have your license," he was told.

Wakil was due to leave for Kunar the very next day. Returning to the ministry was not an option — but standing and screaming at the top of his lungs was.

"WHAT DO YOU WANT?" he bellowed. "ARE YOU ASKING FOR A BRIBE IN EXCHANGE FOR DOING YOUR JOB? IS IT MONEY THAT YOU WANT? FINE — HERE, I WILL GIVE YOU YOUR MONEY!"

People began emerging from their offices

to see what was going on.

"I HAVE BEEN HERE ONE MONTH!" he continued. "WE ARE BUILDING SCHOOLS FOR MY COUNTRY AND YOURS! WHAT IS WRONG WITH YOU PEOPLE?! I AM NOT LEAVING WITHOUT THIS PAPER!"

Eventually, someone produced a key to the filing cabinet and the piece of paper was handed over. When Wakil reached the sidewalk, he took a picture of the license with his cell phone and sent it off to Sarfraz and me.

We were extremely impressed.

Wakil's bureaucratic victory had moved our operation to a new level. The hundred thousand dollars now riding in the pockets of Sarfraz's vest and mine had been withdrawn from our brand-new Central Asia Institute account at the Habib Bank, and our seats on the Faizabad plane had been purchased after the agent confirmed that our names were on the list of authorized NGO representatives.

After several hours inside the air-conditioned shipping container that served as PACTEC's departure lounge, we shuffled up a narrow set of folding steps, ducked through the door of a twelve-seat twin-turboprop Beechcraft, and slowly taxied past a line of aircraft that offered a visual index of Afghanistan's current economic and political crisis. Squatting on the tarmac was an Airbus A310, a gift from the government of India intended to help rebuild Ariana's decimated fleet of planes, which was slowly being dismantled for its spare parts because the Afghan government lacked funds for the plane's maintenance costs. Beyond the Airbus was a collection of white and blue helicopters and fixed-wing aircraft used by the UN and the roughly two dozen international aid agencies that were scrambling to provide the basic services — health care, road construction, communications, and education — that now lay beyond the capacity of Afghanistan's beleaguered federal ministries. About two years earlier, the UN Security Council had warned that due to a combination of violence, illegal drug production, poverty, and dysfunctional government, Afghanistan was in danger of becoming a failed state.

As the Beechcraft took off and roared north toward Badakshan, I reviewed our agenda for this trip in my mind. It had been eight months since my last visit, and during that time Sarfraz had completed nine schools in the Wakhan, with three more projects in the works. This visit would offer a mix of inspection tours, bill-paying sessions, and meetings to discuss new projects. The itinerary called for us to land in Faizabad and head into the Wakhan until we reached the end of the road at Sarhad. From there, Sarfraz would continue proceeding east on horseback until he got to Bozai Gumbaz, where a crew of masons from the Charpurson Valley had begun smashing boulders into the smaller stones from which the foundation of the Kirghiz school would eventually be built. Meanwhile, I was supposed to turn around, make my way back to Kabul, and catch a flight to Britain, where I was scheduled to give a talk to a packed house at London's Asia House and later make an appearance at the Edinburgh International Book Festival with my children.

That was the official plan. The *secret* plan, however, was for me to accompany Sarfraz all the way to Bozai Gumbaz and still make it to London and Edinburgh. A ten-day sortie from Kabul to the far end of the Wakhan and back was almost impossible, but I was determined to set foot in the Pamir. More than anything else, I needed to see, with my own eyes, the home of the Kirghiz people who had first drawn us into Afghanistan.

One hour later, the Beechcraft skimmed over the brown hills surrounding Faizabad, slammed onto a steel runway constructed by the Soviet military, and rolled toward a crumbling one-story building. As we coasted to a stop, I glanced out the window and noted that the plane had been surrounded by three green Ford Ranger pickup trucks containing a dozen men armed with Kalashnikovs.

The leader of the gunmen, a man with dense black eyebrows and a precisely razored beard that was just starting to go gray, was none other than Wohid Khan — the head of Badakshan's Border Security Force (BSF) and the man responsible for hosting the midnight supper on the eve of the Baharak riots back in the fall of 2005 where I had first met Abdul Rashid Khan and drawn up the contract for the Kirghiz school at Bozai Gumbaz. Now forty-two years old, Wohid Khan had begun fighting the Soviets at the young age of thirteen, and like many former mujahadeen whose schooling had been cut short by war, he revered education and saw it as the key to repairing the damage of nearly three decades of fighting. He was passionate about female literacy and building schools for girls — and along with his fellow mujahadeen *commandhan* Sadhar Khan, he had become one of our most important allies in the Wakhan.

Upon receiving word of our arrival, Wohid Khan had raced from Baharak to Faizabad in order to provide Sarfraz and me with the honor of a high-speed escort, a gesture of his friendship. He had also notified the local education authorities, who were eager to see us again. His green pickups — which boasted extended cabs, nine-foot antennae, and an assortment of weaponry including a shoulder-held rocket launcher and a .50-caliber machine gun bolted to the bed of the lead truck — represented a rather dramatic change from the battered mini-vans and decrepit jeeps to which Sarfraz and I had become accustomed.

We roared out of Faizabad, dragging a cloud of dust behind us. The bed of each truck held three armed soldiers, their faces wrapped with scarves to protect them from the dirt and grit, the barrels of their Kalashnikovs wedged tightly between their knees. The driver of each truck was under standing orders from Wohid Khan to push his rig as fast as the horrendous, unpaved roads would allow — forty-five to fifty miles per hour. Speed was essential because Wohid and his 320 men were responsible for patrolling 840 miles of territory where the Wakhan abuts the edges of Pakistan, Tajikistan, and China — and as the only authority in this area, they often found themselves saddled with responsibilities that extended far beyond the normal duties of border agents. These could include delivering emergency food to starving communities in winter, taking sick villagers to the hospital, fixing broken trucks, retrieving lost camels, resolving local disputes, and a host of other problems. Two weeks earlier, for example, the BSF had been called to respond to a tragedy that represented the first major setback for our Kirghiz school project.

Earlier that spring, after some extensive canvassing, Sarfraz and the local *maarif* (education director) had managed to locate two Turkic-speaking teachers in Faizabad who were capable of providing instruction to the children of the Kirghiz. They hired both teachers, then arranged transportation for the men and their families from Faizabad to Bozai Gumbaz, where we were planning to set up a temporary tent school until the permanent structure was completed. About halfway into the Wakhan, near the village of Babu Tengi, the pickup that was carrying the two teachers, their wives, and their four children attempted to shoot through a section of runoff late in the afternoon, when glacier melt is at its highest. The truck became stuck in the middle of the swiftly rising Oxus River, forcing everyone to clamber onto the roof as the water swirled around the vehicle. By the evening, they were prone on top of the cab, clinging to the doorframes and screaming for help. As darkness fell, the driver and one of the families were swept away and drowned. The other family spent the rest of the night balanced on the roof of the truck with their legs in the water as the vehicle rocked back and forth. When word of the incident reached the BSF, Wohid Khan and his men rushed to the site of the accident and managed to pull the remaining survivors to safety.

One of Wohid's primary duties was keeping open the Wakhan's sole road, which serves as a crucial artery not only for his own team but also for the flow of flour, salt, cooking oil, and other staples that are hauled into the most remote communities of the Corridor all summer long to enable these isolated settlements to survive the six-month winter when the roads are sealed with snow. Khan's refusal to tolerate unnecessary impediments became evident one afternoon when, upon encountering a truck stopped in the middle of the road that was blocking several vehicles behind it, the commander got out and walked up to the man working on a broken wheel.

"Driver or mechanic?" he asked.

"Driver," the man replied.

After smashing his fist directly into the man's face, Wohid delivered a reverse swing kick to the driver's solar plexus, knocking him to the ground. Leaning over the man, he told him to finish fixing his axle and never to come back to the Wakhan. Then he got back in the Ranger and we lurched forward and resumed our journey.

We spent the next two days bashing though arroyos, splashing across streams, and blasting through small villages, twisting and wrenching and pounding the trucks as we penetrated further into the most obscure and forgotten corner of Afghanistan. After reaching Baharak and stopping to pay our respects to Sadhar Khan under his walnut tree, we continued heading east. The road threaded through a series of rocky gorges until it reached Zebak, a flat, emerald green valley with a darkly braided delta that bore a vague resemblance to the tundra of northern Scandinavia. From there, the road headed northwest into a barren area of reddish gray rock littered with the wreckage of disintegrated Soviet T-62 tanks. Several miles beyond lay the town of Ishkoshem, which we reached early in the evening of our second day.

Just before the main bazaar, we swerved onto a side road leading to a gravel hilltop and arrived at the crown jewel of our Wakhan program: an unfinished foundation about the size of a football field filled with dirt, stones, and cement — the future home of the Ishkoshem Girls' High School. The completed structure would be two stories tall and would host 1,400 female students. Costing about eighty thousand dollars to build, it was the largest school in the region and the most expensive project the CAI had undertaken to date. It also boasted one of the most magnificent settings for a school anywhere. To the north loomed the Pamirs, a series of rounded, brown, lunar-looking mountains covered with scree. To the south thrust the sharper ridges of the Hindu Kush, armored in ice even in late August. Between them seethed the Oxus, turbulent and churning and laden with a milky gray cargo of glacial sediment.

If Baharak was the gateway to the Wakhan, then this was the front door.

From Ishkoshem, we worked our way into the Wakhan proper, moving from village to village. Since President Hamid Karzai had issued a decree extending the summer harvest-season holiday by an additional week, classes weren't in session. But at every stop where we had a project going there was a meeting with harried foremen complaining of construction delays stemming from the late deliveries of building supplies, laborers falling ill, poor weather, harassment by out-of-town government officials and other NGOs, and a host of other problems. Sarfraz had no sympathy for any of these excuses and pushed his supervisors mercilessly to stay on schedule. At each stop, he also pulled out another brick of cash and doled out the funds necessary to meet the payroll and keep the consignments of cement, rebar, lumber, and other materials flowing in.

As we moved down the road, we were constantly besieged by requests for new projects. Although we have a formal submission process that includes checking in with the local mullah, *tanzeem* (community committee), *shura,* and district government officials, many communities prefer to hand their requests directly to us when we visit the region. In Piggush, where our four-room school was not even finished, the principal had realized that she needed another two rooms in order to accommodate the number of female students who wanted to attend classes. Could we increase the construction budget to meet this need? In Khundud, the elders had convened a *jirga* and decided that the women's center and the girls' school needed a five-foot boundary wall to prevent the women and the female students from being stared at by men in the neighborhood. Was there any additional money to pay for the wall?

There were plenty of other requests, too, needs that had nothing to do with schools. In the tiny village of Wargeant, a two-year-old boy had developed an infection that had caused his testicles to swell to the size of tennis balls. The child had been screaming in pain for several days, and the nearest doctor, back in Ishkoshem, was a three-day walk away. Could we dispatch a pickup truck to get him to a hospital? At the same time, two children in Wargeant had contracted polio over the winter, even though the region had been declared polio free by UNICEF a year earlier. Was there anything to be done, any way we could help?

One of the most painful aspects of these encounters was that Sarfraz and I often found ourselves in the position of being forced to turn down plea after plea — sometimes twenty or thirty times in the course of a single afternoon — because we simply did not have the resources or the time to address them. Early one evening, I was preparing to deliver yet another rejection, this time to a group of women who were submitting a formal request in writing that we consider funding the construction of a ladies' vocational center. Standing before the women, I turned to Sarfraz.

"Your budget for the Wakhan is finished for this year, no?" I asked. We both knew this to be true, but the prescripted exchange would help lay the groundwork for gently and diplomatically turning down the women's appeal.

"Finished," Sarfraz confirmed while pulling out his phone, which had started ringing. He glanced at the number and immediately handed it over.

It was Tara, calling from Bozeman to keep tabs on me.

"Hi, sweetie!" I said.

"The kids are off to school, I'm headed to work, and I just wanted to check in," she said. "What are you up to?"

"Well, right now we're in Ishkoshem, and I'm surrounded by about twenty women who want a vocational center, and they've got this really feisty leader, but I'm afraid we're going to have to say no to them because —"

Sarfraz stared at me quizzically as my wife interrupted and I listened obediently.

"All right, I promise," I replied when she

was finished. "Yes, sweetie. Bye, now."

My next words were directed to the women standing in front of us.

"American wife-boss has announced that we must somehow find the funds for your vocational center," I reported. "Tonight she is attending her women's book club, and if I refuse this project, all the women in my village will be very angry with me — so we will request extra money from our board of directors. In the meantime, wife-boss says that you may wish to consider using your vocational center to start a book club of your own."

The women's expressions of delight at hearing this news were cut short by yet another call coming in on the sat phone. This time it was Suleman Minhas, ringing from Rawalpindi to report an "emergency."

Five minutes earlier, upon answering an incoming call from a number he'd never seen before, Suleman had been asked to hold the line for General Pervez Musharraf's secretary. Stunned, he had pulled his car over, gotten out, and stood by the side of the road with his right hand offering a rigid salute as it was explained that Mr. Greg Mortenson was requested to make himself available on Sunday afternoon for a cup of tea with the president of Pakistan.

This wasn't the kind of invitation that could be ignored, even from the middle of the Wakhan. A month earlier, the government of Pakistan had announced that in recognition of the Central Asia Institute's work during the past fifteen years, I had been selected to receive the Sitara-i-Pakistan, one of the country's highest civilian awards. In addition to being an honor that is rarely bestowed on foreigners, the award would confer special diplomatic and security privileges that would enable us to move around the country far more efficiently than before while simultaneously enhancing the Central Asia Institute's status and reputation. In short, it would make our lives easier and our work more effective — and since the nomination had surely passed across the president's desk for his endorsement at some point during the selection process, turning down a summons to tea would have been both ill considered and rude.

On the other hand, honoring this invitation would involve some challenging logistics. I glanced at the date on my watch to confirm that it was now Thursday evening, and realized I had less than seventy-two hours to get from the Corridor back to Islamabad.

Early the next morning, having spent most

of the night debating the merits of our next move, Sarfraz and I carefully divided up the contents of our jumbo-sized bottle of ibuprofen tablets, said good-bye, and headed off in opposite directions. Clad in his gray *shalwar kamiz,* olive-colored vest, and peacock blue fedora, he would continue pushing east in one of the BSF pickup trucks to Sarhad, where he would secure horses, transfer the rest of the cash — roughly twelve thousand dollars — to his saddlebags, and make his way out to Bozai Gumbaz. Meanwhile, I piled into a second truck with Wohid Khan and started the race out of the Wakhan to Faizabad, then on through Kabul to Islamabad.

Over the next two days, as Wohid Khan and I barnstormed down the same road we had just come up, I worked the phone to set up a special series of charters. In Faizabad, I almost missed my flight but managed to jump aboard at the very last second. As I switched planes in Kabul, Wakil somehow managed to perform a miraculous (and illegal) transfer of the luggage I had left with him through the front door of the airport. That flight took less than an hour, but as we were preparing to make our approach to Islamabad, the pilot turned to let us know that an approaching storm system might force us to return to Kabul. Thankfully, our good friend Colonel Ilyas Mirza of Askari Aviation in Rawalpindi pulled some strings and arranged for a VIP clearance, giving us permission to land. We touched down just a few hours after the Al Jazeera television network reported that Pakistan's parliament had initiated impeachment proceedings, pitching Musharraf into one of the worst political crises of his life.

Although this news came as a bit of a shock, the events that precipitated it had been brewing for some time. In the spring of the previous year, Musharraf had attempted to oust Iftikhar Muhammad Chaudhry, the chief justice of the country's supreme court, on corruption charges — a strong-arm tactic that had triggered a surge of anger at a president who, in the eyes of many Pakistanis, had already done violence to the constitution by seizing power in a military coup in 1999. Attorneys and judges had taken to the streets in major cities, and during the summer a number of protesters had been killed during demonstrations in Karachi while strikes had paralyzed much of the country. Despite this opposition, Musharraf had succeeded in winning a second term as president — but Pakistan's supreme court had refused to confirm the election results until it ruled on the constitutionality of Musharraf's decision to run for president while also serving as chief of staff of the Pakistani army. In retaliation, Musharraf had imposed martial law by declaring a state of emergency, neutralizing the supreme court challenge but turning popular opinion even further against him.

The impeachment demand flowed directly from these events. And although I knew nothing of it at the time, by the following morning when a small black Toyota Camry that had been dispatched from the president's office to fetch me pulled up to my hotel in Islamabad, Musharraf's days in power were drawing to a close.

I wedged into the back of the car with three members of the Dirty Dozen — Suleman, Apo Razak, and Mohammed Nazir, who manages several of our projects in Baltistan. It was a twenty-minute drive to the military section of Rawalpindi where the president lives. We crossed over the bridge where two attempts had been made on Musharraf's life. We passed the set of gallows where Prime Minister Zulfikar Ali Bhutto was executed in 1979, twenty-eight years before his daughter, former prime minister Benazir Bhutto, was assassinated by a suicide bomber in December 2007 in a nearby park. Then we took a hard turn and went down a discreet, narrow road with overgrown brush on the side, where we stopped at the first of four checkpoints. A few minutes later the car deposited us in front of a beautiful old mogul-style residence and Bilal Musharraf, the president's son — who lives in the United States and works as an actuary — came out to greet us.

We were ushered into a simple but quite elegant waiting room adorned with a red carpet and couches upholstered in spotless white linen. Bilal presented us with a tray laden with almonds, walnuts, candy, and yogurt-covered raisins. A butler came in and asked if we wanted tea — green tea with cardamom and mint. And then, all of a sudden, the president walked in and sat down next to me.

"Thank you for taking the time to come and see us," he said. "We've prepared a brunch for you, in the hope that you will stay for a while. *Inshallah,* we may even have time for three cups of tea today."

Musharraf asked a few questions about how our schools were faring in Azad Kashmir and Baltistan, but what he seemed most interested in were my three Pakistani colleagues, and I was more than happy to sit back and permit these men to talk. Apo spoke about working for some of the big Karakoram mountaineering expeditions from 1953 to 1999 and serving tea to numerous dignitaries and military commanders on the Siachen Glacier. Suleman told the long version of the story of how he and I had first met at the Islamabad airport. Nazir, who is shy, was induced to share his assessment of how the Pakistan military had frequently helped us out, and how our artillery-resistant schools in Gultori were holding up.

Eventually, we moved into a dining room, where we were joined by Musharraf's wife, Sehba, and sat down before an elaborate buffet featuring chicken, mutton, dal, salads, desserts, halvah, and a host of other traditional dishes.

The original plan had called for us to meet with Musharraf for about thirty minutes, but at the urging of the president and his wife, we ended up being there for four hours — a development that provoked astonishment and wonder from my coworkers as we rode back to the hotel late that afternoon.

"Most high-level delegations, they only get very short meetings with Musharraf," said Nazir.

"The president of China — maybe thirty minutes?" speculated Suleman.

"George Bush, maximum *fifteen* minutes!" declared Apo.

"No one will ever believe that humble villagers like us were there for four hours," marveled Nazir. "Our families will never believe it. They will all think us mad."

"We have photo for proof," Apo noted, "and Allah also knows all things."

As I listened to my colleagues' excited chatter, I found myself wrestling with a sense of confusion and ambivalence over what had just taken place. On a personal level, of course, the president could not have been more gracious — it was an honor and a pleasure to have made his acquaintance and spent time in his company. I was not entirely convinced, however, that the lengths to which we had just gone and the price that I had just paid in order to attend this meeting represented the right decision.

In order to answer a summons from a head of state, I had abandoned my commitments to the powerless and impoverished people of the Wakhan and flung myself into a five-hundred-mile sprint across the Pamirs, the Hindu Kush, and the Karakoram. In the meantime, Sarfraz, Wakil, and most of the other members of the staff had continued, as they did each and every day, grappling with the unglamorous but essential business of raising up schools and promoting literacy in places that are too small, too remote, and too unimportant to merit the attention of the men and women who shape the affairs of the world.

The contrast between my activities and those of most of my staff seemed to under-score an even larger problem: the extent to which I have been forced to pull away from the aspects of my work that I find personally and spiritually fulfilling in order to attend to what is generally referred to as "the big picture." What would Haji Ali have thought of this? What might my father have said if he were still alive? And what about Abdul Rashid Khan and the other Kirghiz to whom I had made my promise — was this something that they would have understood and respected?

It could be argued, of course, that these developments stemmed from our burgeoning success as an NGO. Yet I was unable to shake the nagging feeling that the values and the priorities that had drawn me into this enterprise in the first place were undergoing a troubling realignment. Certainly it was true that I had been privileged to spend an enjoyable and highly stimulating afternoon in the company of the president of Pakistan. But nine years after having first traveled through the Khyber Pass from Peshawar to Kabul, I still had yet to meet most of the members of the community on whose behalf we had embarked upon our "Afghan adventure."

As if to underscore the possibility that something about this situation was not quite right, a few days later, on August 18, Pervez Musharraf officially resigned from office. Whatever significance our meeting might have held for the Central Asia Institute's future in Pakistan was largely negated. And in exchange for this, I had squandered my best chance, to date, of reaching Bozai Gumbaz.

Now a tenth winter would have to pass before I could even consider making another effort to reach the Kirghiz of the High Pamir.

CHAPTER 15
A MEETING OF
TWO WARRIORS

The Muslim community is a subtle world we don't fully — and don't always — attempt to understand. Only through a shared appreciation of the people's culture, needs, and hopes for the future can we hope ourselves to supplant the extremist narrative. We cannot capture hearts and minds. We must engage them; we must listen to them, one heart and one mind at a time.

— ADMIRAL MIKE MULLEN, CHAIRMAN OF THE JOINT CHIEFS OF STAFF

Admiral Mike Mullen hands out books to CAI students in Afghanistan PHOTO: © 2009 MC1 CHAD J. MCNEELEY, U.S. NAVY

475

In the summer of 2009, the U.S. Marines launched Operation Khanjar, an offensive that involved sending four thousand American troops and 650 Afghan soldiers into the Helmand Valley, a Taliban stronghold where over half of the opium in Afghanistan is grown. The largest U.S. military offensive since the 2004 battle of Fallujah, Khanjar was part of President Barack Obama's decision to send an additional twenty-two thousand U.S. soldiers to Afghanistan — a surge that was prompted, in part, by the fact that the Taliban insurgency was growing increasingly sophisticated and bloody. And by the end of the summer, the Taliban had exacted a stiff price. In late August, the death toll for all foreign forces in Afghanistan rose to 295, making 2009 the deadliest year since the war began in 2001. That same month, the American death toll for the year passed 155 — the previous record for the highest annual casualties, which had been set in 2008 — and then continued climbing.

The Taliban's war on women's education kept escalating, too. By early summer at least 478 Afghan schools — the overwhelming majority of them catering to female students — had been destroyed, attacked, or intimidated into closing their doors, according to Dexter Filkins of the *New York Times*. In addition to the escalating number of incidents, the methods being used to strike terror into girls seemed to exhibit a new level of perversion and psychosis. In May, sixty-one teachers and pupils in Parwan Province were stricken when a cloud of toxic gas was released in the courtyard of their school — the third assault of this kind since the beginning of the year. And on a morning the previous November, six men on motorcycles had used squirt guns to shoot battery acid into the faces and eyes of eleven girls and four teachers as they were walking to the Mirwais Mena School in Kandahar, the heartland of the Taliban.

Unfortunately, two of our schools were affected by this campaign of violence. In the summer of 2008, our school in Lalander had been attacked by a small group of Taliban who sprayed bullets into the teacher's office in the middle of the night. (The local police commander was so enraged by this incident that he later established an outpost on a ridge overlooking the school and set up a round-the-clock guard.) Then, the following July, when two U.S. soldiers were killed in a Taliban attack that took place just below the village of Saw, the Americans gave chase and accidentally killed nine villagers, as well as wounding Maulavi Matiullah, the headmaster. Thanks to the relationship of trust which Colonel Kolenda had established with the village elders before rotating out of FOB Naray, however, an understanding of the incident was later reached at a *jirga* between the military and the village.

To my frustration, I was forced to monitor most of these developments from afar, mainly by phone during my 5:30 A.M. calls to Sarfraz, Suleman, Wakil, and the rest of the Dirty Dozen. Upon my return home after meeting with Pervez Musharraf, the invitations for speaking engagements had continued pouring into our Bozeman office as fast as we could absorb them. Between September 2008 and July of the following year, I gave 161 presentations in 118 cities. In addition to appearances at colleges, elementary schools, libraries, bookstores, and military gatherings, there were two trips to the United Nations, 216 newspaper, magazine, and radio interviews, and a hodgepodge of events ranging from a fund-raising "tea" at the Firefly Restaurant in Traverse City, Michigan, to a talk at the annual convention of the Dermatological Nurses Association in San Francisco.

The appetite of ordinary Americans for learning about promoting female literacy in southwest Asia was beyond anything we had ever anticipated, and the scramble to meet these demands became so hectic that during those eleven months I was able to spend only twenty-seven days in Pakistan and never managed to make it over to Afghanistan at all. It felt as if I saw Tara, Khyber, and Amira even less. In December, *Outside* magazine published a profile in which I was described — with blunt accuracy — as having the weary look of a bear in desperate need of hibernation.

The travel was relentless and exhausting, but there were also some deeply rewarding elements, especially when it came to our deepening relationship with the U.S. military. Perhaps the most gratifying moment in this process took place two days before Thanksgiving when I flew into Washington, D.C., rode the metro to the Pentagon, and padded up to the visitors' entrance, where the recently promoted Colonel Kolenda was waiting to greet me. Ten months earlier, he had returned from Kunar Province in order to serve as a special adviser to help the military make a smooth transition to working with members of the new Obama administration.

Although he and I had exchanged hundreds of e-mails and phone calls, it was the first time we had ever met, and the pleasure was genuine and mutual. After a bear hug and a handshake, he ushered me upstairs, through several layers of security, and, at exactly 8:59, into the office of the highest-ranking military officer in the U.S. armed forces.

Admiral Mike Mullen, the chairman of the Joint Chiefs of Staff, was wearing a navy blue jacket with four stars on the shoulders and was accompanied by a dozen senior officers. After thanking me for coming, he declared, "We gotta make sure we have three cups of tea before you leave my office," and graciously added, "My wife, Deborah, just loves your book." Then, in keeping with the style of a man who had spent the early part of his career commanding guided-missile destroyers and cruisers, he dropped the chit-chat and got straight to the point.

"Greg, I get a lot of bad news from Afghanistan," he said. "Tell me about something good that's going on over there."

So I did. I told him about Sarfraz's schools in the Wakhan and Wakil's schools in Kunar and about the passionate support we receive from mujahadeen commanders like Sadhar Khan and Wohid Khan. I told him that I thought that building relationships was just as important as building projects, and that in my view, Americans have far more to learn from the people of Afghanistan than we could ever hope to teach them. Most important, perhaps, I told him that at the height of the Taliban's power, in 2000, less than eight hundred thousand children were enrolled in school in Afghanistan — all of them boys. Today, however, student enrollment across the country was approaching 8 million children, 2.4 million of whom are girls.

"Those are amazing numbers," replied Admiral Mullen.

"Yes," I said. "They are a testament not only to the Afghans' hunger for literacy, but also to their willingness to pour scarce resources into this effort, even during a time of war. I have seen children studying in classrooms set up inside animal sheds, windowless basements, garages, and even an abandoned public toilet. We ourselves have run schools out of refugee tents, shipping containers, and the shells of bombed-out Soviet armored personnel carriers. The thirst for education over there is limitless. The Afghans want their children to go to school because literacy represents what neither we nor anyone else has so far managed to offer them: hope, progress, and the possibility of controlling their own destiny."

We were supposed to meet for thirty minutes, but we ended up talking for more than an hour — about reading bedtime stories to children, about our families and long absences from home, about Pashtun tribal nuances, about better ideas for collaboration on the Af-Pak border, and about the need for more bilingual education in American schools. At the end of our conversation, the admiral expressed the desire, if his schedule permitted, to drop by and see some of our schools during one of his upcoming trips to the region.

"Admiral," I said, "we have dozens of schools that need to be inaugurated, and we'd love to have you come over and open one of them."

"I promise I'm going to come and do that," he replied. "I'll see you in Afghanistan."

On July 12, 2009, I flew into Kabul on a night flight from Frankfurt that skimmed across Iran and passed over the Afghan border shortly after 4:30 in the morning, just as the tops of distant mountain ranges were being lit pink by the rising sun. As the Boeing 767 began its descent, I gazed out toward the seven-thousand-meter peaks of Afghanistan's Hindu Kush. Beyond their snow-shrouded summits rose the eight-thousand-meter giants of Pakistan's Karakoram. Far off to the right, obscured by shadow and distance, stretched the gentler, greener contours of Azad Kashmir's Pir Panjal. And invisible on the left side of the plane, the peaks of the Pamir Knot brooded over the Wakhan. Down inside the valleys that forked like a network of veins between those serrated ridgelines and ice blue crags lay dozens of villages whose elders were now clamoring for schools for their girls.

The moment we landed, the welcome wagon rolled up and I was reminded that the days when I could blend anonymously into the slipstream of Kabul were now gone. The greetings started at the door of the plane, when I found myself confronted by Mohammed Mehrdad, a Tajik from the Panjshir Valley dressed in a neatly pressed gray jumpsuit with large pockets and a woolen *pakol,* the flat cap worn by the mujahadeen. Mohammed's job involves pushing the mobile staircase up to the side of the plane, and his

484

eagerness to present a salute and exchange an embrace meant that we held up the line of passengers that was attempting to disembark behind me.

Inside the terminal I received another enthusiastic hello from Jawaid, a portly Pathan who spends his day sitting in a brown metal folding chair next to the car parking gate and whose exact job description has always been a bit of a mystery to me. A few yards further on stood Ismael Khan, a baggage handler originally from Zebak, the village several hours from Baharak on the way to the mouth of the Wakhan. Ismael, who is Wakhi, is at least two decades older than me but insists on taking my carry-on and pronounces himself gravely insulted if I so much as reach into my pocket for payment.

A similar reception awaited further into the terminal with Daoud, a Pathan from Jalalabad who had spent most of the Soviet occupation peddling trinkets on the streets of Peshawar as a refugee. Back in 2002, when I had first started flying into Kabul, Daoud had been operating a small pushcart from which he hawked cigarettes and Coke. Recently business had improved to the point where he had been able to upgrade to an air-conditioned store stocked with Swiss chocolates, caviar from the Caspian Sea, and succulent dates from Saudi Arabia. Daoud spent most of his time yakking incessantly on his cell phone, but the moment he spotted me he would hang up and dash from behind the counter with a small gift — usually a soft drink or a candy bar — while shouting *As-Salaam Alaaikum.* Then we would enact the following little ritual.

First I would try to pay for whatever he had given me. Then he would protest and refuse. I would keep pressing and he would persist in his refusals and this would continue until the point where Daoud finally felt that Afghanistan's elaborate hospitality protocols had been satisfied and was convinced that I had been made to feel welcome.

And so it went as I shuffled through customs, baggage, immigration, and several security checkpoints until I had passed through the front entrance, where I spotted Wakil and Sarfraz standing next to the figure of Wohid Khan, tall and dignified in his carefully pressed Border Security Force uniform and polished black combat boots. The requisite exchanges in which each of us inquired after the health and welfare of the others' wives, children, and parents took several minutes.

After my long series of international flights, Wohid Khan would have preferred to escort me back to our hotel for a nap and a bath, but Wakil and Sarfraz had no intention of letting me relax. Much had happened during my eleven-month absence, and there was not a minute to be lost. They bundled me into a hired car and we set off on our first order of business, which involved an immediate review of Wakil's newest project.

During the past twelve months, Wakil had taken on a series of responsibilities whose demands and complexities rivaled even Sarfraz's workload. He had overseen the construction of nine schools in Kunar's Naray district and started another girls' school in Barg-e Matal, a tiny village in eastern Nuristan that had been overwhelmed by Taliban insurgents in July and then retaken by American and Afghan soldiers. As word of these projects spread, Wakil had found himself approached by a series of delegations from more distant regions of the country, including Taliban strongholds such as the Tora Bora area, the city of Kandahar, and Uruzgan Province. In each instance, a group of elders had traveled to Kabul — a journey that in some cases involved an arduous two-day trip on public transport — to petition for a girls' school in their community. As a direct outgrowth of these overtures, Wakil was now planning, with my approval, to embark on building nearly a dozen new schools in 2010, including, remarkably enough, one in Mullah Omar's village of Deh Rawod.

The vision that Wakil and Sarfraz had thought would take twenty years to achieve was unfolding before their eyes.

This exploding interest in female education was not restricted just to school building, however. The previous year, I had encouraged Wakil to think about launching one or two women's vocational centers in Kabul — places where women could gather, as they do in the villages where we have built such centers, to learn skills such as weaving, embroidery, and other domestic crafts. Wakil had decided to put his own spin on this idea, however, by turning the units he was starting up into neighborhood literacy centers — classrooms where older women who had been deprived of the chance to go to school could learn to read and write Dari, Pashto, Arabic, and English. Classes would take place in a private home and would run from four to six days a week, each class lasting two or three hours. The lessons would be taught by teachers moonlighting for extra cash.

In the simple business model that Wakil had designed, the start-up costs were minimal — the main expense was the instruction, which was provided by part-time schoolteachers who would earn about sixty dollars a month. Each literary center would draw its students from the surrounding neighborhood, so that the women would not have far to walk — and so that their husbands were less likely to object to their wives leaving the house for such brief periods. It was a good plan — but Wakil had failed to anticipate the reaction it would provoke.

The first women to attend these classes started telling their friends, who in turn told their friends, and before long applicants were signing up in such numbers that each center had reached maximum capacity. Initially these women came to learn to read and write, but as they acquired these skills, the scope of their ambitions began to expand radically. Some of them started book clubs. Others began to exchange information about dental hygiene and reproductive health. From there, the curriculum spilled into nutrition, diet, and disease prevention. Before long, there were miniature seminars on typing, learning to read calendars, counting money, and the most popular subject of all, for which the demand was simply off the charts: workshops on the rudiments of using a mobile phone.

Wakil quickly realized that this enthusiasm was the by-product of taking a group of women who had been forced to lead restricted and sequestered lives, putting them into the same room, and simply giving them the license to dream. But the chemistry was so combustible that he could barely keep up with the ensuing demands. The idea of women teaching other women was so electrifying that each class rapidly burgeoned from forty to one hundred students, forcing Wakil to set up two, three, and sometimes four teaching shifts to handle the extra load. Normally this would have created budget problems, but under the system he had devised there were virtually no operating expenses except for the teachers' salaries and the supplies — the latter cost being offset by the nominal tuition fees that each center charged. Within a few weeks, Wakil started beefing up his teaching staff, and soon after that the number of centers began to expand.

I knew the general outlines of these developments from my regular telephone briefings with Wakil, as well as from the reports that he e-mailed to me once or twice a week, but I lacked an accurate sense of the actual numbers.

"So how many of these centers have you got going at the moment?" I asked as the car whisked us toward the suburbs south of Kabul.

"Right now we have seventeen centers operating in different parts of the city."

"Well, seven doesn't sound too bad."

"Not seven, Greg — *seventeen*."

"Are you kidding?"

"No joke," he said. "We've got eighteen teachers and 880 students, but the demand is much greater than that. That's why you need to see this for yourself."

When Wakil first went looking for places in which to set up shop, he had concentrated on Kabul's outlying areas, the rougher suburban districts that had been flooded with so many farmers and laborers fleeing the war-ravaged countryside that the capital city's population had tripled since 2001. These neighborhoods lay well beyond the newly paved roads and the glass-and-steel office buildings of downtown, and they bore a closer resemblance to the contours of rural Afghanistan: narrow dirt alleyways lined with open irrigation ditches where the low-slung houses were surrounded by high mud walls and guarded by barking dogs.

Our first stop was the home of Najeeba Mira, who lived on the south side of the city. Najeeba, who was in her forties and had five children, came from a family of illiterate farmers in Logar, a province southeast of Kabul that had seen fierce fighting between the Taliban and the Northern Alliance. She had learned to read and write in a refugee camp in Pakistan, and her specialty was mathematics. For the past two decades, Najeeba had served as the headmistress of a girls' high school in Kabul that is currently bursting at the seams with 4,500 students. With Wakil's blessings, she had agreed to establish a literacy center in her home and teach for four hours a day. For this service, Wakil was paying her a salary of fifteen dollars per week.

We drove through a maze of alleys without sidewalks or street signs and arrived at a mud-walled compound where we were greeted by Najeeba's husband, Mira Jan, a retired veteran, who met us at the door and ushered us in for tea. When the rituals of hospitality had been observed, Mira Jan asked if we'd like to see the literacy center and then guided us around to the back of the compound and into a tiny eight-by-twelve-foot adobe storage room with a dirt floor and one large window. There were forty women inside, packed tightly into rows of five or six, all sitting cross-legged on the floor and facing a whiteboard. Most of these women were in their thirties or forties. Many had young children — the nursing mothers kept their babies with them, while the older children clustered in the back. Najeeba, a diminutive woman whose plain gray *shalwar kamiz* was accented by a black cape that reminded me of a nun's habit, was standing in the front.

A few of the younger women were wearing the white *dupatta* that indicated they were students — which meant they were here to supplement their studies at school. But the bulk of participants wore the drab and ragged *shalwar kamiz* of the urban working poor. Most of their husbands performed manual labor, working twelve or fourteen hours a day at jobs that included brick laying, road construction, garbage collection, and auto repair. They permitted their wives to attend this class in the hope that learning to read and write might eventually enable them to earn additional income for the family. Each night after preparing dinner and attending to their domestic duties, many of these women did their homework together with their daughters.

When we first walked in, everyone shot to their feet and stood silently. Then Wakil said, "Sit down," and introduced me, saying, "This is Doctor Greg, he is from the United States and wants to help with the literacy center. He has a wife named Tara and two children. The money he raises comes from ordinary people in America just like you."

Judging from the writing on the board, we had walked into a Dari class, but the room bore evidence of the women's determination to expand their education beyond vocabulary and grammar. There were nutrition charts on the back wall stressing the importance of eating vegetables and fruits (which most of them could not afford). There were toothbrushes and bars of soap used to accompany hygiene lessons. Glancing at several notebooks, I was struck by the tiny size of the handwriting. Each participant was writing as tightly as possible in order to save space and make the notebooks last as long as possible.

I began interrogating Najeeba, asking how long each class lasted, how busy her schedule was, what subjects her students were studying, and how she felt about their progress. She offered precise, rapid-fire responses in the same businesslike tone that she undoubtedly used with her students. Then I turned to the class.

"This is so amazing — what you've managed to do all by yourselves," I said. "Each of you is achieving something incredible." Then I asked if the teacher or the students

494

had any concerns.

As a matter of fact, they did. Since classes like these were conducted in private homes, Najeeba explained, she and the other teachers were worried about insufficient drinking water, sporadic electricity, and inadequate latrines. As for the students, however, they were willing to put up with those inconveniences, but they were eager to start using computers and cell phones.

"And why do you need cell phones so badly?" I asked.

"Because we all talk to one another and exchange information about how to improve what we're doing," explained Najeeba. "Plus there are many other important things to discuss."

"Such as?"

"Well, the upcoming election, for example. Right now we're all talking to one another about how we're going to vote."

Here was something rather extraordinary. In sixteen years of building schools and promoting girls' education, I had never seen women so on fire. But Najeeba wasn't finished. She went on to explain that each of her students had family members and friends from other provinces, and when these relatives heard about what was going on in Kabul, they had begun clamoring for information on how to establish literacy centers in their own towns and villages. Listening to Najeeba describe the speed with which the idea of a place like this was leap-frogging from one location to another, I was struck by the notion that there might well be a second Afghan insurgency bubbling away beneath the Taliban's uprising — a quiet and hidden revolution of female learning and liberation.

"Perhaps you and your colleagues should consider setting up some kind of co-op or NGO," I said to Najeeba, "an umbrella organization that would assist in the establishment of literacy centers like this not just around Kabul, but also in other parts of the country. Do you think you could get something like that going?"

"Oh, absolutely," she replied. "It would become big very quickly."

And so the idea was born. Three weeks later, Wakil would send word that Najeeba and several other teachers had formed an executive committee and agreed on a name for themselves. By October, the Afghan Women's Co-op, headquartered in Kabul, would already have chapters in five provinces.

"I knew this idea of yours was popular," I remarked to Wakil later that afternoon, after we had toured several more facilities, "but you didn't tell me how many there were or how quickly this concept was growing."

"It's a bit hard to keep count — in another four months, we'll probably have three dozen," he said. "When women take charge, things start to get out of control really fast."

As impressive as all of this was, Wakil's responsibilities did not end with the construction of his new schools in Kunar and Nuristan, his plans to expand into Uruzgan, and the rapidly burgeoning literacy centers. The next morning at 3:00 A.M., he and I set off together with Sarfraz and Wohid Khan to have a look at the final project in his portfolio. Our destination, some ninety miles northeast of Kabul, was the most legendary valley in all of Afghanistan.

Home to more than three hundred thousand people and the country's largest concentration of ethnic Tajiks, the Panjshir Valley was the birthplace and fortress of Shah Ahmed Massoud, the courageous and charismatic mujahadeen commander who successfully repulsed no fewer than nine full-scale Soviet offensives against the valley during the 1980s, earning him the sobriquet "the Lion of the Panjshir." Three years after the Soviets withdrew, Massoud's forces had captured Kabul and he briefly emerged as one of the more promising leaders among the rival mujahadeen factions that divided the country. By 1993, however, widespread looting and unchecked violence on the part of Massoud's soldiers had severely damaged his stature as a national hero — while simultaneously helping to pave the way for the Taliban. He was eventually assassinated by a pair of Al Qaeda suicide bombers, less than seventy-two hours prior to 9/11, and to this day the valley that he defended so staunchly remains a potent symbol of pride for many Afghans. For the staff of the Central Asia Institute, however, the Panjshir held a different significance.

Following the ouster of the Taliban, the Panjshir had benefitted from significant investment on the part of a number of international NGOs as well as the U.S. military, which together had done an impressive job building roads, health clinics, hydroelectric plants, and a number of boys' schools. Although the valley was now one of the safest and most progressive parts of the country, it was sorely lacking in terms of opportunities for girls' education. Moreover, because the Panjshir borders Badakshan to the north and Kunar and Nuristan to the east, the valley represented a gap in the line of outposts of female literacy that Sarfraz and

Wakil hoped to create through the center of Taliban country. If there was eventually to be a continuous ribbon of girls' schools stretching all the way from the Wakhan to Deh Rawod, we needed to plant a few seeds inside the Panjshir.

In the summer of 2008, Wakil had somehow found the time to venture into the valley, establish relationships with local elders, and launch construction on a pair of girls' schools in the villages of Darghil and Pushgur. The Darghil school had opened in 2008, while the Pushgur project — an eight-room structure that would accommodate over two hundred girls — was scheduled to receive its official inauguration at 11:30 on the morning of July 15 with a very special guest.

The road from Kabul led past Bagram Airbase and across the brown expanse of the Shomali Plain to a point where the Panjshir River burst through the mouth of a narrow gorge. For the next ten miles, the road skirted between the river and the cliff until the valley abruptly opened up into an idyllic tableau of beautiful woodlands and irrigated farms, all protected by soaring, 2,000-foot walls of gray, crumbling rock.

We arrived in Pushgur at around 9:30. In the courtyard more than four hundred people had clustered, including several dozen bearded elders, a delegation of provincial officials, most of the two hundred girls who would be attending the school, a platoon of Wohid Khan's Border Security Force troops, and about thirty heavily armed U.S. soldiers. Nearby were several tables laden with food, soft drinks, and bottled water, all of it closely guarded by our friend Faisal Mohammed, the father who had lost his youngest son to a land mine outside our school in Lalander — and who had recently been working informally as Wakil's assistant.

Less than an hour after we arrived, two UH-60 Black Hawks and one CH-47 Chinook flew in from the southwest, circled the area, and then landed, creating an explosion of dust that covered everything. The first man to step out of the lead Black Hawk, clad in desert-camouflage fatigues, was Admiral Mike Mullen.

"Hey Greg," he shouted over the roar of the engines. "I hope you don't mind that I brought some media with me."

As he spoke, the Chinook disgorged a dozen journalists, including reporters from Reuters, the *Wall Street Journal,* the *Washington Post,* NPR, the BBC, and ABC-TV, as well as Thomas Friedman, the Pulitzer-Prize winning editorial-page columnist for the *New York Times.*

After everyone had moved under a large tent and taken their seats, several girls dressed in their new school uniforms presented the admiral with a garland of flowers. Another group of girls recited a prayer while holding U.S. and Afghan flags. Then the speeches began, with extensive remarks being offered by the governor, the district officer, the provincial education director, and a number of other dignitaries. Finally, after thirty minutes, Admiral Mullen stepped to the podium.

To translate the admiral's speech from English into Dari, Wakil had selected one of our brightest students, a twelfth-grader named Lima whose father, a retired petroleum engineer, was so poor that he now fed Lima and her fourteen brothers and sisters by selling firewood in Kabul. Lima was fluent in five languages (Dari, Pashto, Urdu, Arabic, and English) and taught part time in one of Wakil's literacy centers. For four years running, she held the top position among the 3,100 girls in her high school.

With Lima translating, the admiral announced that he was bringing good wishes from the American people, and then spoke with eloquence and passion about the vital importance that education held for the future of Afghanistan. "This school is here because of you, the local people, and your commitment and dedication to start education in your community," he said. "This is a proud moment in which we all celebrate your efforts to build a better future for your country."

It would be difficult to overstate the symbolic impact of witnessing an eight-room school for girls inaugurated by the admiral who served as the principal military adviser to the president of the United States. For Wakil and Sarfraz, there could have been no more powerful vindication of the work to which they had dedicated their lives. For me, however, perhaps the most moving part of that day came when Wohid Khan was asked to stand up and offer a few remarks.

During the past several years, this veteran mujahadeen had demonstrated his passionate dedication to the cause of promoting education in his homeland in more ways than I could count, from helping to transport building materials to our construction sites in the Wakhan to rescuing one of our teachers and his family from the middle of a river. But Wohid Khan is a man of few words, and until that morning in Pushgur, I had never really heard him articulate his feelings in public.

"In our country, our people have suffered

through three decades of war, and as you know many of our fellow mujahadeen have died in these hills and mountains," he began, speaking in Dari. "We have fought hard and we have paid dearly."

He looked up toward the surrounding peaks and ridges.

"A wise man from my home once told me that these mountains have seen far too much suffering and killing, and that each rock and every boulder you see represents a mujahadeen who died fighting either the Russians or the Taliban. Then the man went on to say that now that the fighting is finished, it is time to build a new era of peace — and the first step in that process is to take up the stones and start turning them into schools."

He paused for a moment.

"Having fought for so long under the shadow of war, I believe that the finest service that a mujahadeen can now perform is to build schools and promote literacy. The opportunity to participate in this effort is one of the greatest honors of my lifetime."

Before stepping from the podium and returning to his seat, the Afghan commander then turned gravely to the American admiral and — one warrior to another, one champion of girls' literacy to another — snapped off a crisp, razorlike salute.

■ ■ ■ ■

When the speeches were over, Admiral Mullen met privately for about an hour with the excited students inside the school. Upon emerging, he lingered for a few minutes to shake hands and exchange good wishes, before he and his entourage piled back into the helicopters and departed. Then, as the village of Pushgur sat down to a feast that would undoubtedly take its place in the lore of the Panjshir Valley, Wakil, Sarfraz, Wohid, and I started the drive back to Kabul.

We took our time, pausing to pay our respects at the tomb of Shah Ahmed Massoud and making three separate stops so that Wohid, who loves fresh fruit, could purchase some apples, cherries, and mulberries. Later that afternoon, as we rolled southward along the Shomali Plain, our fingers stained with berry juice, Sarfraz lavished Wakil with compliments.

"You are making even more schools here than we are making in the Wakhan," he exclaimed. "You have achieved much success!"

"It has nothing to do with me," protested our Pashtun colleague. "This is all the will of Allah."

When we finally reached the capital, Wakil

excused himself and raced off to receive yet another delegation of elders from a distant province who wanted to talk about the possibility of starting up a girls' school. Meanwhile, Sarfraz and I turned our attention to our most pressing piece of unfinished business — getting to Bozai Gumbaz.

CHAPTER 16
THE POINT OF RETURN

*And coming down from the Pamir where
the lost
Camels call through the clouds.*
— ANDRÉ MALRAUX, *Les Noyers de
l'Altenburg*

*Kirghiz elders meeting at Bozai Gumbaz to plan new school,
East Wakhan, Afghanistan* PHOTO: © 2008 TERU KUWAYAMA

507

Back in the autumn of 2008, as I was rushing west out of the central Wakhan in order to fly to Islamabad and attend my tea-drinking session with President Musharraf, Sarfraz had slowly made his way east on horseback to Bozai Gumbaz. Once there, he had discovered that his crew of quarrymen was making excellent progress on the task of dynamiting large boulders into smaller pieces that could be shaped with chisels and hammers into the stones that would eventually form the walls of the Kirghiz school. But as he stared at the impressive mound of melon-sized rocks that his masons had created on the flat green meadow next to the glassy lake where the Kirghiz were hoping to locate their school, he found himself grappling for the first time with the practical obstacles we would need to surmount in order to make that vision a reality.

Logistical challenges, of course, are nothing new to us, and over the years, we've been forced to overcome some ludicrously daunting problems. For example, the bridge that we had to build over the Braldu River, which would enable us to carry in the supplies to construct our first school in Korphe in 1996, required two dozen men to haul five 284-foot steel cables wound on wooden spools on their shoulders for a distance of eighteen miles. Similarly, one of Sarfraz's earthquake schools in Azad Kashmir required him to assemble a human chain of more than two hundred men in order to pass cement and other materials by hand around places where landslides had destroyed the roads. Yet even by the standards of our most difficult projects, the Kirghiz school was in a class all by itself.

Bozai Gumbaz had more than enough native stone for the purpose of building the foundation and walls, but there were no commercially available supplies of cement, rebar, glass, nails, corrugated roofing, paint, or any of the other items that Sarfraz's construction crew would need to complete the job. All of that material would have to come from the outside, plus the lumber, too. (There are few trees in the Pamirs.)

In theory, of course, these materials could

easily have been purchased in Faizabad or Baharak and — despite the usual setbacks stemming from muddy roads, landslides, flash flooding, and mechanical breakdown — we could have arranged to have everything hauled into Sarhad by tractor or truck. But how would we have proceeded from there?

From the place where the Wakhan road ends in Sarhad, the journey to Bozai Gumbaz involves a three-day trek along a narrow trail that clings to the cliffs and whose surface is covered in treacherously shifting talus. Along its forty-mile length, this trail ascends and descends a total of 20,000 feet, nearly twice the vertical relief between Everest base camp and its summit. What's more, these ups and downs all take place at altitudes of between ten thousand and fourteen thousand feet, where the oxygen levels make it impossible for conventional pack animals such as donkeys and mules to carry substantial loads. Finally, there are three major river crossings.

To haul all the supplies in from Sarhat would have required a pack train of at least a hundred yaks or Bactrian camels, far more than the number of animals that were available for hire. For similar reasons, a very large yak train leading out of the Charpurson Valley over the Irshad Pass was equally unworkable. On the other hand, perhaps, maybe a supply convoy could have been assembled in western China and punched into the eastern end of the Wakhan, where the terrain was not nearly as rough. But the Chinese-Afghan border had been sealed for more than sixty years — and thanks to the current political unrest among Xinjiang Province's restive Muslim population, the likelihood of Chinese border officials granting a special laissez-passer was less than zero.

As Sarfraz stood beside the mound of freshly chiseled stones scratching his head, he found himself pondering a question that seemed to encapsulate the absurdity of our work: How do you build a school on the Roof of the World when transporting the construction materials from any direction is virtually impossible?

Even by the standards of his own audacity and innovation, the plan that he came up with was magnificently nuts.

In July, Sarfraz had submitted a budget request for the purchase of a used Kamaz, a type of heavy-duty truck that is manufactured in Tartarstan and has a well-deserved reputation for toughness and reliability (the trucks have racked up a record eight victories in the Dakar Rally and are the preferred means of transport for the Russian army). A Kamaz was one of the few motorized vehicles capable of hauling massive loads along the axle-snapping roadbed of the Wakhan without breaking down every few miles, and Sarfraz had calculated that with the money we would save by no longer paying exorbitant fees to have our building supplies brought into the western Wakhan, the truck would recoup its cost in two years. The CAI board of directors had approved the expenditure, and our battered gray Kamaz — which had been freighting construction material all summer long — now emerged as the key to Sarfraz's strategy for Bozai Gumbaz.

Sometime during the next several days, the truck was scheduled to leave the town of Ishkoshem, lumber over a 300-foot bridge into Tajikistan, and make its way north on the Pamir Highway past the ancient ruby mines of Kuh-i-Lal to the Tajik city of Khorog. There, Sarfraz had arranged for the vehicle to be loaded with forty bags of cement and other building materials before proceeding another long day across the aching monotony of the Pamir plateau to Murghab, a town whose name means "river of birds" in Persian.

Meanwhile, Sarfraz had also ordered a

consignment of 190 poplar trees to be cut from the Pamir forests. These logs would be sawed into lumber, and loaded onto the Kamaz when it reached Murgab, at which point the truck — now groaning with its massive load — would continue south for another eighty miles along the valley of the Aksu River, skirting the no-man's-land along the border of western China and the looming hulk of 24,757-foot Muztaghata, the highest peak in the Pamirs.

Eventually the Kamaz would reach a point just above the easternmost end of the Wakhan. There it would cross back into Afghanistan and grind, in its lowest gear, along the remnants of a dirt track that was originally bladed by tanks from the Soviet military and had barely been used since the end of the Soviet occupation. At the point where the track ended, the supplies would be taken off, loaded onto the backs of a herd of waiting yaks and carried the final distance into Bozai Gumbaz, a journey of two days.

Total round-trip distance: just under nine hundred miles.

Time to destination: unknown.

Needless to say, we had never done anything like this before, and setting up the necessary arrangements to enable this unorthodox shipment to move across the heavily restricted Afghanistan-Tajikistan border would have been categorically impossible without the assistance of the man who had emerged as our most formidable ally in the Wakhan.

Several weeks before standing up in front of Admiral Mullen in Pushgur and delivering his "stones into schools" speech, Wohid Khan had approached his counterparts in the Tajik Border Security Force about the possibility of being granted a one-time permit for this special delivery expedition. Despite the fact that Wohid commands deep respect on both sides of the border, the Tajiks were initially reluctant to accede to such an unusual request. (Because southern Tajikistan is plagued by smugglers who traffic heavily in heroin, guns, and even child slaves, its borders are exceptionally sensitive and are placed under extremely tight controls.) The Tajiks' attitude changed, however, when they were presented with a warranty that could not be turned down without giving personal offense: As a guarantee that the conditions of the permit would not be violated, Wohid Khan himself would personally accompany the truck on its entire journey. Doing so would require the Afghan commander to set aside his professional duties for longer than he could really afford. But in the eyes of Khan, there could be no worthier mission for a mujahadeen.

At the moment, there were still a few lingering details yet to be worked out. (The school's windows and doors, which were now being assembled in Ishkoshem, would not be finished before the Kamaz departed for Tajikistan.) Nevertheless, Sarfraz's strategy was clear: Having concluded that access to Bozai Gumbaz from any single direction was impossible, he had decided that the first school to grace the world's rooftop would be assembled by using all four points of the compass simultaneously. The Charpurson masons and carpenters would tromp over the Irshad Pass from the south. The bulk of the cement and lumber would make its way in a daring northern loop through Tajikistan and then be thrust into the far eastern end of the Corridor. And the cash to pay for the final phase of construction, $20,000, would enter the Wakhan from the west in the pockets of my vest and Sarfraz's.

As Sarfraz and I completed our drive back to Kabul from the Panjshir Valley following Admiral Mullen's inauguration of the Pushghur School, we calculated that if we left for Badakshan immediately, we might be able to reach Bozai Gumbaz just before Wohid Khan's yak train arrived, giving us time to conduct a ceremonial *jirga* with Abdul Rashid Khan and the rest of the Kirghiz community. Construction could begin the following day, and with a bit of luck, the walls would be up and the roof would be nailed down before the first big snowstorm locked the Pamirs down for another winter. There was, however, one problem.

"There are no flights scheduled from Kabul to Faizabad between now and the end of the week," explained Sarfraz as we arrived back in Kabul.

"So what are our options?" I asked.

"The roads north are very dangerous," he said. "We must pass through Khundud, and Taliban are attacking. But if you want to reach Bozai Gumbaz on time, we will need to drive all the way."

"Then let's do it," I replied. "It will be just like old times."

We launched our blitz the following morning in a rented Toyota with a driver we knew and trusted named Ahmed. This was the first time I had traveled by road to Badakshan in three years, and I was astonished by the changes. Back in 2003, when I had made my first drive north, the entire landscape had been devastated and scorched by war. The buildings along the highway had been almost totally destroyed, and there were so many land mines buried at the side of the road that it was dangerous even to pull over. Now, however, the countryside was coming back to life. The fields were dotted with villagers tending to their grape vines, orchards, wheat, and barley. It was almost possible to imagine, momentarily, what peace might look like in Afghanistan.

The surface of the highway had been paved, and we made good time. We shot through the Salang Tunnel at 10:00 P.M. and three hours later stopped for tea at Pul-e Khumri, the original home of Abdul, the orphan boy who had repaired our radiator on my first trip north. We asked if there had been any news of him, but nobody knew anything, so we pushed on.

The August night was clear, and the heavens were littered with a spray of stars whose clarity and brilliance I have seen matched only by the skies of Montana. As the hours rolled past and the night deepened, I stared out the window and gave myself over to a floating sense of déjà vu that carried me back to countless similar drives up the Karakoram Highway along the Indus River gorges and into Baltistan during the early years of our work. The names of the mountains and the languages spoken in the villages that were flitting past us in the dark now were different. But everything else — the dull taste of the dust filtering through the open window, the metallic pink glow of the lights above the all-night truck stops beside the highway, the rhythm of the road, and the vastness of the landscape — all of these things drove home the notion that my years in Pakistan and my time in Afghanistan were part of a continuous whole, a journey that was still unfolding and whose final aim remained something of a mystery.

As we dropped off the back side of midnight and entered the early hours of the morning, however, I found myself colliding against the limitation of my own stamina. The endless litany of plane flights and fund-raising appearances across the United States, followed by the whirlwind tour of Wakil's literacy centers and the frenzied preparations for the inauguration of the Pushgur school, now seemed to be catching up with me. Sarfraz, I knew, had been working just as hard, if not harder. And yet, despite the fact that he was a few years older than me, he seemed to draw from a well of energy that was deeper than my own.

Somewhere north of the town of Baghlan, the toll of the past several weeks finally washed over me in a wave of weariness so oppressive that it felt as if someone were smothering me with a wet blanket. Like a long-distance runner who has slipped off the top of his game, I realized that I no longer had the ability to keep up with Sarfraz. In terms of determination, stubbornness, and the pigheaded refusal to give up, the two of us were still remarkably well matched. But when it came to sheer resiliency, my friend and colleague had passed me by and disappeared into the distance.

"Maybe we should rest for a little bit," I suggested as we approached the lights of another fuel station. "Why don't we pull over?"

"No stopping," ordered Sarfraz. "There have been many Taliban in this area recently. We cannot rest until we are past Khundud."

We kept driving, passing through Khundud around 1:30 A.M., and it was not until we reached the safety of Talikan, which lay beyond the furthest advances of the insurgency, that Sarfraz finally allowed our driver to pull into a roadside tea stand and each of us collapsed on a *charpoy,* a short-legged bed whose platform is woven together with coarse rope.

Sarfraz's instincts, it turned out, were as accurate as ever. One month after we passed through Khundud, Taliban insurgents hijacked a pair of tanker trucks, provoking an air strike from NATO fighter jets. The resulting explosion killed more than eighty people, including dozens of civilians. Twenty-four hours after that Stephen Farrell, a journalist working for the *New York Times* who was reporting on the aftermath of the air strikes, was kidnapped, together with his Afghan interpreter. Four days later, a rescue mission by British commandos resulted in the deaths of a British soldier and the Afghan interpreter, whose name was Mohammad Sultan Munadi.

A week prior to his death, Munadi, a thirty-four-year-old father of two, had written the following blog posting for the *New York Times:*

> *Being a journalist is not enough; it will not solve the problems of Afghanistan. I want to work for the education of the country, because the majority of people are illiterate. That is the main problem facing many Afghans.*

Sarfraz and I awoke at just after 5:00 A.M., nudged the driver to his feet and gently prodded him into the rear seat, then pulled back onto the road. With Sarfraz behind the wheel and the sun just beginning to come up, we crossed into Badakshan. The fertile valleys, rugged hills, and broken gorges carried a welcoming sense of familiarity, and the feeling of moving through a landscape to which we belonged was reinforced as we began passing some of our Central Asia Institute schools. First came Fakhar School, followed by Faizabad Girls' School, and beyond that, Sadhar Khan's school in Baharak — where the road south led to the Shodha Girls' School and the Jherum Girls' Primary School. We kept pressing east, skirting above the Eskan Girls' Primary School, the Koh Munjon School, the Wardugh Girls' Middle School, and the Ziabakh Girls' Elementary and Middle School.

On a normal trip we would have stopped at each of these places for tea and a quick visit, but not this time. As we entered the Wakhan proper, Sarfraz kept his foot to the accelerator, and eleven more schools flew past. Together these twenty projects provided visual affirmation of the fact that despite the endless setbacks and delays, we had managed to accomplish something worthwhile during our time in northern Afghanistan. And perhaps I would have given myself over to a wave of pride and self-congratulation, had I not been overtaken by something far more powerful. During my yearlong absence, I had forgotten that the Wakhan, despite its harshness and austerity, is a place of unspeakable loveliness.

Compelling evidence of this fact was on display everywhere. The previous winter had been the worst the Wakhan had seen in twelve years, bringing with it an endless succession of storms that had buried the High Pamir beneath a second mountain range of snow and kept temperatures below freezing well into June. The conditions had been devastating for livestock, and many of the surrounding villages had lost a significant portion of their animals. When the melt-out finally arrived, the hardships had continued with a larger-than-normal wave of avalanches, landslides, and flash floods. Now, however, the Corridor was finally reaping the flip side of the equation.

Thanks to all the moisture from the shrinking snowpack and the glacial melt, the vibrant emerald green colors of late spring were still refusing to surrender to the brown and ocher tones of midsummer. In village after village, every field was bursting with a bumper crop of wheat, potatoes, or millet. Above this shimmering green patchwork soared the double-walled architecture of the Wakhan's unique geologic signature: to the south, the bulwark of the Hindu Kush, blocking off Pakistan; and to the north, across the Amu Darya, the ramparts of the Pamirs defining the edge of Tajikistan. When taken in by the eye in a single, sweeping glance, this dramatic ensemble — the jagged peaks, the foaming river, the orange- and purple-hued rocks, the splashes of color from the wild roses and buttercups, all spread beneath the measureless immensity of the sky — offered a vision of unmatched beauty and grandeur.

On the second day from Kabul, we reached our twenty-first and final school, the Sarhad School, where the road ended and the central reaches of the Corridor began giving way to the colder and more severe lines of the High Pamir. Here, even in midsummer, winter was never more than half a step away. The stretches of flatland that were wedged between the mountains and the river around Sarhad were carpeted in a thick, tightly knotted tundra grass that resembled what one might see in the subpolar latitudes of northern Canada.

Aside from its visual splendor, what makes Sarhad so striking is that more than any other place in the Wakhan, or even Afghanistan, it suggests the possibility that you have arrived in a land where time itself has frozen. Beyond the cluster of low-slung, mud-and-stone houses that make up the village, wild-haired children preside over herds of shaggy-coated yaks and shovel-footed Bactrian camels that look as if they are still part of the Pleistocene. In the nearby fields, which have been fenced off with the bleached bones and the curled horns of ibex and Marco Polo sheep, men turn the earth with plows whose design has not changed in two thousand years.

By the time we arrived, we had been driving almost nonstop for about forty hours. We pulled up in front of the residence of Tashi Boi, the local chief who was in charge of civil affairs in this part of the Corridor and who had been a fierce advocate for literacy and girls' education since he completed a drug-treatment program a decade ago and successfully overcame his addiction to opium, the scourge of so many families in the Corridor. Tashi Boi's home, which he shared with his wife, children, and fifteen members of his extended family, was a traditional Wakhi "hearth house." A hexagonal structure, its interior featured an earthen floor in which a sunken area in the center, which contained the hearth, was surrounded by a raised platform covered with thick blankets and rugs upon which members of the household spent most of their time. The roof was supported by rough-hewn wooden beams, and a touch of modernity was provided by the addition of a support post fashioned from a long steel girder that had once served as the tread cover of a Soviet T-62 tank.

Sarhad was the deepest I had ever penetrated into the interior of the Wakhan, and before stepping inside the house to share a meal of noodle soup, I paused to cast a glance at what lay beyond the end of the road. About fifteen miles to the south rose the escarpments of the Hindu Kush. A day and a half's walk in that direction would take one to the northern entrance of the Irshad Pass. Meanwhile, forty-two miles to the east lay the old Kirghiz burial grounds of Bozai Gumbaz. If Sarfraz and I started first thing in the morning, within three days we could make our rendezvous with Wohid Khan and Abdul Rashid Khan.

I headed indoors with the hope that in less than seventy-two hours, we would finally finish off a piece of business that had been languishing for a decade. It was at this point, however, that fate apparently felt the need to demonstrate the irritating truth that in this place, nothing ever happens the way it's supposed to.

■ ■ ■ ■

One of the benefits of having been raised in rural Africa was that it imbued me with an unusually strong constitution. During my sixteen years of work in Pakistan and Afghanistan, I had only been severely sick twice. When I awoke the following morning, however, my entire body was wracked by chills and my limbs and chest had been overtaken by a fatigue so dense and so heavy that it seemed to have penetrated all the way to the bone. An hour later, my head was spinning wildly and I was locked in the grip of a remorseless fever.

The dizziness and the pounding headache made me think it might be malaria, to which I had succumbed twice as a boy in Tanzania. There were no mosquitoes this high in the Wakhan, however. Whatever it was that had a hold of me, there was no resisting its onslaught, and as Tashi Boi and Sarfraz pumped me full of green tea and piled four or five blankets on me, I slipped into a deep delirium.

Inside the cauldron of my fever, I lost all sense of time, fumbling to the surface only periodically to register what was happening around me. On several occasions, I experienced the blurred sense that someone seemed to be piling yet another blanket on top of me or performing a kind of pressure massage that involved pressing down on my legs and head with two or three fingers, then letting go. In other instances, I could hear the mumbled whispers of Sarfraz and the members of Tashi Boi's household as they discussed my condition and speculated on what to do. Once or twice, I awoke in the middle of the night to realize that a circle of elders was sitting quietly beside me and keeping vigil. The residents of Sarhad were doting and they were worried, and they never once left me alone. Drifting through my illness, I had the sense that people were taking turns sitting beside me and holding my hand for hours.

As the days and the nights melded, my sense of the present slipped away and was overtaken by scenes from my past. I flashed back to my childhood battles with malaria, when I had lost six months of school. I also traveled back to Korphe, where the care that I had received during my first stay in Haji Ali's village seemed to merge with what the people of Sarhad were now doing. At night, over the roar of Tashi Boi's generator, I could hear the yaks clustered outside the house, grunting and mooing in the moon-light — sounds that convinced me that I had been transported back to Montana and was standing on the Great Plains surrounded by a herd of buffalo. At one point, an elderly woman awakened me from my stupor to ask if I wanted to smoke some opium, which she said would take away the pain.

"No thanks," I said, "I've already got some medicine."

As I descended back into sleep, I could hear Sarfraz rhythmically shaking our jumbo-sized jar of ibuprofen like a maraca.

Rattle-rattle-rattle.

Rattle-rattle-rattle.

On the morning of the third day, I awoke with a vast ache over my whole body, but the thoughts in my mind were now running with a coolness and a clarity that mirrored the streams flowing through the fields outside.

The fever had broken.

I sat up, took some tea and some bread, and tried to calculate how long it would take us to reach Bozai Gumbaz.

When he realized what I was doing, Sarfraz, who was sitting on the other side of the room, shook his head wordlessly.

"It's only three days' walk from here," I said, sensing his skepticism.

"You are too weak to walk, and you cannot

keep going," he replied. "We need to get you out of here."

"That's not true. How about if I ride a yak?"

"Greg, you cannot play games with being sick in the Wakhan — there is no medicine here, there are no doctors, there is no way to leave quickly if you get worse. Three years ago I was in the same position you are in now, and I pushed things too hard and almost died. I am not going to let that happen to you. Tara would never forgive me."

"But Sarfraz, we can still make it!"

And then he said something that I had never heard during all my years in Asia.

"I will not take you any further, Greg," he remarked quietly, but in a tone that made it clear that there would be no negotiation.

"I refuse to allow it. We are returning to Kabul."

Later, as Sarfraz and I drove out of the corridor down the very same road that we had just come up, I was struck by the unwelcome thought that after having failed not once but twice to reach the High Pamir, Bozai Gumbaz was beginning to feel as elusive and as unreachable to me as the summit of K2. It also seemed to me that this retreat from the Wakhan bore a disturbing resemblance to my confused withdrawal from K2 base camp down the Baltoro Glacier during the autumn of 1993 when I had wandered off the path, spent the night in the open, and eventually wound up stumbling into Korphe.

In several respects, it almost seemed as if that debacle and this were one and the same. Both experiences had imbued me with a sense of abject failure after having fallen short of an important and meaningful goal. Worse, both forced me to confront the realization that I had let down people to whom I had made a promise. In the case of K2, the pledge I had broken had been made to my sister Christa, in whose memory I had promised to place on the summit an amber necklace that she had once worn. In the case of Bozai Gumbaz, I had failed to keep my word to the Kirghiz. Although we had managed to construct an impressive line of twenty-one schools stretching from Faizabad to Sarhad, one for nearly every village in the Wakhan, the single community we had yet to reach was the one on whose behalf we had ventured into Afghanistan in the first place. Now it looked as if the passing of yet another winter (the eleventh!) was about to mark our continued inability to follow through on the original vow — the vow that had mattered the most, because of all the people at the end of the road whom we were trying to serve, none had needed our help more than the Kirghiz.

As it turned out, however, there were also some key differences between my original failure on K2 and what was happening now. Unlike the defeated mountaineer who had taken a wrong turn on the Baltoro Glacier sixteen years earlier and submitted himself to the kindness of a village filled with people he had never met, I was not among strangers and I was no longer lost. And although I knew nothing of it as Sarfraz and I silently completed our drive out of the Wakhan, despite all the challenges involved in this nearly impossible mission to raise up a school on the Rooftop of the World the Kirghiz were about to be given exactly what they needed most.

CHAPTER 17
THE LAST BEST SCHOOL

The world has turned away from Afghani-stan.
— AHMED RASHID, *Taliban* (2001)

Yaks head to eastern Wakhan, Afghanistan PHOTO © 2007 SARFRAZ KHAN

The first storm of the season struck the eastern Wakhan on September 5, and the eight inches of snow that fell to the ground found Sarfraz back in Badakshan, having completed yet another epic sprint through northern Afghanistan. After bidding me farewell in Kabul, he had flown back to Faizabad to confirm that the Kamaz and Wohid Khan were on their way through Tajikistan. There he had commissioned a second truck to haul an additional forty bags of cement, plus the frames for the Kirghiz school's doors and windows, through Baharak to Sarhad. As Kamaz number two started its journey east, Sarfraz then raced ahead to Sarhad to see if he could round up a dozen yaks — a considerable challenge because the bulk of these animals were still grazing the summer pastures high in the mountains and weren't due to be driven down to the lower elevations for another three weeks.

While Sarfraz concentrated on wrangling his yaks, Wohid Khan was completing his arc through Tajikistan across the top of the Wakhan, and adding items onto the load in the back of the truck with each stop. In Faizabad he purchased an assortment of tools, including trowels, hammers, plumb lines, twine, baling wire, and mason squares. In Ishkoshem he picked up two dozen shovels and several boxes of dynamite, plus eight wheelbarrows. After crossing the bridge into Tajikistan, he worked his way north to Khurog and took on thirty-eight bags of cheap Russian cement, which would be used in the foundation, along with several bags of calcium. The following day he reached Murgab, where he confirmed that the 190 four-inch-diameter poplar trees, which had been ordered two weeks earlier, were now being stripped of their bark and sawn into fifteen-foot-long poles for framing the school roof. Then he and his driver turned south for the Afghan border, where they crossed a barbed-wire fence demarcating the northern edge of the Wakhan and followed the old Soviet tank tracks toward the grazing lands of the Kirghiz.

Together with their horses, sheep, camels, and yaks, the Kirghiz migrate across an area of two thousand square miles. There are

nearly two thousand of them, and they prefer to move in small bands to avoid taxing
the grasslands of the High Pamir. At various
times of the year, however, they congregate
around three primary encampments that are
arranged in a triangle and separated from
one another by a distance of roughly thirty-
five miles. The first of these cantonments, a
few miles south of the Tajik border, lies on
the eastern shore of Chakmak Lake, a shallow body of Windex-blue water that received
its first recorded mention in the writings of
the Buddhist pilgrim Hsuan Tsang, who
passed through the Wakhan on his way to
China in A.D. 644. ("The Valley of Pamir,"
wrote Hsuan, "is situated between two
snowy mountains. The cold is glacial and
the wind is furious. Snow falls even in spring
and summer, day and night the wind rages.
Grain and fruit cannot grow there, and trees
are few and far between. In the middle of
the valley is a large lake, situated in the centre of the world on a plateau of prodigious
height.")

Wohid Khan swiftly discovered that the
tank track was in terrible shape, having received almost no traffic during the previous
twenty years. It took another full day for the
Kamaz to reach the encampment at the center of the world, which the Kirghiz call Kara

Jilga, and which offers almost nothing in the way of amenities. The infrastructure here consists of three crumbling cinder-block buildings, some twenty yurts, and a corral the size of a football field that is surrounded by a low earthen wall designed to shelter the nomads' animals during bad weather and protect them from wolves. But what is truly remarkable about this place — and the reason why the Kirghiz flock to it in such numbers each summer — is the fecundity of the surrounding pastures: an immense carpet of thick-bladed grass so nutritious that even the leanest animals grow fat after ten days of feeding upon it.

In Kara Jilga, the tank tracks ended, and the Kamaz completed the next fifteen miles by bushwhacking across the roadless meadows and bludgeoning through the boulder-strewn deltas until it could go no further. At this point, the load was dropped to the ground and the truck started the long loop back to Ishkoshem. As for the tools and the cement that had just been deposited, another yak train would need to be put together before these materials could complete the final fifteen-mile leg to Bozai Gumbaz.

In the meantime, Sarfraz had managed to assemble his twelve yaks in Sarhad. After loading them with the window and door frames and the bags of cement that had just arrived on Kamaz number two, he started the arduous three-day haul into Bozai Gumbaz from the west. At the same time, yet *another* column of yaks — a minitrain of only six animals that had also been organized by Sarfraz — was ferrying a load of twenty-two-gauge roofing panels over the Irshad Pass from Pakistan.

While all this was taking place, I was back in the United States juggling a spate of university speaking engagements. At odd moments during these twenty-hour days, I would duck into the hallway outside a student seminar or pause before going through airport security to phone Sarfraz for a progress update. On September 10, he reported that his twelve-yak supply train had reached Bozai Gumbaz and he was now rounding up an additional half dozen yaks in order to retrieve the load that Wohid Khan had dumped between Kara Jilga and Bozai Gumbaz. He anticipated returning to the school site at roughly the same time that the roofing panels arrived over the Irshad Pass. Once all of this material had been delivered, the construction crew could get to work in earnest.

Everything seemed to be coming together beautifully, so when my phone beeped on the night of September 15 with Sarfraz's number, I was expecting to receive triumphant news that the project was back on schedule and racing toward completion. Instead, he announced that he was calling from Kara Jilga, where he was sitting at the bedside of a critically ill and possibly dying Abdul Rashid Khan.

Even by the extreme standards of Afghanistan, a country that has endured far more than its fair share of misery and misfortune, it is not easy to find a story more star-crossed than that of Abdul Rashid Khan. Born in the fall of 1937 inside a yurt that his mother and aunts had pitched near Chakmak Lake, the Kirghiz leader had been a witness to one of the darkest periods of his people's history, an era of virtually uninterrupted social disruption and economic decline.

In 1978, the fortunes of the Kirghiz had disintegrated when they were forced to flee their homeland prior to the Soviet invasion of Afghanistan and seek refuge in Pakistan, where they found the climate and the living conditions to be intolerable. At this point, as recounted in chapter 1, the community had split into two groups. The larger faction had decided to accept an offer for asylum from the Turkish government, and in 1982 they embarked on an odyssey known as the Last Exodus to eastern Anatolia, where they remain to this day. Meanwhile, a smaller group of incurably homesick Kirghiz had opted to follow Abdul Rashid Khan back to the High Pamir and resume the migratory lifestyle of their ancestors — a decision that exposed them directly to the chaos that had by now overtaken Afghanistan.

During the final years of the Soviet occupation, Abdul Rashid Khan had played a delicate game that involved cooperating with the Soviet army (which garrisoned approximately a thousand troops in the High Pamir) while secretly channeling provisions and logistical support to the Afghan mujahadeen. By blending diplomacy with deception, he was able to avoid provoking the vicious reprisals for which the Soviets were so hated, while simultaneously benefiting from Russian trade and development assistance. But when the occupation finally concluded and Afghanistan's rival mujahadeen factions plunged the country into civil war, the tiny band of nomads found themselves cut off and, in effect, abandoned by their own government.

As the Taliban clawed their way to power during the mid 1990s and seized control of more than 90 percent of the country, virtually all communication and contact with the world beyond Badakshan ceased. With each passing season, the Kirghiz seemed to slip several notches deeper into poverty and squalor — a slide that accelerated when predatory mujahadeen commanders from Baharak began flooding the Wakhan with opium as a means of financing their war against the Taliban. By the winter of 2001, when the U.S. military retaliation against the attacks of 9/11 finally drove the Taliban into exile, the Wakhan Kirghiz were buckling under the ravages of pervasive drug addiction, chronic malnutrition, inadequate health care, and economic ruin. At this point, Abdul Rashid Khan felt that his only option was to go begging.

When I first met the Kirghiz leader during the Baharak riots in the fall of 2005, he was returning from the second of three grueling and prohibitively expensive trips from the Wakhan to Kabul to beseech members of the Karzai government for schools, medical care, police protection, veterinary services, road construction, a post office — anything to demonstrate that the Kirghiz actually belonged to Afghanistan. On each occasion, elaborate promises were made and later broken — with a single exception. In the summer of 2007, a battered gray van that had been dispatched through Tajikistan along the same route now being traveled by our Kamaz truck had lumbered over the border, followed the tank track across the tundra, and sputtered to a stop in Bozai Gumbaz, at which point the driver got out and walked home. The van — which carried no medical supplies, no nurse or doctor, and no extra fuel — was apparently the federal government's idea of a comprehensive health-care program for the eastern Pamirs. To this day, the only apparent purpose served by this rusting, abandoned vehicle was to offer visual evidence of just how little the Kirghiz mattered to anyone.

By the summer of 2008, when I had cut short my trip to Bozai Gumbaz in order to have tea with the president of Pakistan, the Kirghiz were growing desperate. By now, the only thing that enabled them to survive the relentless Pamir winters was the assistance of their sole outside ally — Wohid Khan, who used his Border Security pickups to deliver sacks of flour, rice, salt, tea, and clothing each fall before the snows arrived. Even with this aid, however, the nomads were playing touch-and-go with starvation and were dangerously vulnerable to illness. The tipping point had finally arrived during the marathon winter of 2008–9, when the Kirghiz began to die in unprecedented numbers. By the time spring arrived, twenty-two people had perished, fourteen of them women who passed away in the midst of either pregnancy or childbirth. Among a population of less than nine hundred adults, losses like these were unsustainable. In addition to saddling the eastern Wakhan with probably the single worst maternal and infant mortality rates anywhere on earth, these deaths upset the ratio between males and females — an imbalance that, thanks to the number of unborn children who had also been lost, would take more than a decade to redress.

Two months later, as the community was still reeling from these events, an Afghan military helicopter had clattered above the alpine grasslands, touched down in Bozai Gumbaz, and deposited a politician named Abdullah Abdullah, who spent several hours shaking hands and asking for everyone's votes in the upcoming presidential election. Yet despite the effort that had been made to solicit the Kirghiz's participation, when election day finally arrived on August 20, 2009, not a single ballot box arrived in the Pamirs. Regardless of whether this failure stemmed from corruption, bureaucratic incompetence, or the fact that the federal election officials had simply forgotten about the Kirghiz, this marked the second consecutive election in which Abdul Rashid Khan and his people had been deprived of their right to vote. (In the October 2004 presidential election, a ballot box did actually make it to the Pamirs — but on the flight back to Kabul, the helicopter that was transporting the box crashed in the mountains and all of the ballots were lost.)

Among a host of other concerns, the ballot-box debacle of 2009 seemed to suggest the humiliating possibility that the Afghan government's apathy toward the Kirghiz might have burgeoned to the point where not even their votes were deemed to have value. Which, in turn, provoked some bleak and troubling questions from the elders to whom Abdul Rashid Khan turned when he was in need of counsel. Was there any reason, these elders demanded, why the entire community should not pull up stakes the following spring, gather together their yurts and their animals, and embark on a Final Exodus? If the government of Afghanistan neither wanted nor cared about them any longer, was it possible that somewhere in China, Tajikistan, or Kirghizstan they might be able to find someone who did? And at this point, did they really have anything left to lose?

During the second week of September, the

hardships and the disappointments of the previous years caught up with the aging Kirghiz *commandhan,* and his health took a severe turn for the worse. When word that Abdul Rashid Khan had taken to his bed reached Bozai Gumbaz, Sarfraz mounted Kazil, his shaggy white horse, and set off on a midnight race to Kara Jilga. Despite the fact that Kazil had been given almost no rest in more than a week, he completed the thirty-mile trip by dawn.

When horse and rider stumbled into Kara Jilga, Sarfraz found several dozen distressed Kirghiz gathered inside and outside Abdul Rashid Khan's yurt. Lying beneath five or six blankets, the stricken leader exhibited the classic symptoms of congestive heart failure: His skin was clammy, his pulse was racing, and his breathing was labored. None of this prevented Abdul Rashid Khan from registering his intense displeasure at seeing Sarfraz.

"Why did you come here when you are supposed to be working on our school?" he croaked.

"I heard that you were ill," replied Sarfraz, "and I needed to find out how you were doing."

"Your duty does not involve fussing over me! If you are not in Bozai Gumbaz, how is our school going to get finished before winter?!"

As he absorbed this dressing-down, Sarfraz realized that the task to which we had committed ourselves had suddenly expanded to embrace a new dimension of urgency and import. Following as it did on the heels of the previous year's tragedies and betrayals, the project at Bozai Gumbaz had now become more than just a schoolhouse. In addition to nurturing a sense of hope for the future of this community, it would offer perhaps the only compelling reason, in the spring of 2010, for the Kirghiz to refrain from abandoning their home and surrendering themselves to a permanent diaspora. To fulfill that role, however, the school first had to be finished — and time was running out.

The following morning, as Kazil was being watered and saddled, Sarfraz called me on his sat phone and laid out what was at stake.

"The situation here is very urgent," he said. "Can you help?"

My first impulse was to drop what I was doing and fly to Afghanistan immediately, but I quickly realized that my presence there would have solved nothing. Instead, I placed a call to Wohid Khan, who began reaching out to his friends within the Afghan and Tajik militaries to find out if there might be a way to extract Abdul Rashid Khan and take him to a hospital. No luck. Then I put the same question to Colonel Ilyas Mirza at Askari Aviation in Islamabad. His response: Without formal permission, the closest point to which a helicopter from Pakistan could fly was a six-day journey by yak from Kara Jilga. Finally, I tried Keyoum Mohammed, a friend from Kashgar in Xinjiang Province, who organized climbing expeditions on the north side of K2 and who had excellent contacts within the Chinese military. Keyoum too came up empty.

Out of options, I did the one thing I had been hoping to avoid: I opened up my laptop and composed an e-mail that formally — and quite shamelessly — attempted to leverage my budding relationships at the very highest levels of the American military.

My e-mail was addressed to two officers: Major General Curtis Scaparrotti, the U.S. commander in charge of eastern Afghanistan; and Admiral Eric Olson, head of U.S. Special Operations Command based at MacDill Air Force Base in Florida. Both men had a personal connection with the Central Asia Institute: Scaparrotti had accompanied Admiral Mike Mullen to the Panjshir Valley in

July for the inauguration of our girls' school in Pushgur, and Olson had made *Three Cups of Tea* mandatory reading for every Special Forces soldier deploying to Afghanistan. After explaining that I had made a promise to myself that I would never burden the U.S. military by asking for help, I laid out the reasons why I was now breaking that promise and provided a few details about Abdul Rashid Khan's location and condition. Then I got to the heart of the matter.

"We also are nearly finished building the first schoolhouse for the Kirghiz, and it would mean the world to Abdul Rashid Khan to be able to live to see it opened by winter," I wrote in my e-mail. "I'm sure this is an impossible task, insane request, and not possible, but I'll ask anyhow: We would be forever grateful if there was a way to get a helicopter to the following location to medivac Abdul Rashid Khan to get him to a hospital in Kabul or Bagram. Please excuse the forwardness of this request, but we've tried all other commercial and Afghan government options and come up empty-handed."

At roughly the same time, I continued pushing a separate request to the U.S. Military at Bagram Airbase to consider dispatching a Chinook into the eastern Wakhan in order to gather up the remaining loads of building supplies and drop them directly into Bozai Gumbaz so that construction could begin immediately. My hope was that the Chinook might serve as a kind of airborne insurance policy: If the initial medivac appeal failed to bear fruit, perhaps the Chinook could scoop up Abdul Rashid Khan before returning to Bagram, thereby killing two birds with one stone.

Both Olson and Scaparrotti responded swiftly with generous assurances that they would analyze their options and do everything they could. Late that night, Olson sent an e-mail to General David Petraeus, head of U.S. Central Command, to inquire about the possibility of getting a medivac into Kara Jilga for Abdul Rashid Khan. The following afternoon, Petraeus forwarded Olson's e-mail to General Stanley McChrystal, the ISAF (International Security Assistance Force) and U.S Forces Afghanistan commander in Kabul. "Stan," he wrote, "sounds like a chance to solidify a key relationship, but know it's a very long way. Doable? Thx — Dave."

Several hour later, McChrystal forwarded the e-mail to one of his key subordinates. "I put great stock in what Greg Mortenson says," he urged, "so let's look hard at the possibility."

With the wheels of the world's most sophisticated military machine now in motion, I phoned Sarfraz.

"Get word to Abdul Rashid Khan and tell him that help is on the way."

If the final chapter of this saga had been written in Hollywood, it would be easy enough to predict what would have happened next. The following morning, the double rotors of a twelve-ton Chinook — the same machine that had performed so many magnificent missions in Azad Kashmir following the 2005 earthquake — would have spooked the living daylights out of every goat, sheep, horse, camel, and yak in Kara Jilga. Having already deposited the rest of the building materials at Bozai Gumbaz, the Chinook would have scooped up Abdul Rashid Khan and made a beeline for the hospital in Bagram. The dramatic image of the chopper receding over the ridgelines of the Hindu Kush would have offered a powerful symbol of the unique partnership that had emerged in the most remote corner of the Wakhan between ordinary Muslims, the American military, and a tiny organization dedicated to the mission of promoting female literacy.

Alas, however, this was not Hollywood but Afghanistan: a place where life is often messy, confusing, and unfair — and where events almost never conform to the script that has been laid out. So here's what happened instead.

A flurry of e-mails flew back and forth among the generals and their subordinates as members of the regional command center in charge of eastern Afghanistan mapped out the options. Then, on Thursday, September 17, General McChrystal received a message from an aviation adviser on his assessment team explaining that things were not looking good. The GPS coordinates pinpointing Abdul Rashid Khan's precise location (which had been transmitted through Sarfraz's sat phone) indicated that the extraction point for a potential rescue mission lay no more than "a 9-iron shot from China" — close enough to a highly sensitive international border to raise concerns about creating a diplomatic incident. Equally problematic, the absence of any nearby fuel depots placed Kara Jilga at the extreme edge of the helicopters' reach, which would increase the level of risk significantly. And finally, after reviewing Abdul Rashid Khan's symptoms, several military surgeons felt that, in light of his age, there was little that could be done for him medically.

A day later, I received an e-mail from

Major General Scaparrotti explaining that the mission had been deemed too difficult and risky to justify, and thus would not go forward. "I'm sorry that we could not be of more assistance," wrote the general. "The flight from Bagram would have been multi-day and high-risk given altitude and lack of basing and fuel en route. My prayers are with Commandhan Abdul Rashid Khan."

This was not the outcome I had hoped for, but as I read the general's message I also understood that it was the correct decision. Although the assessment team's calculus may have sounded somewhat cold, it underscored the most important question to ask: Would it be right to place the lives of two American helicopter crews on the line while risking an international incident on behalf of a patient who was probably beyond help? In my heart, I knew that the answer was no — a decision, it turned out, that was emphatically endorsed by Abdul Rashid himself. "Please know that Commandhan Khan also knows that all of you did your best in consideration of him, and he wishes to extend his profound gratitude," I wrote back to the general.

As I sent off this final e-mail, I hoped that my sincere expression of thanks concealed my equally sincere disappointment over a decision that nevertheless seemed to highlight the wretched fact that in Afghanistan, nothing ever seems to work out the way it's supposed to.

What I did not fully understand at the time, however, was that every now and then in Afghanistan, the strands of messiness and confusion and unfairness manage to braid themselves together and, in the most improbable and miraculous way, offer up a radiant affirmation of possibility and hope that transcends anything that Hollywood, on its best day, could ever hope to imagine.

Which, in a nutshell, is exactly the way this story ends.

EPILOGUE

The birds are gentled in myth. In times of hardship they leave the shrine for havens of their own, and their return is a pledge of peace. Should a grey pigeon join them, it turns white within forty days. And every seventh bird is a spirit.
— COLIN THUBRON,
Shadow of the Silk Road

Kirghiz children at Bozai Gumbaz, Wakhan PHOTO: SARFRAZ KHAN

555

After the snow from the storm on September 5 melted, the weather stabilized and the entire Pamir hung suspended in a golden autumnal interregnum while winter made its final preparations. The sunny days and the cool nights created ideal building conditions while lacing the air with a fierce sense of urgency. Each morning when the Kirghiz awoke, they gazed out at the surrounding wall of twenty-thousand-foot peaks and observed that the snow line had crept farther down toward the valley floor. By the middle of the month, the line of white was at sixteen thousand feet; a days later, it descended to fourteen thousand. When it reached the valley floor, the game would be over.

On the nineteenth, I called Sarfraz to let him know that there would be no helicopters, and found him wrestling with yet another snafu. By now he had completed the job of ferrying all the material from Wohid

Khan's first supply dump to Bozai Gumbaz, but a second load had been deposited at yet another location — an encampment called Gozkhon, which the Kirghiz use mainly in the fall, on the western side of Chakmak Lake about five miles south of the Tajik border. It was a three-day journey from Gozkhon to Bozai Gumbaz, and with the limited number of yaks available to Sarfraz, it could take a month to transfer the entire load, which included the final bags of cement and the 190 wooden poles for framing the roof. At that rate, the school would never be finished in time.

Meanwhile, Abdul Rashid Khan was mired in troubles of his own. As word of his illness spread, men and women all across the Pamir had dropped whatever they were doing and begun walking or riding toward Kara Jilga in order to pay their respects and offer their support. The impulse behind this convergence was touching and appreciated, but it meant that manpower was being drained from Bozai Gumbaz precisely when the need for it was greatest — a conundrum that Abdul Rashid found intolerable. "This is no time to sit around watching an old man die," he railed at his well-wishers, making no effort to contain his frustration. "It is worthless for you to be here when you could be helping to build our future!"

The only peace the ailing leader had was at night, when his family would lift him up and carry him outside the yurt so that he could lie beneath the sky and gaze up at the stars that had once guided his ancestors down from the steppes of Mongolia. And perhaps it was there, in the writing of the constellations, that he found the answer he was looking for.

The next morning, Abdul Rashid summoned everyone together and laid out the situation. Despite the best intentions of the American military, he announced, there would be no helicopters to take him to a hospital or to shuttle the remaining building supplies to the construction site. As far as his health was concerned, he was content to accept his fate and give himself over to the will of Allah. But the school was another matter.

"We live at the edge of the world, and since no help is going to arrive, we have no choice but to do this ourselves," he declared. "This school is our priority. At this point, we have almost no resources left. But starting from this moment, everything that we have will be focused on one goal. *Inshallah,* we are going to finish what we have started."

With that, he issued an edict ordering

every available yak in the High Pamir sent immediately to Gozkhon. The fastest horses were rounded up and saddled, and riders streamed out across the grasslands in all directions. In less than twenty-four hours, long lines of shaggy black beasts were shuffling from the surrounding mountains toward the western shore of Chakmak Lake.

When Sarfraz called on his sat phone to tell me about the Kirghiz leader's proclamation, I thought it was a smart strategy that might help to nudge the odds back in favor of polishing off the school in time. But what impressed me even more were the selflessness and the resolution that lay behind this move. Having already squandered his personal fortune and his health in a fruitless campaign to improve the welfare of his people, Abdul Rashid Khan was now determined to spend the last chunk of capital he had left — the moral force of a dying man's final wish — as a means of rallying the members of his community around a goal larger than themselves. It was an exemplary demonstration of leadership, as well a compelling object lesson in the nobility, tenacity, and grace that is to be found among the people at the end of the road. And it yielded some impressive results.

By September 21, forty-three yaks had arrived in Gozkhon, where they were loaded with cement and lumber, and driven in the direction of Bozai Gumbaz. No one in the Pamir had ever seen anything quite like this. It was the longest yak train in living memory, and more were on their way.

Meanwhile, more than sixty Kirghiz men had rushed to Bozai Gumbaz and flung themselves into the task of assisting the eight masons from the Charpurson Valley who were directing operations. They worked fourteen hours a day hauling water, mixing cement, and roughing out the roof frame, pausing only at at midday for lunch that was laid out by the women in the open. Judging by the descriptions I received from Sarfraz, the scene looked like an Amish barn-raising at the crossroads of Asia.

At the center of it all was the man with the broken hand. By tracing the GPS waypoints registered by Sarfraz's sat phone, it was clear to me that he was everywhere at once: needling the yak herders south of Chakmak Lake to move their animals faster; galloping off to the school to harass the masons; then dashing back to Gozkhon to supervise the formation of a second yak train, and then a third one after that. It took little effort for me to imagine him glancing toward the mountains in the distance, registering the fact that the snow line had descended another hundred yards, and mercilessly thrashing poor, exhausted Kazil into yet another gallop with the trekking pole he used for a horse whip.

Then one evening at about 7:30 P.M., the phone rang in Bozeman. Tara was outside sitting on the front porch with our dog Tashi on her lap, Khyber was practicing the piano in the living room, and Amira was doing her math homework on the kitchen table.

"So?" I asked.

"No problem, sir — the school is finished."

I glanced at the calendar on my desk that sits next to the photograph of Abdul, the orphan mechanic who had repaired our radiator hose on the way to Badakshan during one of our first trips into northern Afganistan. It was Monday, September 28.

Nearly a decade after the original promise had been made to Abdul Rashid Khan's horsemen, the covenant had finally been fulfilled.

I am told that in the heart of a vast, bowl-shaped valley deep inside the High Pamir where the sheep and the goats spend their summers grazing by the hundreds as far as the eye can see, there is a cold blue stream that meanders through emerald meadows until it spills into a small lake that carries the color of the sky, and that the surface of this lake and the surrounding grasslands shiver in unison beneath the movement of a wind that never stops blowing.

About two hundred yards from the edge of that lake, I am told that the ground rises gently and that on the south-facing slope of this incline, positioned at an angle that enables it to absorb as much sunshine as possible, there stands a four-room school-house with an earthen floor and walls that are made of stone. The windows and door frame have been neatly painted in red, and if you stand in that doorway and stare into the distance, apparently you can see the tops of Pakistan's Hindu Kush to the south and China's Tien Shan range to the east, and if you walk around to the back of the school, the slopes of Tajikistan's Big Pamir range will dominate the horizon line to the north.

As I write these lines at the beginning of October, I am told that we will have no further news of Abdul Rashid Khan's condition — whether he lived or whether he died — until next spring, when the passes through the Hindu Kush reopen and when Sarfraz, who must now saddle up Kazil and return over the Irshad to a family in the Charpurson that has not seen him in nine months, can once again ride north to the Pamir. In the meantime — during the six months when the grasslands lie buried beneath the snow and all connection between the Kirghiz and the outside world has been severed — I am told that there will be roughly 200 children who will study at the school; and that the skills they will learn and the ideas to which they will be exposed may usher in changes — some good, others bad — which no one can foresee.

I'm told that Abdul Rashid Khan's people have accepted this uncertainty because they understand that the mind of a child is like the surface of the lake beside the school — and because they know that trying to contain the flames that are lit by literacy can be as futile as dropping a stone onto the surface of that lake and attempting to hold back the ripples with one's hands.

I'm told all of these things, mostly by Sarfraz, because I have never been able to complete the journey to Bozai Gumbaz and see this spot with my own eyes — although a part of me is hopeful that this may be possible someday. It would be enormously gratifying for me to finally stand in the center of the world, at the crux of the old Silk Road, and see how the flower that was planted in the furthest corner of our Afghan garden is

faring. Among the range of emotional pos-
sibilities, I imagine that I might find myself bathed in a deeply satisfying sense of
vindication and pride over what has been
achieved. And that is also why another part
of me suspects that it might actually be best
if I never wind up getting to visit the place
at all.

Like it or not, you see, my reasons for wanting to get a firsthand glimpse of that gem of
a school in the High Pamir are probably not
compatible with the role that I played in its
completion. Because when it really comes
down to it, aside from the service that I performed as a kind of one-man yak train that
faithfully transported the donations of ordinary Americans to the far side of the world,
what was accomplished at Bozai Gumbaz
had nothing whatsoever to do with me. A
fact that for a time, I must now admit, was
not easy for me to accept.

When I first received the news that a helicopter mission to evacuate Abdul Rashid
Khan and ferry the remaining building supplies to Bozai Gumbaz would not be going
forward, I was so terribly dismayed at the
way things had worked out. After all, I had
tried so hard to reach the Kirghiz not once
but twice, and on both occasions had failed.
Now the military had done the same. And

it was undoubtedly my disappointment over these events that blinded me to the rather inconvenient truth that as important as it may have been for us to try, it was even more important for us to fail.

Only a few days later did I begin to comprehend that what the Kirghiz needed was something infinitely more precious and indispensable than whatever assistance might have been rendered by me, the American military, or anyone else who was not part of their community. In place of our help, what they needed most was the sense of empowerment that comes from knowing that they had done it on their own.

And by God's grace, they had achieved that in spades.

Of the 131 Central Asia Institute schools that are now scattered throughout Pakistan and Afghanistan, not a single one of them is more remote or stands upon higher ground than the little four-room structure that the Wakhan Kirghiz, in partnership with Sarfraz Khan, erected on the grassy slope next to the shallow lake in the center of the *Bam-I-Dunya* at 12,480 feet. And aside from our very first project in Korphe, no school is closer to my heart than the one in Bozai Gumbaz, because none was carved so directly and so indisputably from the bedrock of human dignity and self-worth.

By succeeding at an endeavor in which a government, an army, and an NGO had failed, a band of impoverished nomads were able to construct, on the loftiest and most distant corner of their republic, something even greater than a school. They had raised a beacon of hope that called out not only to the Kirghiz themselves, but also to every village and town in Afghanistan where children yearn for education, and where fathers and mothers dream of building a school whose doors will open not only to their sons but also to their daughters. Including — and perhaps especially — those places that are surrounded by a ring of men with Kalashnikovs who help to sustain the grotesque lie that flinging battery acid into the face of a girl who longs to study arithmetic is somehow in keeping with the teachings of the Koran.

Thanks to what the Kirghiz managed to pull off, no citizen of Afghanistan can now look toward the High Pamir without pondering the legend of the ragged company of horsemen who rode over a chain of mountains in search of someone who could build them a school — and who winded up fulfilling the promise that they had been given by

567

finishing that school with their own hands.

Today that legend is inscribed on the stones that were used to build the walls of the school, and as the water falls out of the sky and over those stones, the words of the legend are carried down from the mountains and into the fields and gardens and orchards of Afghanistan. And as the water and the words rush past, who can fail to turn to his neighbor and whisper, with humility and awe — if *this* is what the weakest, the least valued, the most neglected among us are capable of achieving, truly is there anything we cannot do?

Despite everything that has befallen us, do we not continue to hold the destiny of this shattered and magnificent nation, together with the future of all our children — girls and boys alike — in the palm of our hands?

And knowing all of this, is it not time to reclaim the things that have been taken from us?

The answer to those questions reveals the power that a legend can wield — and no one is haunted by this truth more profoundly or with greater anguish, perhaps, than those to whom the privileges of education and literacy have been denied.

If I could somehow have found a way to share the story of the tiny four-room schoolhouse that was nailed together upon the Roof of the World with my old mentor and friend, Haji Ali — a man who never learned to read or write, and who now lies in his grave under the apricot trees next to the barley fields of Korphe — I believe he would have nodded with approval.

He was a man who understood the virtue of small things.

ACKNOWLEDGMENTS

Today, there are over 120 million school-aged children on this planet who remain illiterate and are deprived of education due to gender discrimination, poverty, exploitation, religious extremism, and corrupt governments.

It is my hope and prayer that over the next decade we will do everything in our power to achieve universal literacy and provide education for all these children, two-thirds of whom are girls. Nothing would make me more pleased than if *Stones into Schools* became a catalyst to reach this goal.

It would take another book of the same length as this one to properly acknowledge the thousands of good people who were a vital part of this phenomenal journey over the last sixteen years. I regret that I cannot acknowledge each one of you in this limited space.

Two dedicated writers put in literally thousands of hours to help me bring *Stones into Schools* into the world. Thank you, Mike Bryan, for your perseverance in working nearly every day for an entire year to research and lay the groundwork for this book. And thank you, Kevin Fedarko, for helping me find the most compelling way to construct this narrative, and for your marathon efforts over one hundred consecutive sixteen-hour days to bring this book to the finish line in time for a December 2009 publication. What is most impressive about both of you is your absolute lack of ego and your humility and grace as you passionately steered this story into print. Without your dogged efforts and brilliant skills, *Stones into Schools* never would have happened. I toast you with a cup of the rancid yak-butter salt tea that we shared in the Wakhan and Baltistan. *Baf!*

To the eight incredible women who make up the backbone of our U.S. Central Asia Institute home team — Jennifer Sipes (operations director), Laura Anderson, Michelle Laxson, Lynsie Gettel, Lindsay Glick, Christine Leitinger, Sadia Ashraf, and Genevieve Chabot — there are no adequate words to express my gratitude for your quiet, patient support in running a grassroots organization that has grown exponentially over the last three years. Thanks must also be given to Karin Ronnow, Joel Kaleva, Stefani Freese, CPA, Doug Chabot, Teru Kuwayama, Gretchen Breuner, Shannon Gannon, Billy Durney, Tauheed Ashraf, and the many others who keep CAI afloat when we need to reach out beyond our capacity.

Thank you to the authors who have been a big help and inspiration over the years. These include Khaled Hosseini (and his wife Roya), author of *The Kite Runner* and *A Thousand Splendid Suns,* who wrote the foreword to this book and is a fellow humanitarian helping refugees with his Khaled Hosseini Foundation (www.khaledhosseinifoundation.org); Jane Goodall, author of *Reason for Hope,* who is a dear friend and has and inspired millions of kids with her *Roots & Shoots* program (www.rootsandshoots.org); Thomas Friedman, the author and *New York Times* columnist who has taken a strong interest in our work; Nicholas Kristof and Sheryl WuDunn, authors of the recently published book *Half the Sky,* who share a belief that the empowerment of women can change the world; Fareed Zakaria, author of *The Post-American World,* who believes that education is the most powerful weapon for peace; Ahmed Rashid, author of *Taliban* and *Descent into Chaos,* for sharing his encyclopedic knowledge from madrassas to *mujahadeen;* Rory Stewart, author of *The Places in Between,* who helps the Afghan people with his Turquoise Mountain charity (www.turquoisemountain.org); Doug Stanton, author of *Horse Soldiers;* Nazif Shahrani, author of *The Kirghiz and Wakhi of Afghanistan;* and Kathy Gannon, author of *I Is for Infidel.*

Thank you to the hundreds of public and private schools and universities that I have had the privilege of visiting over the last decade, many of which have adopted *Three Cups of Tea* as a first-year experience, honors program, or common read. Some of the most rewarding experiences of my life have been the enlightening exchanges I've had with the students from these institutions and their teachers. You are my real heroes!

To the dozens of young adults and children who have gone out on their own and started incredible nonprofits, you are an inspiration. These include Garret and Kyle Weiss (www.fundafield.com), Ashley Shuyler (www.africaid.org), Zach Bonner (www.littleredwagonfoundation.com), Anna Dodson (www.peruvianhearts.org), Cambridge (Mass.) elementary-school students (www.cambcamb.org), and Farmington (Mich.) and Danbury (Conn.) students (www.schoolinsudan.org).

Thank you also to the dedicated soldiers who serve our country, often at great risk and for extended periods of time away from their families. Over the last two years, it's been a priviledge to visit and speak at dozens of military bases and institutions and all the military academies. Thank you to Admiral Mike Mullen, chairman of the Joint Chiefs of Staff, who took time out to inaugurate one of our girls' schools in Afghanistan — and to his wife, Deborah, who first put *Three Cups of Tea* in his hands.

A salute also to the following military commanders and their wives, for sharing a cup (and more) of tea, and for inspiring me: General David Petraeus, CENTCOM commander; Admiral Eric Olson, SOCOM commander; General Stanley McChrystal, ISAF/U.S. commander in Afghanistan; Naval Vice Admiral Thomas Kilcline, Naval Aviation commander; Major General Mastin Robeson, MARSOC commander; General James Conway, U.S. Marine Corps commandant; Colonel Stephen Davis, MARSOC deputy commander; Major Jason Nicholson, Foreign Area Officer — Africa; Captain Richard Butler, chief of staff, Naval Air Forces; Major General John Macdonald and Major General Curtis Scaparrotti, both commanders in Afghanistan; and all the officers, NCOs, and enlisted men and women who serve under their leadership.

I also want to especially thank Captain John Kirby at the Pentagon for his encouragement and last but not least, Colonel Christopher Kolenda, who had the foresight to forge ahead and first reach out to the elders of Afghanistan.

In sixteen years, we've never used a dollar of federal government or USAID funds to build a school or buy a pen. But I do owe a deep debt of gratitude to Representative Mary Bono (R-Calif.) who taught me how to advocate for the cause of girls' education in Pakistan and Afghanistan. Thanks also to Representative Earl Pomeroy (D-N.D.), Representative Jean Schmidt (R-Ohio), Representative Denny Rehberg (R-Mont.), Senator Max Baucus (D-Mont.), Senator Olympia Snowe (R-Maine), Senator Mark Udall (D-Colo.), Senator Richard Lugar (R-Ind.) Senator Ben Cardin (D-Md.), Senator John Kerry (D-Mass.) and his wife Theresa Heinz, and also President Bill Clinton, First Lady Laura Bush, Barbara and George Bush Sr., Secretary of State Colin Powell, and Justice Sandra Day O'Connor.

I must thank seven individuals who touched my life and who share my alma mater, the University of South Dakota: Tom and Meredith Brokaw and their incredible family, Lars and Arlow Overskei, Don and Carol Birkeland, and Al Neuharth, founder of *USA Today*.

As a humanitarian, I also thank the dedicated aid workers who fight illiteracy, disease, poverty, wars, environmental degradation, human-rights violations, and more, often against staggering odds.

Thank you to Westside Elementary School in River Falls, Wisconsin, for starting our children's "Pennies for Peace" (P4P) program in 1994, and to the over 4,500 schools who now participate in P4P around the world — you are our real hope for global peace.

Thanks to all the incredible support from the book clubs, women's groups, places of workship, civic organizations, veterans' associations, the AAUW (Association of American University Women), bookstores, libraries, and everyone else who helped both in making *Three Cups of Tea* such a success and in spreading the message about the importance of girls' education.

For their realistic, rock-solid support, I also thank: George McCown, Talat Jabbar, Julia Bergman, John and Ginny Meisenbach, Joy Durghello, Robert Irwin, Nancy Block, Anne Beyersdorfer, Ben Rice, Charley Shimansky, Bill Galloway, Dr. Louis Reichardt, Jim Wickwire, Steve Swenson, Dr. Andrew and Lisa Marcus, David and Eunice Simonson, Ms. Mary Peglar (an octogenarian and my first teacher in Africa, who is now in the UK and still writes sea-shipped letters to me), Jeni and Conrad Anker, Jennifer Wilson, Vince and Louise Larsen, Lila, Brent and Kim Bishop, Jon Krakauer, John and Anne Rigby, Tony O'Brien, Mark (and Sue Iberra) Jenkins, Keith Hamburg, Ricky Golmulka, Jeff McMillian, Andrew Lawson, Susan Roth, Nick and Linken Berryman, Salma Hasan Ali, Sameera and Zahid Baig, Sara Thomson, John Guza, Tom and Judy Vaughan, Sara and Sohaib Abbasi, Angelina Jolie, Pam Heibert, MD, the late Ray Roberts (the original acquiring editor of *Three Cups of Tea*), Jean Hoerni, Patsy Collins, Deidre Eitel, Jim and Margaret Beyersdorfer, Paula Lloyd, and Jose Forquet.

Thank you to my Islamic mentor Saeed Abbas Risvi sahib, who is the most humble man I've known and has patiently taught me about the true virtues of Islam, that it is a faith of tolerance, justice, and peace. May Allah's blessings be with you and your family always.

In Afghanistan and Pakistan my special thanks go to Haji Youssef, Haji Fida Mohammed Nashad, Brigadier General Bashir Baz, Colonel Ilyas Mirza, Captain Wassim Ifthakhar Janjua, Faruq Wardak Sadhar Khan, Wohid Khan, Ghulam Noristani, Abdul Rashid Khan, Wali Boz Ahmadi, Jan Agha, Master Hussein, Shah Ismael Khan, Tashi Boi, Haji Ibrahim, Haji Mohammed Ali, Haji Abdul Aziz, Maulavi Rashdi, Twaha, Parveen, Aziza, Lima, Jahan, Tahera, Rubina, Najeeba Mera, Bibi Raihana, and Uzra Faizad. Two of those I wish to thank who first helped me along the way are no longer with us: Haji Ali and Brigadier General Cahudhry Zakaullah Bhangoo, an angel of mercy who was tragically killed in a plane crash in Turkey in 2007.

A particular debt of gratitude must go to Penguin Group (USA) Inc., which has been instrumental in helping me to bring our cause to the attention to millions of readers through the publication of *Three Cups of Tea* and now *Stones into Schools*. Your offices are a second home, and your tribal chieftains, including Marjorie Scardino, chief executive of Pearson, John Makinson, the chairman and chief executive of the Penguin Group, David Shanks, CEO of Penguin Group (USA) Inc., Susan Petersen Kennedy, president of Penguin Group (USA) Inc., Clare Ferraro, president of Viking, and

Kathryn Court, president of Penguin Trade Paperbacks, are most impressive leaders.

It goes without saying that this book would not have been possible without the guidance of my editor, mentor, and fellow mountain climber, Paul Slovak, the publisher of Viking. It was in his office that my very first visit to the company took place in 2003, when I came in to pitch the idea of a book I was calling *Three Cups of Tea*. Since that time, Paul has been with me every step of the way, and even when I would go off the radar screen for days at a time, he never lost faith in me. His support, wisdom, editorial expertise, and steadfastness have been invaluable.

Several months ago, when Penguin was helping me to organize a party in New York to celebrate the success of the adult and young reader's editions of *Three Cups of Tea* and the children's picture book *Listen to the Wind,* I was astonished to learn that Penguin had calculated that over 440 people at the company had played some role in the publication of my books! I thank all of you for your dedication and devotion, and in particular the following people, who were most closely involved in the production and publication of this new book: Nancy Sheppard, Carolyn Coleburn, Louise Braverman, Noirin

Lucas, Elke Sigal, Courtney Allison, David Martin, Holly Watson, Kate Lloyd, Dennis Swaim, Karen Mayer, Paul Buckley, Jasmine Lee, Jennifer Wang, Hal Fessenden, Sabila Khan, and, working outside of the company, copy editor Hilary Roberts, fact-checker Jane Cavolina and Brynn Breuner, who co-ordinated the maps, photos, and back matter. The other key members of the Penguin team that I must thank include Eileen Kreit, Alan Walker, Jackie Fischetti, Tiffany Tomlin, Jenna Meulemans, Caitlin Pratt, Shanta Newlin, Alisah Niehaus, and Marilyn Hills at the front desk, who sneaks me into the office without authorization. A special shout-out must also go to Penguin's incredible hardcover and paperback sales forces, whose passionate advocacy for my books with the booksellers has made all the difference in the world. And last but not least, thank you to Leoni Atossa, the remarkable lead actress in the *Kite Runner* film, who is the narrator of the audio versions of *Stones into Schools* and the *Three Cups of Tea* young reader's edition. Thank you all!

When I was a child in Tanzania, my parents, Dempsey and Jerene Mortenson, read bedtime stories to my sisters Sonja, Kari, and Christa, and me every evening by lantern and later by electric light. Those stories filled us with curiosity about the world and other cultures. They inspired the humanitarian adventure that has shaped my life. My mother's lifelong commitment to education continues to inspire me. And although cancer took the life of my young father in 1980, his infinite spirit lives on in all that I do. Dad, you are my *baba, kaka na rafiki* (father, brother, and friend). Thanks also to my extraordinary sisters Sonja and Kari, their husbands Dean Raven and Dan Thiesen, and their beautiful families — your love and devotion is a huge inspiration.

Thanks to my amazing kids, Amira and Khyber, whom I love so much; I'm sorry that I missed out on nearly half of your childhoods. That reality is the most painful part of my work and I deeply regret not seeing you first learn how to walk, tie your shoes, or ride a bicycle. You have both given me unconditional love, and not a day goes by that I do not appreciate how wonderful you are and just how hard this has been. Now that I am home more, I am eager to celebrate our precious time together.

Tara, my wife — dear friend, companion, confidante, mother of our children, and the love of my life whom I married six days after meeting you in 1995 — I owe you immeasurable gratitude. During my frequent absences over the fourteen years of our marriage, your support and love has made it possible for me to follow my heart. Thank you for the sacrifices you have made and for being part of this magnificent journey.

Greg Mortenson
October 1, 2009

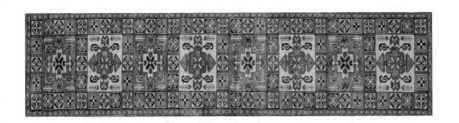

GLOSSARY

AK-47 or Kalashnikov: A Russian semiautomatic assault rifle

Alhamdulillah: Arabic for "Praise be to God"; often used as a blessing to give thanks after meals

Allah: The Arabic word for God

Allah Akbhar: In Arabic, "God is great." This exclamation can be used in prayer, to praise God, or to express approval, excitement, or happiness.

Al Qaeda: An organization that conducts acts of terror, war, and destruction of targets all over the world in order to establish a global Islamic caliphate

Amu Darya: A river in northeastern Afghanistan and southern Tajikistan

arak: Fermented mare's milk, used in central Asia

As-Salaam Alaaikum: In Arabic, "Peace be with you," the standard Islamic greeting

Baba Gundi Ziarat: A shrine at the end of the Charpurson Valley in extreme northern Pakistan

Badakshan: A province in northeastern Afghanistan that includes the Wakhan Corridor

baf: "Excellent" in the Wakhi language

Bagram Airbase: A main air base of the U.S. military in Afghanistan, and also a Soviet base from 1979 to 1989

Baharak: A town in Badakshan Province (in northeastern Afghanistan) with a population of eighteen thousand; site of the first CAI school built in Afghanistan

Balakot: A city in northern Pakistan that was devastated during the October 2005 earthquake

Balti: A tribal group, mostly Shia, that lives in the Karakoram range in northeastern Pakistan

Baltistan: A region in northeastern Pakistan

Bam-I-Dunya: A Wakhi word meaning "Roof of the World," referring to central Asia's Pamir mountain range

Bamiyan: A city in northern Afghanistan

Barg-e Matal: A town in Nuristan Province (in eastern Afghanistan) frequently attacked by Taliban

bida: An Arabic term meaning "corrupting

modernization"

Bozai Gumbaz: A settlement in the eastern Wakhan inhabited by nomadic Kirghiz people

BSF: Afghanistan's Border Security Force

burka: A loose robe worn by some women in Afghanistan and Pakistan that covers the entire body; also spelled "burqa"

bushkashi: A traditional central Asian game played on horseback

CENTCOM: U.S. military Central Command

Central Asia Institute (CAI): Greg Mortenson's nonprofit organization, founded in 1996 with the mission of promoting education for girls in Pakistan and Afghanistan (see www.ikat.org)

chapatti: Flat, unleavened bread similar to a pita or a tortilla

Char Asiab: A valley south of Kabul where the CAI has a school

Charpurson Valley: A valley in northern Pakistan whose name means "place of nothing" in Wakhi

Chokidar: A security guard in Pakistan or Afghanistan

COIN: The acronym for military counterinsurgency operations

commandhan: An Afghan term for a local militia commander

Dari: A form of the Farsi language; spoken in Afghanistan

Deh Rawod: A town in Uruzgan Province, Afghanistan

dua: An Islamic prayer accompanied by a gesture of bringing the palms together and pointing them upward

dupatta: A head scarf worn by girls

Faizabad: The capital of Badakshan Province, Afghanistan

Farsi: The Persian language of Iran

fauji: A term for the military in Pakistan

FOB: U.S. military forward operating base

FWO: Frontier Works Organization, Pakistan's military civil engineering division

Gilgit: A town in Hunza Valley in northern Pakistan

Gundi Piran Higher Secondary School for Girls: A school in Azad Kashmir, Pakistan, destroyed by the October 2005 earthquake

Helmand Province: A Southern Afghanistan province where four thousand U.S. Marines were deployed in July 2009

Himalayas: The mountain range in southern Asia that borders Burma, India, China, Nepal, Tibet, and Pakistan

Hindu Kush: A mountain range in western Pakistan and eastern Afghanistan

Id (also spelled Eid): One of the biggest Islamic holidays, which marks the end of Ramadan, the month when Muslims fast

imam: An Islamic spiritual leader who has had significant training

Inshallah: In Arabic, "God willing"; often used to mean that the speaker hopes something will occur or that he or she will be able to accomplish something, and God's help and blessing will be needed

Irshad Pass: A 16,335-foot pass between northern Pakistan and the Wakhan Corridor in Afghanistan

Ishkoshem: A town in Badakshan Province, Afghanistan

Islam: The Arabic word for "peace" and the world's second-largest religion, based on the teaching of the Prophet Mohammed

Islamabad: The capital of Pakistan

Ismaili: A liberal offshoot of Shia Islam whose spiritual leader is Prince Karim Aga Khan

Jalalabad: A city in Nangarhar Province, Afghanistan

Jalozai Refugee Camp: An Afghan refugee camp in western Pakistan

jihad: An Arabic word meaning "internal struggle," which takes places in two forms: the greater jihad, which is the internal struggle for enlightenment and improvement of one's self, and the lesser jihad, which is the fight against an enemy of Islam

jirga: A village council or meeting

jumat khana: An Ismaili place of worship

Kabul: Afghanistan's capital and largest city

Kali-Panj: A town in central Wakhan, Afghanistan

Kandahar: A city in southern Afghanistan

Karakoram: A mountain range in northern Pakistan containing the world's greatest consolidation of high peaks

Karakoram Highway (KKH): The arterial link road between China and northern Pakistan, completed in 1978

Kashmir: The mountainous region on the border of India and Pakistan

Khundud: A town in the Wakhan Corridor, Afghanistan

Khyber Pass: A mountain pass between Pakistan and Afghanistan

Kirghiz: Sunni nomadic pastoralists who inhabit the eastern end of the Wakhan Corridor, Afghanistan

Korphe: A village in northern Pakistan and the site of the CAI's first school

Kunar: A province in eastern Afghanistan

kwalai: A white skullcap used for prayer by Muslims

Lalander: A village south of Kabul where

the CAI's demonstration school in Afghanistan was built

LOC: The acronym for "Line of Control," the disputed border between India and Pakistan

Logar: A province southeast of Kabul, Afghanistan

lunghai: A type of wrap-around turban worn by Pashtun tribal people

madrassa: An Arabic word meaning "educational institution"

maktab: Dari and Pashto word meaning "school" used in Afghanistan

Mardhan Shar: The capital of Wardak Province, Afghanistan

Mazar-i-Sharif: A city in northern Afghanistan

Mi-17 and Mi-24: Soviet military helicopters used in Afghanistan

muezzin: A chanter in a mosque who intones the call to prayer

muhajir: The term for "refugee" in Pakistan and Afghanistan

mujahadeen: An Arabic word meaning "struggler" and the name given to the Afghan freedom fighters

mullah: A community Islamic leader

Muslim: A person who practices Islam

Muzaffarabad: The capital of Azad Kashmir, Pakistan

naan: A type of thick bread commonly eaten in Afghanistan

nanwatey: The Pashtun code affording the right of refuge and protection to all guests

Naray: A district in northern Kunar Province, Afghanistan

Neelum Valley: The epicenter of the 2005 earthquake in Azad Kashmir, Pakistan

nemek choi: The Wakhi word for salt tea mixed with goat's milk and yak butter

NGO: The international term for "nongovernmental organization"

night letter: A threatening letter delivered under cover of darkness by the Taliban

Northwest Frontier Province: A tribal area in northwestern Pakistan; one of Pakistan's five provincial areas

Nuristan: A province in eastern Afghanistan

nurmadhar: An Urdu term meaning "village chief"

Operation Enduring Freedom: The official U.S. military designation for the war in Afghanistan started in 2001

opium bride: A daughter sold into slavery to pay for an opium habit

pakhol: A Dari and Pashtun term for the woolen hat often worn by mujahadeen

Pamirs: A mountain range in Afghanistan, Tajikistan, and China known as the Roof of the World

Panjshir: A province and valley in northern Afghanistan

Pashto: The language spoken by Pashtun tribal peoples, who live along the Pakistan-Afghanistan border

Peshawar: A city in Pakistan near the Afghanistan border

pir: A Wakhi/Tajik term meaning "elder"

Pul-e-Khumri: A town in northern Afghanistan

purdah: An Urdu and Hindi term meaning "curtain," which refers to the cultural tradition of women covering themselves in public

Qayamat: An Urdu term meaning "apocalypse"

rupee: The unit of money used in Pakistan, India, and other countries

Salang: A strategic pass and tunnel north of Kabul

Sarhad: A village at the end of the only road through the Wakhan Corridor

shaheed: An Arabic word meaning "martyr"

shalwar kamiz: Loose, pajama-like pants and top worn in Pakistan and Afghanistan

Shia: The second-largest Muslim denomination worldwide, at 17 percent

shura: A word used in Afghanistan meaning

"an elder"

SOCOM: The acronym for the U.S. Special Operations Command

Sunni: The main sect of Islam, representing 82 percent of Muslims worldwide

Swat Valley: An area in northern Pakistan ruled by the Taliban for two years until 2009

Tajikistan: A mountainous country north of Afghanistan

tanzeem: A word used in Afghanistan and Pakistan meaning "village committee"

Uighur: An Islamic people who live in far western China

ulema: An Arabic term for Islamic religious leaders

Urdu: The national language of Pakistan

Uruzgan: A province in southwestern Afghanistan

USAID: The acronym for the United States Agency for International Development

Waalaikum-Salaam: An Arabic phrase meaning "May peace be with you also"

Wakhan Corridor: A 120-mile-long corridor in northeastern Afghanistan

Wakhi: A Persian tribal people who live in the central Wakhan and northern Pakistan

Waziristan: A region of western Pakistan located in the Northwest Frontier Province

Xinjiang: A province in far western China with a significant proportion of Uighur ethnic Muslims

Yardar: A hamlet near the town of Baharak in Badakshan Province, Afghanistan

zalzala: The Urdu term for "earthquake"

Baharak school girls, Badakshan Province, Afghanistan GREG MORTENSON, 2009

INVESTING IN GIRLS' EDUCATION YIELDS HUGE RETURNS

INCOME GROWTH

Girls' education leads to increased income for the girls themselves and for nations as a whole. Increasing the share of women with a secondary education by 1 percent boosts annual per-capita income growth by 0.3 percent. That's significant, since per-capita income gains in developing countries seldom exceed 3 percent a year.*

Educating girls also boosts farming productivity. Educated farmers are more efficient and their farms are more productive, which leads to increased crop yields and declines in malnutrition.†

MATERNAL AND CHILDREN'S HEALTH

Educated women have smaller, healthier, and better-educated families.

The better educated the women in a society, the lower the fertility rate. A 2000 study in Brazil found that literate women had an average of 2.5 children while illiterate women had an average of six children.[‡]

The better educated the women, the lower the infant mortality rate. "The mother's education is often the single most important influence on children's survival. . . . Educated mothers learn how to keep their children healthy and how to use health services, improve nutrition and sanitation, and take advantage of their own increased earning capability. Girls who stay in school also marry later, when they are better able to bear and care for children."[†]

By increasing health-care knowledge and reducing the number of pregnancies, female education significantly reduces the risk of maternal mortality.[*]

Educated women are more likely to insist on education for their own children, especially their daughters. Their children study as much as two hours more each day than children of illiterate mothers and stay in school longer.[†]

WOMEN'S EMPOWERMENT
Educated girls and women are more likely

to stand up for themselves and resist violence: "In poor areas where women are isolated within their communities, have little education and cannot earn much, girls are often regarded as an economic burden and women and girls sometimes suffer deliberate neglect or outright harm."[†]

Educated women channel more of their resources to the health and education of their children than men do.[†]

Educated women are more likely to participate in political discussions, meetings, and decision making.[†]

Studies show that education promotes more representative, effective government. As women are educated and approach parity with men, research shows that "governments and other institutions function better and with less corruption."[†]

Girls who become literate tend to teach their mothers how to read and write, much more than do males.[§]

When vegetables or meat wrapped in newspapers are brought home from the bazaar, women often ask their literate daughters to read the news to them and can understand more about the dynamic world around them.[§]

*The World Bank
†The Council on Foreign Relations' *What Works in Girls' Education: Evidence and Policies from the Developing World*
‡UNESCO
§Greg Mortenson

KEY INGREDIENTS IN SUCCESSFULLY BUILDING GIRLS' SCHOOLS

The Council on Foreign Relations' *What Works in Girls' Education: Evidence and Policies from the Developing World* spells out several critical elements for successful girls' schools, many of which Central Asia Institute has incorporated:*

Build schools close to girls' homes. School-age children are 10 percent to 20 percent more likely to attend school if they live in a village with a primary school. Proximity also increases parental involvement.

Insist on community involvement. Community schools tend to meet culture norms and use local language. Community-based and community-supported schools gener-

*The Council on Foreign Relations' *What Works in Girls' Education: Evidence and Policies from the Developing World*

ally have higher enrollment and quality and lower dropout rates.

Build "girl-friendly" schools. Girls' schools must have private latrines and boundary walls. In some cases, it's most appropriate to build separate schools for girls.

Provide female teachers. Recruit locally. Even very young women can teach programmed curricula effectively if they are trained and supported.

Focus on quality education. Ensure that a school has enough teachers, ongoing teacher training, heavy emphasis on math and science, and adequate books and supplies.

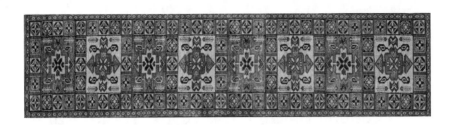

TAKE ACTION

1. Visit www.stonesintoschools.com for more info, book reviews, events, and ideas.
2. Suggest *Stones into Schools* to a friend; colleague; book club; women's group; church; civic group; synagogue; mosque; university or high school class; military friends or families; or a group interested in education, literacy, adventure, crosscultural issues, Islam, or Pakistan and Afghanistan.
3. Check if *Stones into Schools* is in your local library. If not, either donate a copy or suggest to the library that they add *Stones into Schools* to their collection. Ask your friends or family in other states to do this also.
4. Ask the book editor of your local newspaper or radio station to consider letting you review the book.

5. Pennies for Peace, www.penniesfor-peace.org, is designed for schoolchildren. Get your local school involved to make a difference, one penny and one pencil at a time. Since 1994, more than two hundred million pennies have been raised through Pennies for Peace.

6. If you want to support our efforts to promote education and literacy, especially for girls, you can make a tax-deductible contribution to our nonprofit organization, Central Asia Institute, PO Box 7209, Bozeman, MT 59771, phone 406-585-7841, www.ikat.org. It costs us $1.00 per month for one child's education in Pakistan or Afghanistan, a penny to buy a pencil, and a teacher's salary averages $1.50 per day.

7. Please direct media or *Stones into Schools* inquires to info@stonesinto schools.com or call 406-585-7841.

For more information contact:
Central Asia Institute
PO Box 7209
Bozeman, MT 59771
406-585-7841
www.ikat.org
info@ikat.org

ABOUT THE AUTHOR

Greg Mortenson is the director of the Central Asia Institute. A resident of Montana, he spends several months of the year in Pakistan and Afghanistan. He is the author of the *New York Times* bestselling title *Three Cups of Tea.*